Salmon Fishing
on Small Rivers

Charles Bingham

Salmon Fishing on Small Rivers

Scottish river section by
Rob Wilson

BLANDFORD

A Blandford Book

First published in the UK
1994 by Blandford, a Cassell imprint
Villiers House
41/47 Strand
London WC2N 5JE

Distributed in the United States
by Sterling Publishing Co, Inc
387 Park Avenue South, New York, NY 10016-8810

Distributed in Australia
by Capricorn Link (Australia) Pty Ltd
2/13 Carrington Road, Castle Hill, NSW 2154

British Library Cataloguing-in-Publication Data
A catalogue record for this book
is available from the British Library

ISBN 0–7137–2479–X

Typeset by Litho Link Ltd, Welshpool, Powys, Wales

Printed and bound in Great Britain by The Bath Press, Avon

Contents

Acknowledgements

I am indebted to all who helped in the preparation of this book.

My especial thanks go to Rob Wilson, of Brora, Sutherland, for his contribution on the small rivers of Scotland. Rob Wilson also provided the photographs in this chapter.

My reports on the River Derwent in Cumbria were made possible by the introductions arranged by Dr Jack Abernethy, Julian Shaw and Bill Waldron.

James Hardy of House of Hardy gave of his experiences, made fly rods and reels available and introduced me to Alan Bagnall, head bailiff of the Northumbrian Anglers' Federation.

John Garside extended to me the hospitality of the Brigands Inn on the River Dovey, and arranged a meeting with Emyr Lewis, head bailiff of the New Dovey Fishery Association and Captain of the Welsh National Fly Fishing Team in 1990.

Charley Bateman, Con Waldron, Roddy Rei, Ray Burrows (who is Hon. Sec. of the Bodmin Anglers' Association) and John Nolan, and Neil Barnett of Wadebridge Anglers gave generously of their time and knowledge. I thank them all.

I also thank the *Sunday Telegraph* and *Trout & Salmon* for permission to reprint my articles.

Conversion table

Length

1 in		= 25.4 mm
1 ft	= 12 in	= 0.3048 m
1 yd	= 36 in	= 0.9144 m
	= 3 ft	= 0.9144 m
1 mile	= 1760 yd	= 1.6093 km

Weight

1 oz		= 28.350 g
1 lb	= 16 oz	= 0.454 kg

Temperature

To convert °F to °C, deduct 32 and multiply by 5/9.

Introduction

There he stands, in spring, dressed in Norfolk jacket, breeches and short leather boots; stark as a dead tree upright on the bank. He casts at 2 minute intervals and between each throw takes two paces down the river. The 15 ft greenheart rod rolls out a long line of silk, which sinks, carrying down the single No. 2/0 hooked, feather-dressed fly at the end of the gut cast. His man waits a short distance from the water, leaning on the shaft of his gaff. At the end of the day, two or three fish of two or three sea-winters are carried to the hut and weighed. Later, back at the 'big house', our angler, after refreshment, pink-cheeked and bewhiskered, collapses into a tub of hot water in the pine-panelled bathroom, his back nigh broken by the casting. The year – c. 1900.

Move into the twentieth century. Arthur Wood now takes his turn upon the high bank of the Aberdeenshire Dee at Cairnton. His garb has altered from Victorian years only to the extent that he wears a trilby hat and his baggy trousers are thrust into short rubber boots. The gillie weathers the storms in a three-piece plus-four suit of tweed and the gaff he holds is mounted on a 7 ft shaft. To the casual glance little has changed. But scrutinize the great man's tackle for he is sweeping his forbears aside. His rod is single-handed and 12 feet in length; split cane the material. The silk line, with grease upon it, floats. The flies are different too; they are much smaller, on Low Water hooks, and some of the shanks are bare of all but red or blue paint. Wood is doing something different, he is ushering in the greased-line era: c. 1920s.

Three generations pass. It is July, August or September. An angler is now fishing a little river, the Dee being too expensive and the waiting list too long. The gaff has gone; a gillie is rare. The fisherman has a Gye net slung on his back. The rod he uses is short, between 9 ft and 12 ft long, his line is of a man-made fibre and floats without grease, being lighter than water. Hair has replaced feather as dressing on the flies and the hooks of these are trebles. Fishing alone, searching for lies, he wears polarized spectacles, thigh boots and a 'breathable' waterproof jacket. It is not easy to see his clothes because he moves stealthily below the bank with his 'fore and aft' just visible. The year is 1990.

This book is written for those who would fish the narrow waters and stalk their salmon in secret hidden valleys. If you can drop your fly under the far bank without a false cast, using a rod of 10 ft 6 in., then you are on a small river. There are 14 small rivers in the south-west of England; a number in the valleys of Wales; and in Scotland there are more of them than oats in a plate of porridge.

It is a personal quest, seeking a fish from the pots, holes and frothing runs of these little waterways. Hope is around each corner. Rod low, head too, knees bent and fly searching, one fishes these intimate pools until . . .

Today, more anglers seek salmon than in the past. Fifteen years ago, in my work as a game-fishing instructor, the demand for trout tuition exceeded that for salmon and sea trout by a substantial margin. This is not the case today. I find my time consumed in instructing those who wish to fish their local rivers, in many parts of the country, for salmon. The little rivers await them. The cost need be no greater than a day at trout. This book is for you. May it bring success.

Publisher's Note

There is an inevitable delay in book production between receiving the author's manuscript and the publication of the finished work. In this case, the main body of research and interviews were carried out by the author over a period of time up to December 1990, so the reader may find some specific salmon fishing results since that date are absent.

Part 1

Fishing techniques

1 The salmon

When I arrived at the river, a green car, ancient and rusty, was tucked away under the trees bordering the water. Inside were a jack, a sack and worthless rubbish. There was no sign of the owner, but the tyre tracks in the mud were fresh. I took the registration number. (Cars may be confiscated by the police if used for salmon poaching.) Old vehicles of little value are often used and therefore, in November, at salmon-spawning time, an old car by the river raises suspicions.

I parked my car nearby, let out the dogs and set off down the river, thumbstick in hand. The owner of the car was some way off when his hat became visible, moving from right to left as he walked behind the wall which flanks the salmon-spawning stream. With his head below the level of the stones, he could not see me as I moved up to the wall. A glance over and there he was, hands and hat brim shielding the light as he peered into the river. Crouching the dogs silently in the rushes, I leaned on my stick and watched him from a distance of 100 yd, with just my head above the wall. There was no mistaking his interest; he was searching for salmon redds – and then he saw me. Whirling about, he lit a cigarette and started in alarm as the dogs, tension overcoming obedience, ran forward to investigate.

Off he went. I looked where he had peered. Salmon redds were there – light patches on the river bed of gravel and small stones – and salmon too, swimming in alarm about the pool. Some tucked their heads under the banks and others made off to deep water. At home I telephoned the head water bailiff. Later, when a policeman called to discuss my shot-gun certificate, I told him the registration number of the car and he fed in the information over his radio. Within a minute there came a reply. 'That's F-----,' he said. 'Known for poaching. His family have three old cars and a motorcycle. A difficult man to catch. The fact that you've disturbed him may move him on elsewhere. Otherwise he'll be back when the moon is full or with a lamp.'

I have never been able to see the point of poaching salmon on their spawning beds. The fish are debilitated and the flesh pale and tasteless, which only adds to the crime of it being illegal to offer to buy, sell, or offer to sell fresh salmon between 31 August and 1 February. Perhaps they go into the poachers' deep-freeze and are brought out in the spring. Even so they would make a sorry sight on any slab and be tasteless on a plate.

Salmon on moorland spawning beds in December.

The life cycle of the salmon

Two days later I visited another stream with a black pool at its head. The pool is nowhere deep, the blackness on the bed being a sediment washed down from peat bogs on the hill. The pool was full of fish. They leaped, splashed and glistened in the late November sun. Two streams feed the pool, their beds of small stones cleared of silt by the water-bailiff's digger and kept clean by the current. The southern stream twists up and away to where the sun sets behind the hill. The stream arriving from the west is the one. There, as I watched, tails cut the water skin and backs curved above the surface as cock fish lifted over the piled-up gravel ridge behind each redd. Over or around the ridge, the cock fish moves to lie beside his chosen hen. At intervals they curve and quiver, ejecting ova and fertilizing milt. If you return next day, the *redd* which they have cut, that trough 6 in. deep, 24 in. wide, and longer than themselves, will have been smoothed, the pair having gone elsewhere to repeat the process and spread the risk to the survival of their eggs. A hen of 10 lb may extrude 7000 eggs, in three or four places, over several days. Then she and her mate are done, exhausted, and will almost certainly die. Known as *kelts*, they do their best to swim downriver to the sea, but few succeed.

Visit the stream at the end of December and you will witness a distressing scene – salmon on their sides, just bodies, white with putrefaction, on the river bed. The winter floods break down the weakened bodies until all that is left is a jaw bone stranded on a sandbank, a tattered skin wrapped about a fence wire by a bank-submerging spate, and the backbone remnant of an otter's meal. Some hens, just a few, swollen with eggs they are unable to extrude, may remain in the river for several months. These fish are known as *baggots*.

The small area cleared of stones beneath the water on the river bed is a salmon redd.

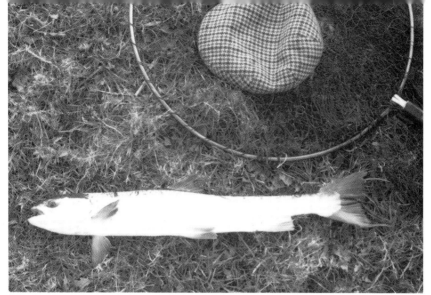

A kelt. Note the thin body. The eye of this living fish looks down; the eye of a dead fish looks out. Kelts are returned alive to the river as required by law.

In 1968, when I first caught one of these salmon, I was unaware of the state of my catch, gaffed it and knocked it on the head. It could not have been returned in any case, because of the use of the gaff, which I no longer employ. My fishing diary records the event:

17 April 1968 About noon, hooked a fish of about 10 lb in tail of Bush Pool. Fish lost when it ran out of the bottom of the pool. Rained in afternoon. River rose 1 in. 4.00 pm. Top of Bush Pool. 15 lb salmon. No. 4 Thunder & Lightning. Fish found to be full of well-developed roe.

The colour of this hen's belly was yellow. Whether the salmon estimated at 10 lb was a cock which had run up in the spring, and now accompanied the baggot, I shall never know.

Roes of 10 lb hen salmon taken in June. (Note the clean head.)

Roes of 10 lb hen salmon taken in September. (Note the dark head of stale fish.)

Let us return to the headwaters where life is stored in mid-winter beneath the stones of the river bed. Ova are there; eyed ova to carry on the cycle of life. In 90 days or thereabouts, depending upon the temperature of the water, they hatch. *Alevins* are released, complete with a sustaining yolk sac attached beneath their chin. The yolk lasts them for a month and then, as *fry*, they start to feed. In May, you may see these tiny 1 in. fish if you disturb the shallow places with your boots or just stand still and watch the river bed. I have seen another thing when the hawthorn is in flower: a small, webbed-pad imprint on the mud where only large prints were before. The owners of the pads, the otters, do little harm for they love eels, frogs and furry creatures more than trout and salmon.

The next stage in a salmon's life lasts for the best part of 2 years, the length of time which it takes for the fish, now known as a *parr*, to grow to 7 or 8 in. long in an acid stream. Parr mature more quickly in the alkaline rivers of the chalk stream areas where food is more abundant. The parr is hungry; it feeds voraciously and may take the fly of the trout fisherman. Release it with care, with wet, cold hands, because a parr scalded by the heat of hot, dry fingers may die. Over this period of 2 years, parr move slowly downriver and may end up in the lower reaches, where I have often had to remove them from my trout fly. In the early years of this century, when trout fishing held sway on the premier chalk streams of the south of England, parr were not always welcome. C. Ernest Pain (1934) wrote:

It has been claimed that, as salmon do not feed in fresh water, the presence of the large fish cannot harm trout fishing. But parr feed in fresh water; they do nothing else but feed in fact – except for an occasional light interlude spent in annoying the trout angler by chewing his flies – the voracious little beggars.

A parr can be distinguished from a small brown trout by the adipose and anal fins. Both are clear in the parr, but the adipose fin of the trout is brown or red, and the leading edge of the anal fin is white. This small fish is the food of all the river predators. Many times I have seen a mink galloping down the bank with one held in its teeth, no doubt for a maturing litter of cubs. Cannibal brown trout take them, and the large stocked trout of the chalk streams may hold victims in their stomachs. Herons fish by day and in moonlight; I have seen them glide down to the river edge on wide, silent wings at dusk as I wait for the light to go before starting after sea trout. The otter takes a few and, if pike are present, they will also grab a parr. And so, despite the 7000 eggs laid by our 10 lb hen fish, the numbers hatched continue slowly to decline. This is accelerated at times by pollution, abstraction of water from the river, and disease.

If our samlet survives its nursery months in the river, it takes on a silver sheen in April or May 2 years after hatching. It 'smoltifies' and swims downriver to the sea. Smolts are greedy. Several times, in a fit of over-ambition, one has hooked itself upon my Devon minnow or Mepps spoon as I have been spinning the lower river for spring salmon; grasped underwater they can usually be returned unharmed and sent upon their way. Down they go, over the weirs and through the salmon ladders. But the dangers continue in the lower reaches of the river. John Potter, whose family have been connected with the Nursling salmon fishery at the mouth of the River Test for generations, told me in 1989:

In the Little River at Nursling in the spring of 1988, a couple of days after we had put in 7500 or so young fish, we caught a brown trout of about 3 lb that took a salmon bait. Inside this trout were five, micro-tagged smolts.

The North Atlantic accepts and hides the smolt, although numbers continue to reduce. Lost to us it travels far, and here we must rely on other men to tell us where it goes. Clearly the distance which may be covered, and thus the location of the feeding grounds visited, depends upon the length of time it spends in the sea. The earliest it will return is the end of June of the following year. These are known as *one-sea-winter fish*, or *grilse* and they may have travelled as far as the Faeroe Islands. In June and July, these entrants to the rivers of their birth weigh between 3 and 5 lb. In September, the later arrivals may pull down the spring balance to 7 lb and, if the season on a river extends to November or December, the weights of even later arrivals may reach double figures. The grilse is an athletic fish of so slim a configuration, particularly in the tail, that special attention must be paid in the matter of its landing, as we shall see later.

If the fish returns after two or three sea-winters, having fed perhaps off the coast of Greenland, it may enter the river during January, February and March, and then onwards throughout the season. It is unwise to give average weights for full salmon, for these may be peculiar to individual rivers.

10 lb 8 oz spring salmon of two sea-winters taken 5 miles above the tide.

If pressed, I might put forward that a two-sea-winter fish is likely to weigh between 7 and 20 lb and a three-sea-winter entrant over 20 lb. To illustrate that these are only approximations I have personal knowledge of a 20 lb three-sea-winter fish and a 24 lb cock salmon kelt of two sea-winters. Neither of these salmon showed previous spawning marks on their scales, which were read in the laboratories of the National Rivers Authority (NRA).

The fishing year

Having traced the life history of the salmon, we ought now to consider fishing in relation to the time of year and the likely yields, as well as the section of the river to which our effort should be applied as the season progresses. When one sallies forth upon the business of catching a salmon, and to achieve this purpose entails many miles of motoring and many days of fishing, one likes to know the chances.

Success in the spring is not so likely as it was 15 or 20 years ago. Consider first the months of January to May, during which period great changes take place in the methods we apply, as we shall see. The fish we seek will be two-sea-winter salmon with a sprinkling of three-sea-winter specimens. The body temperature of salmon is directly related to that of the water. Consequently they are cold and lethargic at this time and neither leap nor ascend high obstacles, such as weirs or steep falls, until the water temperature reaches a figure close to 40°F. A warm spell in February may encourage fish to run 10 miles upriver, but they are still likely to be within the lower reaches. At this time, fishing is therefore confined to these sections. Due to the reduction in numbers of two-sea-winter fish in recent years (their place being taken later in the season by grilse), catches will not be numerous – but the salmon will be of good size and excellent quality.

In April, the water temperature will reach 50°F, rising to the higher 50s in May. With greater energy resulting from the warming of their bodies, salmon are no longer deterred by obstacles and will swim for many miles in a single dash. In this upriver migration, they may cover as much as 20 miles in 2 or 3 days. We know this because sea lice have been found on fish that distance from the estuary, and sea lice drop off a salmon after 2 or 3 days in fresh water. This is the time to fish the middle reaches of a river.

In June, towards the end of the month, the first of the grilse arrive, and they run far and fast. In many small rivers, other than those which are chalk-based and spring-fed, grilse rely *mainly* on spates to move up the valley. I say *mainly* because, in my experience, small grilse, even those of up to 6 lb in weight, will ascend *spate* rivers in small numbers in conditions of drought. In 1989, towards the end of the worst drought since 1976, I knew of two 6 lb grilse taken in a spate river, from the same pool, 6 miles above the sea. One fell to a No. 8 Black Lure in moonlight during a spell of sea-trout fishing on the night of 21 August, and the other was taken on 10 September. This second grilse fell to a Toby which was cast upstream just before the first rains fell. Large sea trout swim up rivers in times of low water, and often weigh as much as grilse.

You will not be wrong if you credit salmon with the ability to anticipate the arrival of a spate before a drop of rain has fallen. A farmer whose land borders a deep pool in a salmon river told me that, in September 1989, after 4 months of drought and many hours before the arrival of first water following the rain, salmon started to leap in an excited manner in the pool. At the same time, the water bailiff observed fish run a salmon ladder 5 miles below the farmer's pool which they had previously refused to ascend. They knew a spate was coming. They also knew the extra water might not last and made the most of the time available. Within a matter of 24 hours they were jumping a weir 6 miles above the tidal waters at the rate of one every 2 minutes. Swimming on through the lower stretches of a river, they moved rapidly into the upper waters.

When planning a holiday on a little river, timing is critical for consistent success. You should choose a month when many fish are present and go to an area of river which they habitually frequent.

In recent years there has been a reduction in the numbers of two-sea-winter salmon and an increase in the runs of grilse in many rivers. Furthermore, from early spring, when the first entrants swim in from the sea, the population of salmon of all ages builds up continuously in a river until, and beyond, the end of the season. The later the month, the greater the number of fish. My choice, if no regard is paid to the flesh quality of salmon, would be September, followed by August and then July. If urged to pick a single time, I would choose the second half of August, when salmon are still in good condition. July is a hot, brassy month with a heat-wave risk. In August, the evenings draw in and one may fish until dusk without exhaustion. September presents the angler with an unhappy dilemma – whether to return or keep a gravid fish. I doubt whether many people would persuade a novice to return his first salmon if it was gravid. Indeed, with no one to advise him, he might not even recognize a hen with a swollen belly. But I can report the righteous glow that fills the experienced angler when he does the right thing: he will have contributed to the future of the salmon race. Such a return will be at little cost to himself because hens filled with roe are not worth eating.

The table below is given to support the July, August and September suggestions, and to draw attention to the increasing numbers of grilse in total salmon populations. The figures have been compiled from the rod returns of the 17 recorded rivers in the South-West Water area (now under the auspices of the NRA).

Fifteen years ago, the numbers of grilse and salmon caught in July, August and September would have been in the region of 35 per cent of the total. Today, reflecting increased grilse runs and reduced numbers of two-sea-winter salmon, the July, August and September catch is nearly 50 per cent of the total rod take.

Entries of salmon from the sea, their upriver progress and subsequent rod catches are dependent not only on months but also on water temperature and volume. Nevertheless, the grilse late-entry trend is showing an increase according to my experience, which is supported by the figures. Whether this trend will be reversed is not possible to predict, but it may happen due to the recently arranged cessation of the netting of two-sea-winter salmon off the coast of Greenland.

Percentage of summer rod catches in seasonal total

Year	July/Aug./Sept.	Season total	July to Sept. % of total
1974	1673	3318	50
1975	1138	3211	35
1976	616	1809	34
1977	567	2688	21
1978	555	1762	31
1979	1053	2252	47
1980	1753	3861	45
1982	538	1661	32
1983	736	1816	40
1984	531	1652	32
1985	2039	3173	64
1986	2294	3763	60
1987	1333	2641	50
1988	3054	4579	66
1989	924	1868	49
1990	725	1717	42
1991	588	1255	47
1992	1915	2659	72

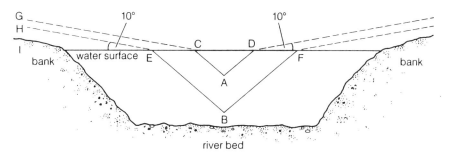

Windows of vision: (a) position of trout; (b) position of salmon; (c/d) trout's window; (e/f) salmon's window; (g/i) angler standing; (h/i) angler kneeling. The kneeling angler is almost invisible to the salmon; the standing angler's shoulders are visible. Neither is visible to the trout.

The senses of the salmon

Sight

At short range, say up to 10 yd, the salmon's sight is excellent but must be considered poor beyond that distance because of the light-scattering effect of water and suspended sediment in the river water. Salmon certainly see our flies well enough at normal distances if they are well presented, but the fly must be close to the fish in thick water.

The sight of salmon in poor light and at night is better than our own. This is due to the presence of a 'mirror' behind the light-sensitive cells of the retina (the *tapetum*). This mirror consists of a layer of cells (*iridocytes*) comprised of silver-coloured guanine. Incoming light passes through the retina, hits the tapetum and is reflected back through the retina. This 'double pass' use of the light is efficient at night but may be too effective for comfort by day. At high light intensities, a pigment discolours the tapetum, rendering it ineffective. What does all this mean to the angler? Probably that a salmon is able to see a fly, or other lure, in conditions of poor light which would defeat an underwater human.

There is no doubt that salmon have colour vision, and that this is enhanced in good light. They are most aware of colours at the red end of the spectrum (red, orange and yellow). Striped objects also attract attention. The success of black flies, fished off a floating line, can probably be attributed to the fact that black provides the greatest contrast to the sky. What the salmon sees of the angler and other above-surface objects is discussed on p. 86. But even at this stage, let me advise you to adopt a stealthy crouching approach on a little river.

Hearing

Whether a salmon is able to hear as such I do not know, but it is certainly sensitive to vibration. I take sound into consideration only as part of the general caution with which an angler ought to fish. A fisherman who shouts may also walk tall along the bank and stamp his feet – and we must take account of vibration. This is sensed by the nerve cells along the lateral line of the salmon. It is not unusual to see an angler, wearing thigh boots with studded soles, jump down off a bank onto the gravel bordering the edge of the river. The vibration caused by such an action scares salmon and these insensitive persons hook few fish. On the other hand, the vibration of an artificial spinning bait may attract salmon.

Smell and taste

The salmon has a tongue and two nostrils, which leads me to the conclusion that it has senses of taste and smell. Indeed, it is the sense of smell that, on the salmon's return from the sea, leads it to the river of its birth. Investigation may follow one of two paths: laboratory studies and observation whilst fishing.

Scientists have established that the nostrils contain receptors which are connected by the olfactory nerve to the olfactory lobes of the brain, where smell information is processed. There are taste buds on the tongue and also on the surface of the body in front of the mouth and in the back of the inside of the mouth; these report to the brain. So, as it has the ability to smell and taste, we should take care not to scare salmon by smells which they find deterrant and, equally, ensure that natural baits are tasty!

Women, because they emit pheromones, chemical messengers, which are attractive to male salmon, are at an advantage in the offering of tasty baits. Men are at a disadvantage: their hands, held in the river, deter salmon downstream of the angler.

I have had some success in catching both salmon and moles and have come to the conclusion that they both have a well-developed sense of smell. This has led me to camouflage any aroma emanating from my hands when fishing. Before setting a trap for a mole, or attaching a prawn to a mount, or threading two lobworms on a hook, I always rub my hands through earth. I cannot honestly say whether I catch more fish because of this precaution, but I do catch fish! With the fly or minnow it is a different matter. These lures are taken at speed, with no opportunity for a salmon to take a sniff. Worms, prawns and shrimps are seldom taken at speed, but they are inspected and, I suspect, sniffed. This is not hearsay. Whilst fishing the Test for salmon in the 1970s, I spent much time watching salmon confronted with a worm or prawn. Looking down through the clear water from the bough of a tree, their cautious approach and careful investigation of my bait was visible.

At the river bank we may observe the senses of the fish in action. Visually stimulated, the salmon moves to take the lure. If this is artificial, a metal Devon minnow, tube fly or plastic prawn, the object may be taken quickly into the salmon's mouth. After a moment, it will be ejected, which is why we strike to set the hook before the salmon spits out the lure. On the other hand, if the bait is natural, a *fresh* shrimp or lively worm, the bait will be taken into the mouth, punctured by the teeth, savoured and, after an interval, swallowed. That is why, when worm fishing, we have to give the salmon time to assess, chew to release the juices of the worm, and swallow. If you refer to p. 105, it will be noted that taste in fish has been a factor in angling since the seventeenth century, the years of 'old Oliver Henly', fishing companion of Izaak Walton. Care in natural bait preparation is still taken today.

Dick Haston, doyen prawn angler of the lower River Test, told me: 'The finest bait you could have would be to go down (to the sea) and catch the prawns alive, then cook them on the river bank. If you see a salmon at a prawn you will notice that he mouths it . . .' Dick also stated that stale prawns are almost always rejected.

It can be stated categorically that salmon do not feed in fresh water. I clean all the fish we catch and have yet to find a full stomach or, for that matter, anything inside at all. It is true that salmon take natural fly from time to time, and that they will toy with worms and prawns, but not to the extent that weight will be gained in the river or its loss arrested. I am often asked the age-old question: 'Why does a salmon take a fly?' The reason might be found among the following: a river feeding memory; aggression; curiosity; and a surprised automatic response to the sudden disturbance of its state of torpor by the appearance of an unusual moving object.

Head of 5 lb cock salmon. Note the kype (hook) on the lower jaw and the rear of the eye, which is in line with the rear end of the maxillary bone.

Distinguishing salmon from sea trout

The weight of grilse is in the region of 5 lb. The weight of large sea trout in pounds may reach double figures, and a 5 lb specimen is not uncommon. It is necessary to distinguish between salmon and sea trout, both of which may enter a river at the same time, because the start and finish of the open season for these fish may differ. A salmon caught in the River Teign in February may be retained whereas a sea trout must be returned to the river. The season for salmon opens on 1 February but that for sea trout opens on 15 March. On the River Camel, the salmon season extends to 15 December, but the last day of sea-trout fishing is 30 September.

To identify the fish three physical characteristics should be examined.

The head

The eye of a sea trout is wholly forward of the rear edge of the maxillary bone. In salmon the rear edge of the eye is in line with the rear edge of the maxillary bone. The head of a sea trout is more hunched than the streamlined head of a salmon.

The tail

The tail of a sea trout is square, although little sea trout (in the 12 oz – 1 lb range) have forked tails. The tail of a salmon is concave.

Scale count

Count the scales in a line from the rear of the adipose fin to the lateral line. There will be 13 or more in a sea trout. A salmon has 9–12 scales.

Head of 3¾ lb sea trout. The eye is forward of the rear end of the maxillary bone.

Salmon tail. The rear edge is concave.

Sea trout tail. The rear edge is straight. Note the seal tooth marks. Stream Foot, River Coquet, Northumberland.

I counted the scales on two sea trout and a salmon taken from my deep-freeze, with the following result:

Sea trout: 3 lb 12 oz = 16 scales

1 lb 6 oz = 15 scales

Salmon: 10 lb 4 oz = 11 scales

2 Characteristics of small rivers

Not all small rivers are spate rivers. Some salmon waters run down steep and fast from the moors and rocky places; these are the true spate rivers. Others spring in steady volume from chalk aquifers, or wind slowly through areas of gently sloping agricultural land, woods and forests. We are aware that, in order for salmon to leap weirs and other obstructions and to ascend to the higher sections of a watercourse, spate rivers must have rain even though salmon may enter the lower river in times of drought. But in chalk and agricultural waters, rain is not needed in the short term for salmon to ascend the river, unless there is some great obstruction to be overcome. These rivers flow more steadily in times of drought, losing volume only slowly. But both types need rain in order to *fish* well. This greatly depends upon resting salmon being stimulated by the addition of oxygen to the water by raindrops, and flow increases have a more marked effect than is the case in a great river. Even in a major river rain helps; in a small one it is almost essential.

Spate rivers

These are numerous on the west coast of the British Isles, where the land is rocky, often with a steep decline to the sea. Not only are these waters numerous on the Atlantic shores, but there are also many more of them than of the agricultural type. It is no exaggeration to say that the arrival of salmon in the upper reaches and spawning areas of these rivers is entirely dependent upon rainfall.

In times of drought, which may last for 1 or 2 months, or even longer, those fish which have entered the river are held in a state of torpor in small pools linked to each other by a shallow flow, trickling over stones. Not until rain falls on the hills and moors, bringing the feeder streams, brooks and ditches to life, will these stickles be covered to a depth which enables a salmon to move up to the next pool and beyond.

For the first half an hour of a spate, salmon are responsive to the many methods available to the angler. At the height of the spate they may also be taken in those places where they rest momentarily at the top of a demanding ascent, e.g. in the wide, slow tail of a pool which they have just entered. Finally, there are the golden hours when the river is dropping back.

A stranded tree top shows the height reached by this small river in a recent spate.

In between rainstorms, fish become 'potted' and difficult to catch. They are by no means uncatchable, as we shall see, but the chances are reduced. In drought, the worm, shrimp and twilight fly have terminated the freedom of many fish. The dry fly too may appeal. But, for a run of fresh, eager salmon, the angler must look to rain.

A small number of two-sea-winter fish will enter in early spring, in March and April, and a few of these may be caught. Throughout April, a steady drop in water level is the normal experience. By May, we may be in the situation of isolated pools, deep enough for the well-being of residents, and the chances are that this state will persist until mid-June. The Coronation of Queen Elizabeth II took place during the first week of June 1953, because records showed this to be almost always dry. The fact that it rained continuously on the day goes to show that, for Coronations and salmon fishing alike, one should never say 'never', and never say 'always'! Spates are likely after the middle of June and, as I write in June 1990, it is raining and has been for some days. Yesterday, after 3½ dry months, the following entry was made in my fishing diary:

24 June 1990 Salmon 10 lb. U/S No. 4 Mepps. Air 56°, water 53°. Level 2 in. below bottom of gauge after a good spate 2 days before, following 3½ months of drought. At a water temperature of 53°F a salmon will rise up to take a Mepps of large size thrown upstream. This fish took first chuck into neck of Luncheon Pool. Many swallows and swifts about. Damp and wet. Alison fell in and borrowed my spare trousers. We found a dipper's nest under a bank and the shuck of a hatched dragonfly. [U/S = upstream]

An earlier June entry reads:

24 June 1986 Cloudy and wet. Used sink-tip line. 1 in. Black Dart tube fly. 9 lb in Saucepan Handle and 9 lb under sycamore below Rock Hole.

It is not worth fishing the tail of this pool unless water circles this boulder in a spate.

Salmon lie immediately in front of weirs in high water.

Note that the fish in these two entries were two-sea-winter salmon, it being before the time of the first run of grilse. This run of one-sea-winter fish may start in the final week of June or early in July, depending on rainfall. The chance of success therefore increases in July, August and September, as we have seen in Chapter 1. This is confirmed by the many occasions on which family seaside holidays are swamped in August! On the final day of August 1974, and for the first 6 days of September, I took a mixture of grilse and two-sea-winter fish on fly from a small spate river: 6 lb on No. 1/0 Hairy Mary; 10 lb, 15 lb, 6 lb on the same fly; and 6 lb on No. 2 Hairy Mary on a lower water level. Then back to the No. 1/0 for two fish of 9 lb each in a full river. The conclusion to be drawn is that fishing visits to strange spate rivers should take place in August and September. In addition, remember that the equinoctial gales arrive in the third week of September and a stiff upstream wind is almost as helpful as rain. If I ignored flesh quality and had to choose 2 weeks likely to bring a full reward they would be the final fortnight of September – but the gravid hens should be returned. Some of these rivers continue their open seasons into October, November and the middle of December. The Tamar complex fishes until 14 October:

13 October 1982 Oak Tree Pool. Nicola again took a ciné film of a 9 lb salmon being played and netted by me. No. 2 Mepps. A great deal of water this month has brought up a number of fish.

The Camel, Fowey, Plym and Yealm in the south-west of England have their main runs of fish in the late autumn and early winter. These are spate rivers, but rain is likely in the final months of the year.

Lies in spate rivers

The water in these rivers is usually acid, which discourages the growth of weed. Furthermore, the violent flushes to which they are subject keeps the bed clear of mud. We thus have a river of jagged features, where salmon take up station in lies formed by faults in the bedrock, at the sides of turbulent pool necks formed of slate or granite, and where the current is diverted around boulders. It is rare to find salmon resting behind an obstruction because they dislike the water turbulence. Look for them in front of a boulder, just above the lip of a weir, or in a trough in the river bed. In high water, the tail of the pool is favoured, in front of the first stones and boulders forming the start of the next stickle.

A salmon likes to have 4 or 5 ft of water over its back; it follows that the lie at the tail of a pool will be vacated as the water level drops and the depth reduces. As the spate continues to fall away, salmon move up the pool to a lie in the centre, and then again to stations forming the sides of the pool run-in, where they will remain until the next spate, protected from view by bubbles and turbulence and where there is a good supply of oxygen. Thus, in a pool 75 yd long, there may be only three or four favoured resting places, each only a few feet long and a yard in width.

Unless a gillie with detailed knowledge of the particular river is employed, it will take an angler years to acquire an intimate knowledge of these lies. Due to the permanent nature of the river bed, the lies seldom change but are individually attractive only at specific water levels. The build-up of knowledge of fruitful places in a river takes years; it follows that it is best to learn one river in detail rather than have a sketchy knowledge of many.

A lie in front of a small waterfall.

Mark the water level with a stick on arrival at the river.

In his book L.R.N. Gray (1957) wrote:

It makes such a lot of difference to the catch if those fishing know the river well. Two average local rods would catch twice as many salmon here as half a dozen good visitors.

You should always have a water-level gauge of some description at the point where you reach the river after leaving the car. This need not be a post marked off in feet and inches; a natural feature is just as good. You may then tell at once whether a pool half a mile distant is fishable without having to

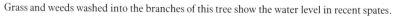

Grass and weeds washed into the branches of this tree show the water level in recent spates.

This boulder was covered within 1 hour of spate commencement. When water just washes over the top, the level is right to fish the tails of pools on this beat; if higher, the river becomes unfishable.

walk there to look and, in addition, which particular lie is likely to be occupied and which size of bait or fly will be seductive. In my own case, a land-drain pipe juts out of the opposite bank. If the pipe is covered, the river is too high everywhere; between the top and half-way down the pool tails will be best; one quarter up leads me to the rocky runs and pool necks, and so on. In another river, I inspect a large boulder which slopes into the river at the downstream end and take my guide from that, or from whether a bed of gravel which I can see from my car is submerged.

To illustrate the 'hour by hour' character of little spate rivers, consider the following account. For 2 days, Thursday and Friday, there was half a dustbin lid of rain outside my study. Early on Saturday, I went to the river to find it had not moved, the dry ground of several days having absorbed the rain. By Saturday evening, another half lid had been tipped out. On Sunday, at 7.00 am, the lid was once again half full. I drove to the river to find it in flood, swollen by the run-off from the saturated ground, and had to return home. At 10.00 am on Sunday, the rain stopped and no more was forecast. A dilemma confronted me: would the water have fallen by 1 ft by 6.00 pm, enabling me to fish in the evening, or would it be better to make an early start on Monday? Free time could not be made for both. The fear was that the water might have run away by Monday, but that is when I decided to go. One reason behind this decision was the date – 1 July; there were, as yet, no grilse in the river, only a few two-sea-winter fish. Grilse would not have time to run up by this particular day but might have arrived by the morrow, because July is the start of their season.

From this timetable it is clear that the local angler has an advantage in 'catching it just right'.

To continue this story. On Monday morning, on arrival at the river, the water level was low, confining fishing to pool necks. No grilse were seen but one salmon turned under the fly. This fish was in rough water at a pool run-in. It was tried with a number of flies, including a surface lure, but refused to come again. The water temperature was 53°F and the air 59°F. The water temperature may have been too low for a surface lure.

Before leaving this description of spate rivers, let us consider the effect of acidity on fish. When the first spate comes down after a dry period of several weeks, it is more acid than the normal flow; it carries debris and crumbled peat and the water is likely to be dark in colour. I always go out to fish in such conditions because volume of water is an over-riding factor, and some success is usually achieved (as has been seen from the diary quotes). But the second and subsequent spates are better. The water will be cleaner after the first washout and more fish may have arrived. Many anglers hold that the acid, dirty water of the first spate sickens fish, making them reluctant to take the fly. I believe this to be true, but there are always exceptions!

At the present water height, salmon will only lie 2 yd downstream of Lara Bingham's hand in this pool which is 100 yd in length. When water reaches the level indicated by the white 1 ft ruler, salmon will be caught as they pause in the tail of the pool.

Chalk and lowland rivers

These are not so numerous as the spate waters and, in the case of the chalk streams, the water is alkaline. Because of the slow flow and meandering nature of the river, mud is deposited on the bed and weeds are a common feature. The upriver migration of salmon is not subject to the vagaries of rainfall unless an obstruction has to be overcome.

In a dry period, I recall seeing salmon move up the River Frome; they progressed at a walking pace close to the bottom of the river. On the lower Test, at Broadlands, grilse arrived in July unless the water was running at a very low rate of flow, and even then one or two appeared. The same observations apply to the little Dorset Piddle which, despite its brook size, used to hold some large salmon. On that river, a lie in front of a hatch may be vacant and then, when inspected through polarized spectacles the following day, a fish may be seen waving his tail in front of the wooden boards and opening and closing his jaws from time to time. More consistent fishing may thus be had on these rivers than on the spate streams; a natural bait is particularly effective when there is no exciting flush of fresh water. If you have a weekly rod on such a water you should attend at weekly intervals regardless of the rainfall. Sooner or later a salmon will be yours.

These observations are meant to suggest not that more fish will be caught on chalk streams than on spate rivers, but that it is always worth trying.

One might sum up the comparison as follows: chalk streams, many days with few rewards; spate streams, few days with many rewards.

Lies in chalk and lowland rivers

The lies on these rivers are subject to alteration from year to year. Beds of mud and gravel shift in winter floods and where, one season, fish lie in front of a mud bank, by the following spring that bank may have been washed away. You generally have to look to the deep holes, bends in the river where fish lie under the outside bank, the long gaps between trailing weeds on shallow chalk stickles, and in front of the rising tail of a pool for fish. Beneath a bankside tree whose roots have been washed out is always worth a try and, in hot weather, the brassy days of July, your fly should pay attention to the streamy runs.

Many of these rivers have man-made groynes of wood jutting into the river; these are provided to afford lies, temporary resting places for travelling fish. Do not expect to find a fish in the turbulence behind the boards of which they are constructed; expect it to lie a yard or two off the groyne and slightly downstream.

Each type of river has individual charm, but the angler must adopt the methods suited to the water. Fly, spinner, and worm and prawn if we accept the latter two baits, are at our disposal. We shall see which to adopt and where.

3 Playing salmon

The process of exhausting a hooked salmon starts the moment the line tightens and the rod tip bends. The majority of salmon hooked on the fly will be downstream of the angler, as will those hooked when spinning deep in cold water. In warm water, the fish is more likely to 'take' opposite or above the angler when he is fishing the worm, shrimp or prawn, or casting a large Mepps or Toby upstream in summer and retrieving fast. In the latter case, the angler may stay in the position from which he cast but, if the fish is below him, he ought to move to a position opposite or below it. A salmon will not tire rapidly if it is downstream of the angler, even if his rod is well bent, because the pull exerted by the rod is counteracted by the assistance given to the fish by the current. Therefore, when a fish has been hooked in the downstream position, the angler ought at once to move down opposite the fish unless it is in the tail of the pool. If the fish has been hooked just above the pool run-off, the angler ought to do his best to persuade the salmon to move into the middle of the pool; in that position, the angler may then place himself opposite to the salmon. The majority of salmon hooked in the tail of a pool will acquiesce to a steady upstream draw, sliding forward without fuss *if they have not seen the angler*.

As well as positioning himself opposite or below the fish, the angler ought to stay out of sight. The hooked salmon does not understand what has happened when it is hooked. It does not know about human beings, rods, lines and salmon flies. All it knows is that something strange is attached to its jaw and that this insignificant thing is making maintaining its balance in the currents of the river difficult. It does not know in which direction to swim, or whether to move at all, in order to relieve itself of this attachment. But everything changes if it sees a threatening object, you, moving on the bank – it rushes away, up- or down-river. Therefore, on hooking a salmon, it is advantageous for the fisherman to remain out of sight. I like to play a salmon from behind a bush, whilst kneeling on the bank, or wading tucked below the skyline. If this concealment is maintained, a steady pressure may be exerted on the fish without getting a violent response. This pressure should be maintained for as long as possible with the rod over the river and the line 'up and down'. The salmon will counteract this upward pull by putting its nose on the river bed, and it will tire itself in its endeavour to keep in that position.

The salmon of 20 August 1988 (p. 63)

The prominent positions of these two men will frighten a salmon to further effort. The netsman should be tucked under the bank. The rodsman should be on his knees or also under the bank.

above right: The netsman is holding the net correctly now that the fish is inside (no weight on aluminium shaft). The salmon should have entered head-first, not tail-first.

below: The head of the salmon should be at the bottom of the net.

As soon as it feels its strength ebbing, it will move. It will also shift if subjected to side strain. If the angler lowers his rod and, at the same time, swings it towards or over his bank upstream of his stand, he will exert side strain on the fish. To counteract this pull, the salmon will point its head upstream towards the far bank. The river will now press upon the flank of the salmon closest to the angler and the fish will swim upstream. So, off it goes, up and across, with the angler maintaining a steady pull. If too much pressure is exerted, it will either leap or turn and run downriver.

Aerial gymnastics are to be avoided. Leaping is cut to a minimum if the fish is not handled roughly and visibly. Firm pressure, constant but not excessive, should be your aim. Of course, there will always be the exception, the occasional leaper. After all the Latin name for the salmon, *Salmo*, means 'the leaper'. Although general advice can be given in the controlled playing of salmon, there are fish, like human beings, which refuse to accept the normal paths of life. One such springs to mind:

1 May 1987 10 am. Half-way down The Bend. Ran out of top of pool, then came back. Jumped five times. 11 lb. 1¼ in. Black Dart tube fly. Floating line.

That fish was violent. And strong too. And helpful. If you cannot have a quiescent fish, opt for one which runs hard and fast upriver. It will soon be breathless. A fast upriver rush against heavy water and a firm pull from the rod knocks the steam out of any fish. For this particular fish, it was even worse; it jumped five times on the way, each crash a solar plexus punch. The fact that it did not come unstuck is evidence of the desirability of dropping the rod point when a salmon leaps. This is an old controversy: tight line *v.* slack line whilst the fish is in the air. I am a slack-line man. When a salmon jumps, down goes my rod point, to be raised immediately the fish is back in the water. In my early days, I hung on tight, all the time, and lost the fish! Today, I slacken, the hook rarely comes away and the nylon is never broken if it is of 15 lb BS (breaking strain). A fish of two or three sea-winters will give about 2 seconds notice of its intention to leap by a violent underwater acceleration. Those seconds are sufficient warning. A grilse may leap without notice, flinging up and twisting as it goes. The grilse gives no warning. Even so, I do my best to see that it does not twist against a tight line or fall back on a taut leader.

So far we have considered the leaper and the helpful fish that fights upstream of our position. The fish that runs downstream, and sooner or later they all try, must be persuaded otherwise by guile. You cannot just hang on or the hook may bend open or tear free.

Consider first the fish which turns downriver, swimming fast for the tail of the pool. Keep a tight hold on it until it is within about two rod lengths of the run-off, then let the line go slack. This slackening may be achieved by dropping the rod point of a fly rod and simultaneously stripping 3 or 4 yd of line from the reel. If you are using a spinning rod with fixed-spool reel, flip over the bail arm for 3 or 4 seconds; with a multiplier, click off the check for the same interval. The removal of all pressure will prompt the fish to turn about; it will face upstream and thus be able to breathe, as the water flows through its mouth and washes out through the gills. You can successfully stop a salmon in this way in about four cases out of five, but all depends upon acting in time. If the salmon reaches that area where the water is being sucked down to the next level, you are too late and it will continue on, helped by the current.

After the 3 or 4 seconds slack-line interval, tighten on the fish gently and 'walk it up', it will follow quietly, sliding upstream through the water. 'Walking-up' is simple. It is a smooth way of moving a salmon out of danger from a position near the tail of a pool to a safe area in the middle or top.

Hold the rod out horizontally and at right angles to the bank, then walk slowly upriver without using the reel, just holding the line tight against the butt of the rod. At first, the salmon may barely shift and the rod will become well bent, but then it will follow, unresisting, supine, its smooth flanks and nose sliding through the parted water. As soon as safety is attained the angler should shorten his line and again position himself opposite or below the fish.

At times, a salmon will set off for the sea and be almost unstoppable. Out of the tail of the pool it goes. Now you bless your backing and the unresisting needle knot which joins it to the line. You should also let the line go slack and prepare for a wetting. The fish will probably halt in the next pool if it feels no drag; in fact a slack loop of line, pressed downstream by the current, will pull from behind, possibly causing it to move upriver again, but this is optimistic. Slack line, washing about, is dangerous. It may snag. It has to be risked. So, there you are on the bank, there is a static salmon in the water, and between you 50 or 60 yd of river. Follow the fish along the bank. But if there is an obstruction – a bankside tree with branches sweeping the water – what then? With a steady pull on the line, it might come back, or it might not. Provided that you are not reckless, a salmon warrants a wetting. Take the wallet from your hip pocket and place it on the bank, not forgetting to preserve your flask, descend into the water and flounder on. Such excitements are worthwhile, a part of fishing in little rivers, but not to be entered upon lightly if the flow is fast and deep.

15 June 1980 No spate since last week of March. Now a good flood. 1.15 pm. Rock Hole. 8½ lb. 1½ in. Black Dart tube fly. This fish went down almost to Tailer Pool 200 yd below. I had to follow, soaked to chest in crossing river. Netted from opposite bank.

After 10 weeks of drought that fish was important. It must be harvested. In I went. Out he came. All the way down the river, the Gye net remained on my back as my thigh boots filled. Full boots are not heavy whilst in the water and they protect your knees and shins from sharp rocks and solid boulders. Washed on, I landed on a flat rock on the far side, trapped the fish in the net and knocked him on the head with the priest, which was safely held on the cord around my neck. I lay down flat on this wet rock whilst my heart beat went down from an estimated 125 beats per minute to a normal 70. I raised my legs to allow the water to cascade from my boots onto my waist. It was warm water. It didn't matter. After putting a cord around the salmon's tail and through its gills, I struggled back across the river to my home bank.

A final point on playing a salmon: don't allow it to reach the point of absolute exhaustion in heavy water. It ought to be netted whilst still able to hold its own against the current. A heavy fish, totally unable to control itself, may be swept downriver and lost if it no longer has the strength to respond to 'walking-up'.

The salmon of 30 July 1990 (p. 74)
Lara Bingham correctly cuts her silhouette . . . the salmon can now see her . . .

. . . and make a greater effort . . .   . . . in vain.

A two-sea-winter salmon
of 10 lb can be lifted
by a hand grip on the tail
wrist with hand
up or down.

4 Landing salmon

The three stages – hooking, playing and landing salmon – are each fraught with the danger of loss, but landing carries the least risk. The salmon has a say in whether or not it is hooked, and it may cunningly snag the line during the fight. Your actions will only be partly responsible for the successful accomplishment of the first two stages. But, once you have fought your fish to a standstill, a loss at the end will be your fault. The methods discussed below apply whether you are fishing the fly, the worm, the prawn, or sallying forth with a spinning rod and Devon minnow. To a limited extent, the choice of landing method is governed by the physical characteristics of the river and any regulations in force on that water. The gaff, for example may not be allowed at all, or only between certain dates. Time of year is also a factor, for grilse run from July onwards and with them only certain methods are successful.

The Gye net

I never go salmon fishing at any time of the year without a 24 or 25 in. Gye net held across my back by a peel sling. A 30 in. diameter Gye is also available but, in my opinion, unless you are fishing a river known for very large salmon, the advantage of the added size is more than offset by the

A 24 in. Gye net and peel sling. The shaft is cut short at the top by 6 in. Pull the Velcro tab at the bottom to release.

A salmon should be netted head-first . . .

and the net then lifted at the bracket joining net and shaft . . .

. . . or dragged ashore.

encumbrance of carrying so large a piece of equipment along the bank. I have yet to lose any salmon, my own or anyone else's, at the net, and am happy to be a hostage to that statement! Confidence will attend you if the netting is carried out correctly. It is easy to lose a salmon at the net through faulty actions; it is difficult if you adopt the following techniques.

Let us first consider netting your own fish. This is much easier than netting someone else's or having a third party net yours. Act as follows. Wait until the fish has had its say and is at the wallowing stage, having shown its white belly several times. In other words, it is tired and incapable of making a further run. Then, and not until then, pull the peel-sling Velcro tab to let the net drop down with your hand on the rubber grip at the end of the shaft. Put one foot into the net ring and draw out the sliding shaft. Stand in the river so that you are on the same level as the fish and place the net beside you on the bank. With both hands on the rod, work the salmon upstream of your position, pick up the net with one hand, then turn the fish and swim it head-first downriver into the net. The head of a salmon is heavier than the tail. Once the head, followed by the body, has slid down into the bag it will be held there by the current. If you are fishing from the right bank, the net would be held in the right hand, which would be downstream of your body; if on the left bank, the left hand is used. Once in the bag, do not lift the net by the aluminium shaft, which may bend; drag the fish ashore. To lift it up onto the bank, grip the metal bracket at the shaft/ring junction.

There are pitfalls which may be encountered. Do not attempt to haul your fish upstream to the net. The salmon's nose will be the first portion to touch the meshes of the net ring and, if a hook point protrudes from its mouth and catches in these meshes, the hook may be pulled out and the fish lost. This is particularly so when using a treble hook, of which one point may be standing proud. Do not attempt to bring the net up from behind the fish, scooping at it tail-first with the salmon pointing upstream – it only has to swim ahead to escape. In slack water, a salmon may be drawn towards you into the extended net, but its head must be kept above the level of the net ring in case a hook protrudes. Do not slide a salmon over the net rim in shallow water or a hook may catch in the meshes – choose a knee-deep place.

It is hard to net a salmon in fast water, which may sweep the extended net into the bank. Try to find a slack bay; lack of current will confuse the directional awareness of the salmon, and you can hold out the net. The late Robert Pashley, doyen salmon angler of the River Wye, used to stamp about with his boots in a bay to raise clouds of mud; once enveloped by this thick soup, the salmon lost direction and floundered at his mercy.

If netting someone else's fish, be sure to tell the angler to slacken the line the moment the fish enters the net. To this end, the rodsman must position himself where he can see when the net has engulfed the fish. I have twice nearly lost salmon when netting for another angler who has pulled the fish out of the net; in both cases the rodsman could not see that the fish was already in the bag. One of these experiences involved a fish of 20 lb. I managed to push two or three fingers into its mouth, grip it around the wrist of the tail with the other hand, lift it onto the bank and, for safety, sit on my squirming victim until I could use the priest. If anyone doubts the presence of teeth in the mouth of a fresh-run salmon I can assure him they are there – my fingers were lacerated!

Gye nets have polished metal rims. The flash of bare aluminium may stimulate a salmon to a final effort to escape. Paint the rim a dull colour. Additionally, the net bag ought to submerge at once and not float on the water surface. To assist rapid sinking, drop a stone into the bag or twist a strip of lead or copper permanently onto the bottom meshes. A further point. When in the carrying position the shaft is across the net ring. The handle then protrudes towards the ground, and the end of the shaft extends by 8 in. beyond the ring, poking out above the shoulder. These two ends will stop you scrambling under branches, or climbing through a riverside tree when following a fish. Shorten the end of the shaft by 6 in. then split the shaft end with a hacksaw to enable the stop plug to be re-inserted.

Do not rely on a small net. Small nets only accommodate small fish. Avoid nets with Y-shaped folding arms; they may fail to open if the ends of the arms catch in the net mesh, and a salmon may slide out over the sagging cord which joins the arms.

The gaff

On some rivers, the gaff may be used throughout the season. On others, it may be prohibited before 15 April, to conserve kelts attempting to return to the sea, and, after 30 August, to allow gravid hens to be returned so that they can continue their upstream journey to the spawning beds. On my home river, the gaff is illegal at all times, a prohibition which has my full support because it is a cruel instrument which defaces a beautiful fish.

If a river holds fish of 25 lb or more, a case may be argued for carrying a telescopic gaff on your belt, in addition to any net on your back. Such specimens are a challenge to any net, but rare. The chances are that the gaff might be carried for 10 years and never used. Speaking for myself, I have ruled out the gaff entirely. There are no absolute figures but it is unlikely that a salmon of suitcase size will be encountered on a little spate river because the size of salmon tends to be relative to the size of the water. There is no doubt that a salmon may offer a chance to the gaff before it is ready for netting, in other words before it is played out. A quick snatch at the fish as it swims by may succeed, but there is a risk if the gaff touches the leader. Also, if you miss, the fish will then know what it is all about and fight harder.

A telescopic gaff.

A tailer in use.

When it is in use, place the extended gaff beside you on the bank as the fight comes to a conclusion. Then, with the fish almost stationary in front of you, place the shaft, hook down, across the salmon's back at the point of balance. Aim to pull in the gaff point, which should be needle-sharp, below the dorsal fin, draw the fish towards the bank and then lift it onto the grass or heather. There must be no pause; one continuous movement will ensure that the salmon does not slip off the hook. If a metal telescopic gaff is used it may then be snapped shut, reversed, and the salmon hit on the head with the handle. In my early salmon-fishing days, I shattered the cork handle of my gaff by administering the last rites to more fish than it could stand. But, the gaff is no longer for me.

The tailer

Three facts may recommend the tailer to you: it is easy to carry; the wire noose may land a large salmon; the fish may be returned unharmed. Let the emphasis be placed upon the word *may*, for the method is a sure way, sooner or later, of losing a salmon. In addition, it is unsuitable for grilse. These slim fish of 4, 5 or 6 lb in weight, and at times more, have no knuckle to the tail so there is nowhere for the wire noose to settle and tighten. No, the tailer loses fish. All the same, it is humane and could be carried for the rare chance of a large salmon on a big fish river in addition to the net.

When a fish has been played to a standstill, slide the brass ring at the end of the thin wire to the end of the metal shaft. Together with the thick, twisted cable, withdrawn from the hollow handle, a bow will be formed which may be placed over the tail. Move this noose up the body to just behind the dorsal fin, then pull smartly at right angles to the body. The noose will slide back down the body, tightening as it goes, and settle just above the tail – if you are lucky! If unlucky, you will be left with a dangling wire in one hand, the rod in the other, and a frightened salmon renewing its fight for freedom.

Whilst it is unwise to rely on a tailer after grilse arrive in mid-June, it may be carried in the spring when only two- and three-sea-winter fish are in the river. These fish have substantial tails. Twenty-five years ago I did not possess a Gye net, relying instead on a tailer in early spring and in the autumn, and the gaff in the intervening months. The first time I used my tailer was as follows:

15 March 1967 River Taw. Fox & Hounds Hotel. Beat No. 8. Millers Pool. 3.30 pm. 2 in. Yellow Belly. 9 lb. Tailed in a slack backwater.

The memory persists of surprise and relief when this untried device worked and the fish was dragged across a sandbank onto the grass.

Beaching

On each pool of your beat be aware of shelving beaches where a fish may be drawn ashore. If you do not know the area, it is advisable to inspect in advance the water you are to fish and to memorize danger spots as well as landing places. Have a plan ready.

Beaching is simple and safe. Play out the fish and head it towards the beach whilst you walk backwards over the ground, keeping an eye on the salmon. When its head touches the sand or gravel and it lies on its side, walk down to one side, reeling-up as you approach, until you are behind the salmon. Grip the wrist of the tail with the circle of the thumb and forefinger, with the palm of your hand over the tail, and push it up the bank.

Beaching is a safe method. Push from behind and then lift the fish up the bank.

The commonest way to lift a salmon is with the little finger towards the tail. The position of the hand may be reversed if the angler is in the water and wishes to hold the fish high.

A grilse has no knuckle to the tail. It may be lifted by placing the hand on top of its head and pressing in the gill flaps.

The hand

If a beach is not available and you have no landing equipment, all is by no means lost. A satisfactory experience awaits you. A two-sea-winter salmon may be lifted out of the water in the grip described above. If you are standing in deep water, reverse the position of your hand and lift with the palm towards the salmon's head; the salmon may then be held level with the shoulder as you step ashore. Grip will be improved if you wipe your hand over mud, earth or sand. A grilse cannot be lifted out of the water by the tail which, having no knuckle, will collapse and slide through your hand. Instead, place the hand over the head of the fish, with the palm and forearm lying back along his body, and press in the gill flaps with the thumb on one side and two or three fingers on the other. Squeeze hard; the gill flaps will collapse, the fingers and thumb will obtain purchase under the skull, and the fish may be lifted out of the river. It is of little help to be told by an onlooker: 'Get your fingers in his gills'. Try it on a squirming fish and it will probably twist free.

Fifteen years ago, I lent my net one day to a Dutchman who had forgotten his. No sooner was he out of sight and recall than I hooked a grilse. With no place for beaching, and being ignorant at that time of the head hold, I tried to grip its tail. It squirmed and was away. Contrast this with the following short diary entry:

19 August 1988 First stickle below Stoney Pool. 1¼ in. Black Dart tube fly. 4 lb 8oz. Net fell in river. Landed fish by grip across top of head. Retrieved net.

What actually happened was that a bramble caught in the peel sling, pulled open the Velcro tab and released the net, which fell into the river as I leaped from rock to rock whilst playing this fellow in and out of the boulders. Some 20 yd downstream, the fish was picked out by the head grip, tapped on the skull with the priest, then placed with the rod in safety on the bank. The net was recovered from 3 or 4 ft of water.

Pushing a grilse onto a rock. The water is too fast to hold out the net.

A thought which may save you embarrassment. It is unwise to volunteer to land a salmon for someone else. He may be incompetent and you will be blamed for the loss. Assist only if requested. Stand back. Enjoy the fun. A novice landing a salmon is a situation not lacking in surprises – and sometimes humour!

5 Fly-fishing tackle

Rods

It would be possible to fish a little river throughout the season with a stiff, 9 ft trout rod, provided that it had a butt extension to support the wrist when playing a salmon. This assumes that you could spin in the cold water of early spring instead of fishing the fly on a sunken line, for this would be beyond the capacity of a rod of this length. If wooded valleys are to be included in the scene, where the river runs through an arch of branches, this may be the longest rod for which there is room.

There are advantages as well as limitations to single-handed fly rods, but the limitations are few when using a floating fly line on a narrow river. The advantages are clear:

1 Room to cast in restricted spaces.
2 Less vertical height, meaning less of the length of the rod will be visible to fish.

You could get by covering open water with a 9 ft rod if you remember my definition of a small river: 'If you can drop your fly under the far bank without a false cast, using a rod of 10 ft 6 in., then you are on a small river'. It will be remarked at once that the 9 ft rod is shorter but, even so, the fly would not fall far short of the far bank and the fish might be at your feet.

Home-made rod-racks in the author's garage.

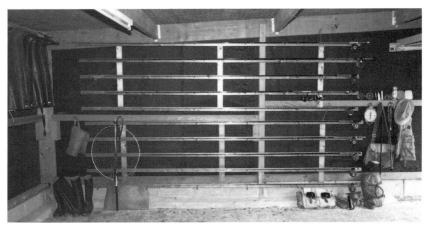

I do not advocate fishing solely with so short a rod; it is better to have a selection. What is put forward for your consideration is that you can *always* use a short rod, whereas you might knock the top off a long rod on overhanging trees. Long rods have their place on a wide river, about which there is little to be written in support of the single-handed outfit. In selecting a rod, we seek the following:

1 The ability to present the fly, if necessary against the wind, and mend the line.

2 The power to control, tire and, if necessary, hold an exhausted fish against the current.

3 The length to lift the line over bankside bushes and clear a snagged line from an underwater boulder when playing a fish.

4 A short length for use in restricted places.

5 A light rod weight and a well-balanced action.

Clearly, one rod cannot meet all these requirements, although all should fulfil the first three. Ideally one would have a selection of three rods to cope with different rivers and changing water conditions and, if you are a normal angling squirrel, you will soon acquire them! They should be purchased in the following order of priority if little rivers of all types are to be fished but you cannot afford to buy all at the same time:

1 9 ft o in. plus a butt extension.

2 10 ft 6 in. plus a butt extension.

3 12 ft o in. double-handed.

Nothing written above alters my view that you should always use the longest rod possible, up to a maximum of about 12 ft on a little river, provided that it is suited to the conditions under which you are fishing. It is river conditions which limit rod length. What are these limitations and how may we cope with them? When should the three rods be used if we possess them all?

The 9 ft rod

This is the minimum length with the power to control a salmon and to enable you to carry out your wishes. An 8 ft 6 in. or even an 8 ft spinning rod could be used but these are stiffer than fly rods. It is true that you might kill a salmon on an 8 ft 6 in. trout rod, but the fight will be longer and the chance of losing the fish greater. The 9 ft rod should be used only where you are forced down to this length by a canopy of overhead branches, and where growth on the opposite bank of a narrow stream makes casting hazardous. You will almost certainly be wading inside the canopy and the rod will be able to reach halfway to the far bank. The risk of a salmon going around an underwater rock and snagging the line is thus not great, because the rod is long enough to clear the line. Neither is additional length needed to lift the line over bankside bushes when playing a fish – all the bushes are at your back and above you.

9 ft Hardy Farnborough No. 1 plus butt extension. Line No. 7/8. Leeda Dragonfly 100 reel.

This rod should be made of carbon fibre or fibreglass. With split cane, power will only be available if the rod is stiff, and thus heavy. We need a lightweight rod for single-handed use. Before purchasing a single-handed rod, make the following assessment. Hold the rod with the thumb of your casting hand on top of the cork handle, stiffen the wrist and, with the rod horizontal, test the action. This should be done without fitting the reel and line. From the curve as the rod flexes, it will at once be apparent if it is soft and thus unsuitable. If you have to purchase by mail order, look for a line rating of No. 7/8 on the AFTM scale (see p. 52). Hardy market rods of this description, but be sure to order the butt extension.

The 10 ft 6 in. rod

This is the most versatile of the three. If rated at AFTM No. 7/9, it has the power to kill any salmon likely to be met on the rivers under consideration, and to do so with authority. The length is sufficient to:

1 Keep the major portion of the line out of the water when playing a salmon (much drowned line is a major cause of fish loss).

2 Lift the line clear of an underwater boulder around which the fish has taken a turn.

3 Lift the line over a bush on the bank if you have to follow a fish by running along the bank.

In addition, the extra 18 in. ensures improved line mending – it is easier to move the fly from side to side over a salmon, or draw it upstream and let it drift back. Such a rod, in the language of a Devonshire man would be described as 'a proper job'.

When fishing in low, clear water conditions, you are constantly dogged by the requirement to exercise stealth, to creep forward on your knees, to wade under the bank, to cut your silhouette against the sky. Not only you – also the rod!

The higher the rod in the vertical plane, the greater the visible length to the fish. With this rod, 18 in. less of the rod top will appear in the salmon's window than with a 12 ft rod – and if you keep the rod tip low, this may mean none at all! The description 'daisy-cutter' applies to a ball bowled along the ground in cricket; we might adopt the description 'dipper-swatter' for horizontal casting, because this bird rarely flies more than a foot above the water in its journeys up and down the river.

This rod has the power to fish a sinking line and the delicacy to fish a wake fly across the river surface. It is not out of place in a spate in a medium-width river. Recently I purchased a carbon-fibre weapon of this length, a Bruce & Walker tubular rod described as the single-handed AFTM No. 7/9 Salmon and Sea Trout. A 4 in. butt extension was supplied to screw into the socket which normally accommodates the rubber button. At my request the rod was finished at the factory with matt varnish to reduce light flash when casting. I chose a tubular rod because I do not like the light reflection of the flat surfaces of a hexagraph section rod of split cane or carbon fibre. Goddard and Clarke (1980), using underwater photography, cleared up many of the mysteries of 'what the fish sees'.

We conducted a number of tests using gloss-varnished and matt-varnished rods in conditions of bright sunlight, at different distances from the window [the trout's vision window]. In every case, when a gloss-varnished rod (particularly a flat-sided split-cane rod) caught the sunlight, it heliographed its presence to the observer below the water.

For a single-handed rod of this length, carbon is the material to choose. At one time I fished with a 10 ft Sharpe's Sea Trout Special of resin-impregnated split cane. The rod had a built-in 2 in. cork extension behind the reel fitting and would handle a salmon with ease. A superb rod for the superman with steel wrist and palm of well-cured leather!

10 ft 6 in. Bruce & Walker, Salmon and Sea Trout plus butt extension. Line No. 7–9. Hardy St John reel.

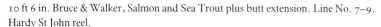

12 ft Hardy Graphite. Line No. 9. Reel Hardy Perfect 3¾ in.

Allow me to tell you of the first time I used my new 10 ft 6 in. rod. The fact that the victim was a peal does not make the event any less exciting than the playing of a grilse. A heavy peal in the dark is the equal of any grilse. The diary entry reads:

19 June, 1990 Peal 3 lb 12 oz. 1 in. Alexandra tube tied by Lara [my youngest daughter]. Right in the tail of Cottage Pool. Moonless after a little rain. One savage take. A great fighter which leaped with a fearful crash under the far bank. Before dusk I saw a hobby flash along the river after swallows or house martins.

[The hobby is a small, rare, migrant falcon which arrives in this country from Africa in the spring. It nests in the southern counties of England.]

The 12 ft double-handed rod

For the first 25 years of my salmon-fishing life, I possessed only one rod, a 12 ft A. H. E. Wood, No. 2 split cane with steel centre by Hardy. This killed salmon from Sutherland in Scotland to the rivers of England's south coast. Its retirement was forced by overwork and many stressed landings. The diary reads:

28 September 1975 Test. Rookery. River high after much rain. Water coloured. 2 pm. Rookery Pool. 8½ lb. No. 1/0 Hairy Mary. Broke rod top when netting fish. 6 pm. Ash Tree. 7 lb. Same fly. Tony one on prawn.

The top of the rod was snapped off because my thigh boots stuck in the mud of the river bed and I sat down whilst netting the salmon. The rod struggled on for another two or three seasons with the spare top, but the cane had become soft and would not put out a line into the wind. That is one of the deficiencies of split cane: it does lose resilience with use and the passage of years.

I still enjoy using a 12 ft double-handed Sharpe's impregnated split-cane rod, which is in three sections, spliced together and bound with insulating tape. The cane is impervious to water, needs no maintenance, and the matt finish is dull and non-reflective. The action is slow but delightful, and the weight of 15 oz is not excessive. You would have to buy one secondhand, for they are no longer made.

So, carbon fibre it ought to be for lightness (about 10 oz for 12 ft) and a long, resilient, maintenance-free life. But when would we use a 12 ft rod when all the time our need is to keep low? Why, in a spate. When the river runs full and stained, the flow is powerful and aids the fighting fish – that is when we bless the length and strength of our 12 ft rod in an open moorland river.

Later in this book (p. 127–37) a visit to the River Coquet in Northumberland is recorded. Close to the river is the town of Alnwick, headquarters of House of Hardy. I took the opportunity of visiting the factory where I selected three rods suited to our needs; all are made of carbon fibre. James Hardy arranged for these to be fitted with suitable reels. These are the particulars:

1   12 ft 6 in. Favourite. AFTM No. 9. Double-handed.
Marquis No. 1 Salmon reel of 3⅞ in. diameter.

12 ft 6 in. Hardy Favourite. Hardy Marquis No. 1 Salmon reel.

below left: 10 ft 6 in. Hardy De Luxe plus butt extension. Reel Hardy St John.

below: 9 ft 6 in. Hardy Sovereign with built-on butt extension. Hardy Marquis No. 10 reel.

2 10 ft 6 in. plus 4 in. screw-in butt extension. De Luxe. AFTM No. 7/8.
Single-handed.
St John reel of 3⅞ in. diameter.

3 9 ft 6 in. Sovereign with permanent, built-on butt extension. AFTM No. 7/8.
Single-handed.
Marquis No. 10 reel of 3¾ in. diameter.

Fly lines

When fishing a little river you do not require a great variety of fly lines.
Each of the rods listed, even the longest, will perform satisfactorily with an
AFTM No. 8 double-tapered line. Let us suppose you possess all three rods.
In this circumstance, all you need is one reel with three interchangeable
spools, on each of which should be placed 100 yd of 20 lb monofilament
backing. The backing should be joined to the fly line by a needle knot which
will run smoothly through the rod rings. Monofilament is preferable to
braided backing, which creates greater water drag when playing a fish and
has to be joined to the fly line with the more bulky Albright knot. The three
spools will accommodate a floating line, a fast-sinking line, and a floating line
with a sinking tip. I do not suggest that this minimum of equipment is ideal.
You would be forced to cease fishing if the single reel broke down. Two or
three reels would be better if you are contemplating a holiday in the Hebrides
away from the postman and the tackle shops! But it demonstrates that
floating, sinking and sink-tip lines, all on the same size of reel and of the same
AFTM line rating may be interchanged between the three rods.

The AFTM Scale of line weights must be understood. Clearly a line of steel-
hawser weight will break any fly rod. At the opposite extreme, if the line is
made of button thread, sufficient weight will not be available to flex the fly
rod. The weight of the line must match the power of the rod. This power is
not governed by the length of the rod but, to put it simply, by its stiffness.
The AFTM Scale enables us to match the line weight to the capacity of the
rod to propel that line through the air. We might have two single-handed rods
each 10 ft long. One could be rated for lines of AFTM No. 4 or No. 5, and
the other for No. 7 or No. 8. The first would be a gentle rod, suited to fishing
fine nylon and dry flies with delicate hooks at medium range and, in its
'bendiness', to accommodate the stress of a take without the fine tackle
breaking. The second rod would enable the angler to cast the heavier line a
long distance and, if necessary, against the wind, but would snap fine nylon if
a large trout made a smash take.

The AFTM Scale is based upon the weight of the first 30 ft of the fly line,
excluding, in tapered lines, the thin 2 ft tip. This length is used on the
assumption that 30 ft is the average length of line false-cast by the average
angler. In other words the rod is capable of maintaining that length of line in
the air without stress. It is not necessary to know the actual weights in grams

or grains, you only need to appreciate that, in the Scale, the smaller the number, the lighter the line, and vice versa.

Suitable line weights are as follows:

1 No. 4 and 5 for light trout rods.

2 No. 5 and 6 for trout rods in general use, No. 6 being the most common line on the chalk streams of the south.

3 No. 7 and 8 for distance casting on a lake or reservoir with a stiff rod.

4 No. 8 and 9 for light salmon rods.

No. 4 is the line of lightest weight listed here, and No. 9 the heaviest. The Scale includes lines outside this range: No. 11 will match a 14 ft salmon rod, and a No. 3, a 6 ft delicate trout wand.

Manufacturers of rods usually inscribe the AFTM Scale weight which they consider most suitable upon the butt of each rod – again based upon a 30 ft length to be false-cast. If you are habitually fishing a shorter length of line, e.g. within a small, restricted tunnel between trees, it would be sensible to increase the line weight by one number on the Scale. Likewise, in the open, where a length of line greater than 30 ft may be lifted into the air, the line weight might be reduced by one number. The fact that line weights can be so finely adjusted does not alter my view that a No. 8 line will suit most conditions encountered by the angler with our three rods in the rivers already described.

It is the momentum of the fly line when travelling through the air which carries out the fly. This momentum is the product of line weight and speed. For lines to possess weight they need to be more substantial than the nylon leader which joins them to the fly. The centre section of a No. 8 floating line may be $\frac{1}{16}$ in. in thickness, whilst the diameter of a 15 lb BS leader will be about $\frac{15}{1000}$ in. or $\frac{12}{1000}$ in. for a 10 lb leader. Such a disparity in diameter between line and leader at their junction does not favour good fly presentation – the likely result of such a combination being that the fly would fall back over the fly line as both landed on the water. The American fly-line makers, Scientific Anglers, state:

The lowest cost line today is the level line. With a uniform diameter throughout its length, it is much less versatile than other lines. Casting with the level line is more difficult and less delicate.

We need a line which tapers down to a thin tip or, preferably, one which tapers to a thin tip at both ends of its 27 yd length. Such a line is known as a 'double taper' (DT). It has the advantage that, when one end is worn, the line may be reversed and the other end brought into use. The double taper is suitable for overhead, roll and Spey casts. Again I quote Scientific Anglers:

The double taper has a long level centre section which tapers down to a fine point at each end and it makes a delicate presentation of your fly. It is also the best taper for those situations where you need to make roll casts.

There is only one other line profile which we need to consider, the weight forward (WF). Scientific Anglers state:

The most popular line is the weight forward. It makes long casts much easier than level or double taper lines. Two features make this possible. The weight is placed in the forward section of the line, whilst the rest of the line is mostly a light, small diameter running line that slides easily through the rod guides.

We do not need to make long casts, but the weight of the line, being well forward, makes this line suitable for casting the shortest distances, i.e. in restricted spaces, where little length of line is outside the rod tip. But the lack of roll-casting ability leads us to choose the double taper. We need three of them:

1 DT8F – a double-tapered floating line.

2 DT8s – a double-tapered fast-sinking line.

3 DT8F/s – a double-tapered sink-tip line.

The floating line will be used from about the middle of April until the end of October. These months will see water temperatures above 50°F. (The use of floating and sinking fly lines at different water temperatures will be discussed on pp. 73 and 75).

The floating line of today floats because it is lighter than water. It will not float any better if it is greased; in fact the application of grease may damage the plastic coating of the line, causing it to crack, deteriorate and sink. In the first half of this century, until about 1960, fly lines were made of silk and had to be greased to make them float. This is the origin of the term 'greased line fishing'. The method was the same as that employed today with our plastic lines. The greased silk line was a delight to cast. Being thinner than the lines of today, it cut into the wind with less effort on the part of the angler. Casting with it was one thing; living with it was another! It had three disadvantages:

1 It had to be greased at least twice a day. This grease rubbed off onto the leader which had to be kept clean by rubbing with wet mud or Fuller's earth.

2 Wet mud scratched the leader, making it more visible.

3 If you transported the rod to the river on the roof of the car, with the leader and fly attached and lying alongside greased line, the leader had to be cleaned before starting to fish or it floated on the water surface.

A final disadvantage could be added: the rigmarole of drying the line each evening after use to prevent it rotting. Arthur Wood of Cairnton on the Aberdeenshire Dee had wooden wheels of about 1 yd in diameter upon his rod-room walls – on these he dried his lines. We may leave the plastic line of today upon the reel for the whole season and it will not deteriorate as a result of being left damp with the reel still upon the rod. This shortens the time lapse between the end of the day's fishing and the raising of the whisky glass upon returning home!

The sinking line will be used in the cold water of early spring and late autumn if you do not wish to spin or are not allowed to do so. It may also be used in hot weather to seek salmon lying on the river bed. Fly lines sink at different rates: fast, intermediate and slow. In running water, the fly will not be carried far below the surface with anything other than a fast-sinking line.

I sometimes use a sink-tip (F/S) fly line. This line floats throughout its length, with the exception of the first 10 or 15 ft, which sink. It has a place in fast water to hold the fly beneath the surface and thus prevent 'skating'.

A Black Dart tube fly (enlarged).

Colour of fly lines

I use a dark green sinking fly line on the basis that most materials found under the surface in a river are dark in colour, with the exception of chalk. Many stones are slate-grey, black or brown; weeds are green; washed-out tree roots resemble black rope. A dark fly line fades into the underwater scene. My floating lines are light green in colour and thus visible to me on the water surface, pointing to the position of the underwater fly. On dark water, a dark floating line is not readily discerned by the angler, who will tire his eyes searching constantly for the location of his fly. White floaters should be avoided. They flash in the sky and underwater photography has revealed that they are clearly visible from below on the water-surface mirror. I have a friend who regularly fishes a small, heavily bushed salmon river. His clothes are drab, his face sunburned and on his head there rests a hat of disreputable Irish tweed. The Royal Marines could take a lesson from him in camouflage. But his line, oh dear, his line is white. Seeking him from a distance, my eyes directed a few feet above the undergrowth, he reveals his presence as the white line cuts a startling path through the air above the bushes on the back cast. What the salmon think about the forward throw may be left to the imagination!

Fly reels

Fly-reel design leaves us to make a choice between:

1 Small-diameter reels with a wide drum.

2 Large-diameter reels with a narrow drum.

In the first category are the new Prince and Sovereign reels of House of Hardy. These are of the highest quality with a price tag to match. At slightly less cost one may purchase reels in the Leeda System Two range.

In the second category is the Hardy Marquis No. 8/9 and No. 10, and the bargain-priced Leeda Dragonfly 100; this is the only reel of the five mentioned which is made of carbon fibre.

The reel with a wide drum recovers line at almost the same rate when 15 yd of line has been drawn off as it would when full, because the level of line in the spool sinks slowly. The large-diameter, narrow drum recovers line more rapidly when almost full than the small-diameter, wide drum, but the rate of recovery reduces markedly as line is stripped off and the level falls on the spool.

Which to choose? With the short length of line to be cast on a little river, I favour the large-diameter narrow drum, although there is little to choose between the designs in our situation. But, and it is an important *but*, choose the size of reel larger by one grade than the manufacturer suggests will hold a double-tapered No. 8 floating line and 100 yd of 20 lb BS monofilament backing. In this way you will always have rapid line recovery – and it will look as though you only pursue large fish!

Do not resort to the multiplying reel. Use sound, simple tackle. Any item of equipment which incorporates a lot of moving parts is more liable to break down than one of few pieces. If grit finds its way into a single-action reel, the spool may be removed and the whole washed out in the river. Not so the multiplier, which may require the services of a screwdriver to dismantle the pieces – and if one screw drops in the sand or water . . .!

If I had to make a new start in my salmon-fishing life, on limited means, I would buy the Dragonfly reels and spools. They are not of the highest quality, that cannot be expected at a price one-third or one-quarter of the other reels suggested, but they are made in England, at Falmouth in Cornwall, and they are reliable. I have used one constantly for all my floating-line, still-water trout fishing and night sea-trout adventures for 4 years, and nothing has gone wrong. This must be a soundly based recommendation because I fish 3 or 4 days a week.

Ease of acquisition and cost may govern your choice, and lead to the purchase of new reels, but a look at the secondhand market is rewarding if you have the time. Three of my reels are old favourites. We have been together for many years and taken many fish. They are:

1 For the 12 ft double-handed rod: Hardy 3¾ in. wide-drum Perfect with DT8F line.

2 For the 10 ft 6 in. single-handed rod: Hardy 3⅞ in. narrow-drum St John with DT8F line. Hardy 3⅞ in. narrow-drum St John with DT8S line.

The St John DT8S will also be used on the 12 ft rod when necessary. Of course, instead of two St Johns, a single reel with spare spool will suffice.

3 For the 9 ft rod, the more recent carbon-fibre reel was selected:
Leeda Dragonfly 100 with DT8F line.
Leeda Dragonfly 100 spool with DT8F/S line.

A search would have to be made for a secondhand Perfect because these reels are no longer made in a size above 3⅝ in., which is insufficient for a DT8F line. Both the St John and the Perfect are on the heavy side, but are strong, reliable reels, incorporating spare ratchet springs. A reel with a single spring which breaks will bring your fishing to a standstill. All three reels have an adjustable drag which may be set to a light resistance when using fine nylon. A spring ratchet adjusts the Hardy reels; the Dragonfly incorporates a disc brake of simple construction.

Finally, make certain that the line and backing fill the spool. If they do not, you might as well have purchased a smaller reel. The best way to ensure this when fitting a new line is to wind the line on first, and then fill to capacity with the backing. The whole has then to be reversed. Of course, because a sinking line is of smaller diameter, and thus takes up less room than one which floats, it may be necessary to place 10 or 15 yd of old fly line beneath the backing to ensure a full spool. Do not use string for this purpose because it will rot; old, plastic fly line takes up plenty of room and will last for ever as a filler.

Nylon leaders

Three seasons ago, half-way through the summer, I lost a salmon when the nylon leader broke, an event so rare that the previous breakage cannot be recalled. The fish, of medium weight, perhaps 10 lb, decided to make for the sea in heavy water. It was too close to the pool run-off for me to persuade it to turn by slackening the line and dropping the rod point. Such tactics usually cause a salmon to swing about to face upstream. That point had been passed. With the rod dangerously low, an attempt was made to stop it by brute force because I could not follow because of a bankside tree. Suddenly the rod straightened and the line flew up into the overhanging branches. I pulled down the line to find the 15 lb Platil Strong leader had snapped at the hook attachment knot, a tucked half blood.

Now, Platil Strong, which is no longer made, was a nylon of smaller diameter than most other monofilaments of the same breaking strain. I had great faith in the brand, always using 17.6 lb with my 1 in. tube flies and never, literally, suffering loss through breakage. Then the manufacturers ceased to make 17.6 lb, substituting 20 lb and 15 lb. I chose the latter and it proved satisfactory until the event described, which may have been due to a roughened eye on the treble hook weakening the nylon. From that moment, I decided to fish my 1 in. weighted tubes on the 20 lb marque. Fearful that my efforts might be spurned by salmon because of increased visibility, I cast without full confidence. But lo, by the end of September, nine grilse had not objected!

I gave a spool to a friend and asked him for his comments after 2 or 3 weeks. 'Yes', he said, with a smile. 'It's jolly good, the fish don't mind at all, and I can pull fair-sized branches off the trees when the fly gets caught.'

The point is this. Fish with the strongest nylon that circumstances and fly size permit. It is entirely unsporting to fish finer than necessity demands, for the line to be broken, and to send a salmon away with a hook in its mouth and a yard of nylon trailing behind.

There are many excellent monofilaments on the market. One cannot test them all and they are hard to compare in field conditions, which vary constantly. When Platil Strong came off the market I decided to try Maxima Chameleon which is made in Germany. The manufacturers state of this product:

Inbuilt chemical reagents make this line change colour in water and daylight (not artificial light). The rays of light are absorbed but not reflected. That makes the line invisible to fish and results in more catches.

On the basis that 20 lb Platil Strong had a diameter of $^{15}/_{1000}$ in. I decided to try 15 lb Chameleon, which is of the same diameter. This choice has proved satisfactory, not only in the 15 lb rating for my weighted, socketed tube flies fished in spate conditions, but for salmon dry fly at 10 lb BS. I also use this brand for sea-trout fishing at night, making up a 9 ft tapered leader as follows:

1   Butt section – 3 ft of 20 lb.

2   Middle section – 3 ft of 15 lb.

3   Point section – 3 ft of 10 lb.

It is not suggested that 15 lb Chameleon suits all weights of fly. If used to fish a No. 8 Low Water single or tiny Stoat's Tail tube with No. 14 treble, the fly would not swim in a lively manner, but stick out like a sore thumb at the end of the leader. For small, lightweight flies one might reduce to 12 lb, or 10 lb if there are few rocks or weed beds in the river. If using 10 lb nylon, one should set the reel drag at a light pull.

A long leader of 10 ft is only necessary when one is fishing in clear water and sunlit conditions, where line shadow is the concern. A leader longer than this would only be necessary when casting downstream with the sun shining down the river. In these adverse circumstances, the line shadow on the river bed precedes the line. In sunk-line fishing, the leader could be reduced to 6 ft in length, after all, we spin with a trace of 3 ft between the bait and the weight at the line/trace junction.

I carry spools of the required strengths in my pocket, and then choose to suit the size and weight of fly. A blood bight loop is tied at the end and about 9 ft are pulled off and joined to the fly line with a sheet bend. This bulky knot is helpful when fishing the floating line – movement indicates a 'take' by a fish – but it should only be used when fishing with 12 ft or 10 ft 6 in. rods. There is no danger of winding this knot through the top ring of these rods when netting a fish because the rod is longer than the leader. When using the 9 ft rod, it is advisable to needle knot a short length, perhaps 12 in., of 20 lb nylon to the ends of the fly lines on the Dragonfly reel and spool. This short length may then be joined to the leader with a blood knot. Both blood and needle knots will slide in and out of the top ring of the rod when landing a salmon.

I usually draw a fresh length of nylon from the spool for each day's fishing, or if I have already caught a brace of fish. Used nylon should be taken home, then wound in a tight coil around the fingers, cut through into short lengths 2 or 3 in. long and discarded in the dustbin. Birds and animals may become entangled in the line when lengths of several feet or inches are discarded on the river bank. Monofilament on the spool will keep in supple condition for 2 or 3 years if stored in the dark, but will deteriorate if exposed to strong light. Never leave a spool on the dashboard of your car.

Ancillary equipment for all fishing methods

In addition to the rod, reels and lines, I always carry the following when fishing:

Gye net and peel sling	Rod licence (in England and Wales)
Midge cream (summer)	Thermometer
Pocket knife (to cut nylon)	Tin of beer and sandwiches
Polarized spectacles	Twine to carry fish
Priest with a neck cord	

Waterproof clothing: hat, fishing coat (or waistcoat with thin waterproof folded into the back pocket), mittens (early spring)
Thigh boots or cheap thigh boots cut down to knee length (summer)

In my car, there will be:

Bin bags for salmon	Spare polarized spectacles
Binoculars (to view the river from a distance)	Spare twine
Hand tools (screwdriver, pliers, etc.)	Thermos packed with ice to hold
Insulating tape	spare bait (if prawn or shrimp
Plastic container of drinking water	fishing)
Spare clothing	Plasters

According to the method of fishing, I also carry the following items:

When fishing the fly:
50 yd spools of 12 and 15 lb Maxima Chameleon
Flies in fly box of six compartments

When spinning:
50 yd of 12 and 15 lb Maxima Chameleon for traces
Tin of weights and swivels
Plastic (non-rattling) box of spinning baits

When using natural baits:

50 yd spools of 10, 12 and 15 lb Maxima Chameleon for traces
Tobacco tin of prawn mounts, prawn and shrimp pins, sliced hooks, Thamesley Sure-
   Shot SSG, weights, treble hooks in sizes No. 6 (prawn) and No. 12 and No. 14
   (shrimp), fine pink wire, thin lead wire
Tin with pierced lid for worms in moss
Flat tin of prawns and shrimps packed between flat pieces of sponge to prevent
   breakage of legs and whiskers.

Thigh boots and clothing

In cold weather, to keep myself warm and dry, as well as being able to wade,
I wear lightweight thigh boots inside which are Long Johns and two pairs of
woollen socks. The straps at the top of the boots are not attached to the belt
holding up my trousers. Instead, each strap is fitted at the end with a split
ring for attachment to a pair of special braces. This suspension system is just
an elasticated strap, adjustable for length, with a dog-lead clip at each end.
The strap passes behind the neck, comes down each side of the front of the
chest and clips to the split rings arising from each boot.

My boots have cleated soles. Teaching many dozens of anglers each season,
some of whom bring their own boots with studded soles, I am certain that
metal studs are not non-slip. Studded soles clatter on rocks, are heavier than
cleated or felt soles, and damage the linoleum on the kitchen floor. Felt is
light in weight, silent in use and, whilst no sole is completely safe, felt slides
less than other materials.

Thigh boots become hot and damp at the thighs, knees and calves in summer
because of perspiration. In these conditions, I purchase a cheap pair of thigh
boots and cut them off level with the back of the knee. This provides 6 in. of
length more than a gumboot and allows the legs to breathe. I wear a waxed,
Hardy fishing jacket as an outer garment in cold weather, but the lining
becomes wet with perspiration on hot days. In the summer, my coat is a
lightweight, waterproof, breathable jacket of Grenfell cloth, made by
Haythornwaite & Sons. A hood, press studded onto the neck of the coat, cuts
off sound reception and you no longer whirl around to spot the place where
a salmon splashed. In wet weather, wear a waxed hat with a circular brim
which extends beyond the collar of the coat. The coat itself should be long
enough to cover the tops of the thigh boots. Pockets ample in both size and

 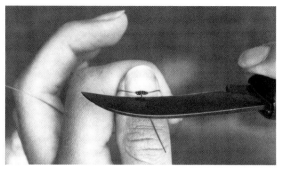

left: Fullers Earth and washing-up liquid on a damp cloth wiped over a nylon leader will cause it to sink and thus be less visible. Carry the mixture in a 35 mm film-spool container.

right: A sharp knife will cut nylon against a thumb nail.

number are essential. The poacher's pockets in my coats contain a single, folded, plastic bin bag; the bag will hold a 10 lb salmon, tied head to tail, and this can be placed in the pocket, which will remain clean.

In dry summer weather, comfort and freedom of movement are provided by a sweater and fishing waistcoat. In the wide back pocket of my waistcoat is a thin, unlined plastic mackintosh. In an emergency, a polythene bin bag will keep the body dry: cut three holes at the closed end for your head and arms. The bag will also keep your dog dry: put him inside, head protruding, and tie your salmon-carrying cord around his neck.

Mittens are a comfort in cold conditions, but absorb water in rain – and fish hooks catch in those of hand-knitted wool. The Orvis Company of Stockbridge will send, by mail order, 'Non-Absorbing Fishing Mitts', which they describe as: 'Made from warm, non-absorbing polypropylene, when they get wet you wring them out or shake them – their insulating qualities are instantly restored.'

6 Salmon flies

'I have often had salmon take the floating knot which fastens the line to the cast, which annoys me pretty badly! One cannot help it though; they will take anything.' So said Arthur Wood of Cairnton on the Aberdeenshire Dee, who experimented, and achieved success in summer, with bare, painted hooks: his 'Redshanks' and 'Greenshanks'.

When fishing the prawn, I have seen a salmon rise and take the Hillman lead in preference to the bait. One month ago my daughter took a 10 lb 8 oz fish on a 1½ in. tube fly at a water temperature of 65°F, when we are all taught that small flies should be used in warm water. I have taken three grilse from the clear water of the Test on a No. 4 Silver Doctor at a water temperature of 68°F when they would not look at a smaller fly.

In April, in the high level of a minor flood on a spate river, my hands white with cold, I grassed two salmon of 12 and 15 lb on a No. 6 Low Water single-hooked Hairy Mary. Custom ought to have dictated a 2 in. tube fly. Three years ago a friend took over 40 salmon and grilse, mainly from June onwards when the water would have been warm, on a 2 in. tube fly. This scruffy, hair-winged offering is on the dull side in colour. His comment at my astonishment: 'I always use them. Smaller flies don't suit me.' Salmon will take a strip of orange peel: try it yourself! A keeper on the Test told me of a salmon which took the red-painted hooks of a prawn mount on which there was no prawn.

I once caught a 9 lb salmon in mid-June on a No. 5 Mepps thrown upstream in clear water. The generally accepted practice is that one fishes a small lure in warm water and something large when the river is cold.

What, then, are we to make of these 'against the rules' incidents and, in the case of the 40-salmon man, constant practice? One might reply: 'Whatever one ties on gives a chance', and this is almost true. Between 1960 and 1966, from early April onwards, in high or low water, fishing a floating fly line, I caught all my salmon on one fly, a No. 6 Low Water Hairy Mary single. There was one exception, a 13 lb salmon on a No. 6 Low Water Blue Charm single. There would be nothing remarkable about this if I fished only in conditions of water temperature, clarity and volume which suited that fly. That was not the case. When I caught fish, others caught them at the same time on monstrous, carrot-sized creations. But, I might have caught more, and so might they, if we had conformed to the accepted principle of matching fly size to water conditions.

I think I have written enough to make plain that salmon are not particular. They will take most lures if in the mood. It is the angler who should be particular: he must satisfy himself. L. R. N. Gray (1957) described the man who constantly changes his fly or spinning bait as a 'tackle fiddler'. Avoid this label, and avoid wasting time by satisfying yourself that you are fishing a 'good' fly. Then, throughout the season, your needs will be met by four or five patterns. Before I give my choice, let me put before you the characteristics of a 'good' fly: a fly which we shall not need to change frequently and one in which we have faith.

1 The fly must be sufficiently attractive for a salmon to see it and take it into his mouth.

2 The hook must stand a better chance of taking hold than any other hook we know.

3 The salmon must stay hooked until landed.

Colour

It is now common knowledge that fish see in colour. It is thus open to us to dress our salmon flies to incorporate the shades seen most clearly. The fact that a salmon, which does not feed in fresh water, is readily able to see your lure does not mean it will take your offering into its mouth – but it does have the option. If it did not see the fly you could not catch the fish.

Scientists tell us that fish see colours at the red end of the spectrum (red, orange and yellow) more clearly than the greens and blues. We are also advised that stripes are readily noticed. Adding my own findings to those of the scientists, I would also advocate the colour black, which is silhouetted stark against the sky. If a black body is ribbed with gold or silver tinsel, to produce a striped effect, so much the better.

Awareness of these facts should lead us to incorporate the most effective colours into our fly dressings. We ought not to doubt the researchers: their findings were confirmed in advance of their experiments by the success, since the early years of this century, of one or two outstanding wet-fly patterns. You only have to take a Peter Ross out of your fly box to be convinced. Look at that fly: the black and white stripes of the teal-feather wing; the black-tipped, orange tail of golden pheasant; the silver-and-red body, striped with silver ribbing. These, with a black throat hackle waving in the current, are enough to catch the eye of any fish.

The Black Pennel has my support, and the Connemara Black. Both have a black body and the striping effect of silver tinsel ribbing. The Connemara Black has the added attraction of a golden-pheasant crest-feather for the tail, this feather being yellow in colour.

20 August 1988 Grilse 6 lb. Came upon a young man playing a salmon on a trout rod. 4 lb nylon. No. 12 Connemara Black. Hill Pool. 3.15 pm. Heavy water. His father had run back to the car for a large trout net, but I lent my 24 in. Gye. He lost another on same fly when nylon broke as salmon went into weeds.

But, beating all the black flies in summer is a small, silver-ribbed Stoat's Tail tube!

So, the attractors are: red, orange and yellow; bodies striped by ribbing and striped feathers, such as teal and jungle cock; the starkness of black.

The tube fly versus the single hook

It is rare for me to fish the fly in any form other than as a tube. The outstanding attribute of this form is that a treble hook is employed and the hook may be replaced after each salmon. If the tube has a socket in the tail, the round eye of the treble may be inserted; the hook will thus stay in position instead of hanging down and perhaps catching back on the leader. If the tube has no socket and is of small-diameter polythene, such as a ballpoint-pen tube, a needle-eyed treble may be pressed into the end. The ease with which a tube may be dressed, when mounted on a darning needle held in the fly-tying vice, is another advantage.

As already stated, the salmon must be hooked and stay attached until landed. There can be little doubt that a treble hook with points turned out (the Partridge 'outbend'), gives the best chance of hooking a fish. The high-carbon-content wire is strong and the barb is small and close to the point, ensuring that the hook penetrates beyond the point of no return almost at once. A further advantage of the barb being close to the point of the hook is that the throat of the hook is deeper, giving a deeper hold.

At the initial 'take', a treble is more likely to find a hold in the mouth of a salmon than a single. This must be so; three hooks give more chance than one. If you inspect the mouth of a 'back-end' cock salmon, you will find that a single hook has plenty of room to pass out of the gap that has developed between the upper and lower jaws. We all spin with treble-hooked lures and discard the hooks or minnow mounts if one point is broken. It is thus illogical to fish with double or single hooks, unless you find it difficult to ensure that a tube fly swims without skating on the surface.

Staying attached

The shanks of Partridge x1 and x3 outbend trebles, which I use in tube flies, are shorter than single or double hooks of the same gape. Put the other way around, the single and double shanks are longer. If the shank protrudes prominently outside the mouth of a hooked fish it will be subject to the pull of the nylon leader from various directions during the playing of the fish. This pull is likely to lever out the hold. The shortness of the treble shank cannot transmit the same leverage and thus the hooks break out less frequently. The only difference between the x1 and x3 is that the former has a round eye and the latter a needle eye. The round eye will be held in place by the socket at the

Alison, Alex and Angela with the 10lb salmon
of 24 June 1990.

A 10lb salmon to the author.

From the tail of a pool in high water – an 8lb salmon, 29 July 1988

Lara Bingham about to net a 10½lb salmon taken 'backing up', 30 July 1990.

Salmon should be cleaned before being frozen.

Opposite above: Spin deep in early spring.

Opposite below: Bob Sinclair-Taylor using every scrap of cover.

John Mill's first salmon, weighing 8½lb, 16 April 1987.

Gye-net shaft cut short does not protrude above the shoulder.

Dr Tom Owen fishing in a spate.

The River Cocker, Cumbria.

tail of a Type 'B' Slipstream tube (see pp. 66–7); and the needle eye may be pressed into the polythene of a socketless tube. You also have to consider hook breakage, particularly in rivers with snags, weeds and boulders. A long-shanked, Low Water single may snap at the bend if a salmon takes a turn around a rock. In 1966 I named one pool 'Broken Hook Pool': the shank of a fine-wired No. 6 Low Water Hairy Mary snapped when I hung onto a salmon in heavy water as it attempted to dash out of the tail of the pool.

You may well ask whether there is a place for a single-hooked fly. I must answer that I do not carry large, heavy singles: No. 2, No. 1, No. 1/0, 2/0 and larger sizes. The iron is hard to drive into a salmon's jaw and the risk of losing fish is great. The Low Water single has a place in my armoury because it swims well in fast water. In other words, it does not skate on the water surface. It carries the risk of shank breakage, but this is reduced if Partridge Code N hooks are used in preference to their lightweight Code 01 Wilson, which was originally intended as a dry-fly salmon hook.

The Waddington

If I cannot have a tube fly, my next choice would be a Waddington. This is a length of wire, on which the fly is dressed, with a loop at each end. The leader is tied to one loop and the other loop passes through the eye of a round-eyed treble. The sole advantage is the treble hook. Disadvantages are that the whole fly has to be discarded if the hook is damaged; the wire may lever out the hook-hold; the hook may dangle unless held in line with a short length of bicycle-valve tubing. Hooks can be replaced in the case of the Partridge Waddington Shank, in which the shank is comprised of two parallel wires, one of which has a gap for hook replacement. This gap has to be bound over and closed with fine wire to retain the hook. It is clear that the Waddington has complications which are not present in the tube fly.

Doubles and up-eyed trebles

I cannot advocate double hooks, or those up-eyed trebles with long shanks, such as the Esmond Drury or the Partridge x2b, on which the fly is dressed, unless they are of small sizes with correspondingly short shanks. Hooks in sizes larger than No. 8 have shanks of a length where leverage is again a problem. At one time the Esmond Drury was marketed in only two sizes, the larger of which was the No. 2. Flies on this hook were unpleasant to cast. They entered the river with a plop, and unless using the Spey cast, you expected to see your right or left ear take flight as the lure whistled past.

Fly dressings

Those conditions which govern the choice of fly – water temperature and the height and clarity of water – are discussed in detail on p. 62. I will now give the dressings of six flies which satisfy all my needs. I fish two of the flies, the

Black and Copper Dart tubes, under most circumstances when a river is in spate. The Hairy Mary tube, the Low Water Hairy Mary, the tiny Stoat's Tail and the Shrimp are employed in rarer circumstances. The Type 'B' Slipstream socketed tube is available from E. Veniard Ltd of Croydon.

Black Dart

Tube: Type 'B' Slipstream socketed 1¼ and 1½ in.
Hook: No. 8 Partridge x1 outbend treble
Tag: No. 16 oval gold tinsel
Body: Black floss over close turns of fine lead wire
The lead is stopped short of the head where the bucktail wing is to be tied in
Rib: No. 16 oval gold tinsel
Wing: Orange bucktail
Cheeks: Jungle cock – a long feather, three-quarters the length of the tube – one on each side
Head: Black varnish
Silk: Black Naples

If a fly longer than 1½ in. is required, it is not necessary to stock a 2 in. tube in your fly-dressing cabinet: increase the length of the orange bucktail to overlap the hook by the fancied length.

A socketed tube is fat and thus liable to skate on the surface of the water. The lead wire counteracts this tendency.

To dress the fly:

1 Place the pointed end of a darning needle of a diameter which will grip the tube in the jaws of a rotating vice. Slide the tube onto the needle, with the socket at the jaws end.

2 Run Naples silk in side-by-side turns from the head of the tube to within ¹⁄₁₀ in. of the end of the socket, where the gold tinsel is tied in. Take eight turns towards the head and tie down but do not cut off.

3 Tie in the black floss and then, fractionally towards the head, wind on ¹⁄₁₀₀ in. (0.37 mm) lead wire, in side-by-side turns to within ⅕ in. of the tube head. Tie it down and cut off. Add the floss silk on top of the lead, tie down at the head and cut off.

4 Pick up the gold tinsel and wind in three or four ribbing turns, in a spiral, stopping short of the end of the tube by ³⁄₁₀ in., and cut off.

5 Rotate the tube on the needle and lay on sparse tufts of bucktail at the head, and glue in each tuft with a small spot of clear varnish. The bucktail surrounds the head. Trim off just behind the flange at the front of the tube. The length of the bucktail should exceed the hook by about ½ in.

6 Tie in one jungle-cock feather on each side; the feather should almost reach the gold tinsel tag. Whip off, and paint the head with black varnish.

Copper Dart

Tube: 1 in. Type 'B' Slipstream socketed
Hook: No. 8 Partridge x1 outbend treble
Body: Close turns of 0.40 mm copper wire over a single layer of black Naples silk
Wing: Orange bucktail
Cheeks: Jungle cock. A short feather about 10 mm in length, one on each side
Head: Black varnish
Silk: Black Naples

To dress the fly:

1 Place the pointed end of a darning needle of a diameter which will grip the tube in the jaws of the rotating vice. Slide the tube onto the needle, with the socket at the jaws end.

2 Run Naples silk in side-by-side turns from the head of the tube to just above the socket where the copper wire should be doubled under and tied in.

3 Take silk back to the head in wide turns.

4 Wind the copper wire in side-by-side turns to just behind the head and tie down just short of the point where the bucktail is to be tied down. Cut off the wire.

5 Rotate the tube on the needle and lay on sparse tufts of bucktail. Glue in each tuft with a spot of clear varnish. The bucktail surrounds the head. Trim off just behind the flange at the front of the tube. The length of the bucktail should exceed the hook by ½ in.

6 Tie in one jungle-cock feather on each side; the feather should reach half-way down the copper body, the intention being to resemble an eye. Whip off, and paint the head with black varnish.

Hairy Mary tube

Tube: 1¼ in. type 'B' Slipstream socketed
Hook: No. 8 Partridge x1 outbend treble
Tag: No. 16 oval silver tinsel closest to the socket and two or three turns of yellow floss above
Body: Black floss over close turns of fine lead wire
Rib: No. 16 oval silver tinsel
Wing: Natural brown bucktail
Head: Black varnish
Silk: Black Naples

To dress the fly:

1 Place the pointed end of a darning needle of a diameter which will grip the tube in the jaws of the rotating vice. Slide the tube onto the needle, with the socket at the vice end.

2 Run Naples silk in side-by-side turns from the head of the tube to within 1/10 in. of the end of the socket where the silver tinsel is tied in. Take six turns towards the head and tie down but do not cut off.

3 Take three turns of yellow floss to occupy the next 1/10 in. above the silver tinsel. Tie it over the loose end of the tinsel and cut off.

4 Tie in the black floss and then, fractionally towards the head, the $^1/_{100}$ in. (0.37 mm) lead wire, which should be wound in side-by-side turns to within $^1/_5$ in. of the tube head. Tie down and cut off. The black floss silk follows on top of the lead and is tied down at the head and cut off.

5 Pick up the oval silver tinsel and wind it in three or four ribbing turns, in a spiral, stopping short of the end of the tube by $^3/_{10}$ in. and cut off.

6 Rotate the tube on the needle and lay on sparse tufts of bucktail at the head. Glue in each tuft with a spot of clear varnish. The bucktail surrounds the head, and should be trimmed off just behind the flange at the front of the tube. The length of the bucktail should just exceed the hook. Whip off and paint the head with black varnish.

Low Water Hairy Mary

Hook: Partridge Code N Low Water No. 6 single
Tag: Oval silver tinsel and yellow floss
Tail: Golden-pheasant crest and Red Ibis
Butt: Black ostrich herl
Body: Black floss silk

Rib: Oval silver tinsel
Hackle: Blue cock
Wing: Brown bucktail
Head: Black varnish
Silk: Black Naples

To dress the fly:

1 Place a Low Water hook in the rotating vice.

2 Wind the silk from the head to opposite the point of the hook. Tie in the silver oval and make a half hitch.

3 Wind the silver oval for $^1/_{10}$ in. Tie, leaving oval hanging.

4 Tie in the yellow floss and wind the silk forward over the oval for $^1/_{10}$ in. Make a half hitch.

5 Wind the yellow floss for $^1/_{10}$ in. towards the head. Tie and cut off.

6 Tie in a small golden-pheasant crest and a tuft of Red Ibis and make a half hitch.

7 Tie in black ostrich herl and wind three turns towards the head. Tie and cut off.

8 Tie in the black floss and form body to head leaving room for the wing. Tie and cut off.

9 Spiral the oval up to the head, tie and cut off.

10 Turn the vice over and tie in a tuft of blue-cock hackle. Tie and trim the ends.

11 Return the vice to normal and tie in a tuft of bucktail for the wing. Glue into place with a drop of clear varnish.

12 Trim the ends, form the head with whipping and black varnish.

Stoat's Tail

Hook: No. 12 Partridge x2B for the fly dressed directly on to the treble hook. Partridge No. 12 outbend x3 needle eye in conjunction with a ballpoint pen tube.
Body: Black floss silk.
Wing: The long hairs from the tail of a stoat.
Black Labrador is a good substitute.
Head: Black varnish
Silk: Black Naples

This may be dressed directly onto a treble hook or onto a short piece of the polythene tube of a ballpoint pen with separate small treble.

The hook shank or the tube may be left bare, but dress if desired with black floss which may be ribbed with optional silver tinsel.

To dress the fly:

1 Run Naples silk from the head to just above the treble division, and there tie in floss and silver tinsel.

2 Take Naples silk in wide turns to the head, wind on the floss, tie down and cut off. Spiral rib, tie down and cut off.

3 Tie in a single tuft of stoat's tail of a length to the bend of the hooks and glue in place with a single spot of clear varnish. Trim off stubs of hair and whip off allowing room behind the eye for the nylon of the Turle knot. Paint head with black varnish. If dressing on a polythene ballpoint-pen tube, a tuft of hair may be placed on each side or all around.

Shrimp

Hook: No. 12 Partridge x2B
Body: Tail half in red floss, front half in black floss
Rib: No. 16 oval silver tinsel
Throat hackle: Hot orange
Cheeks: Two small jungle-cock feathers
Wing: Orange bucktail
Head: Red varnish
Silk: Hot orange Naples or Gossamer

If dressed on a hook smaller than No. 12, the whole of the body may be of red floss.

To dress the fly:

1 Run silk from the head to just above the treble division. Tie in floss and silver tinsel.

2 Take silk to the head in wide turns, wind on the floss, tie down and cut off. Spiral rib, tie down and cut off. With both the floss and tinsel, allow a short space behind the eye of the hook for the single loop of a Turle knot.

3 Tie in a short tuft of hot orange dyed hen-hackle at throat.

4 Tie in a single tuft of orange bucktail of a length to the bend of the hooks. Glue in place with a spot of clear varnish. Trim off stubs of bucktail.

5 Tie in two, small, jungle-cock cheeks. Whip off, allowing room behind the eye of the hook for the Turle knot, and varnish the head.

7 Fishing the fly

Casting

I am firmly of the opinion that the four casts – overhead, roll, single Spey and double Spey – cannot be learned from a book. This statement is based upon my many years of casting tuition and the considerable number of pupils who have come to me after failing to make progress from diagrams and written instructions. A day of casting on a river under a qualified teacher will enable those who aspire to cast with a double- or single-handed fly rod to achieve their object. This is particularly true with the double-handed rod, which is easier to master than the single-handed. The names of qualified instructors may be obtained from the Register of Experienced Fly Fishing Instructors and Schools (see pp. 203–4). You would not expect to play golf, tennis or learn to ski without practical tuition. The same applies to fly casting. I intend to assume that you have taken this instruction and know how to execute these casts, and confine myself to their application.

The overhead cast

On an open river, with plenty of room on the banks for the back cast to extend, this is the most widely used cast with a floating fly line. The line will cut into an adverse wind more effectively than with roll and Spey casts. It is inadvisable to rely upon this cast when fishing a sinking fly line and heavy fly because:

1 The fly line will probably have to be rolled up to the water surface by a roll cast before lift-off into the back cast.

2 Following lift-off into the back cast, the weight of the fly makes it difficult to control in the air; thus it may take your hat, or, worse still, your ear, with it as it passes on the forward movement. A sunk line is better coped with by a Spey or roll.

So, imagine that you are using the overhead cast on an open little river. You will have no difficulty in placing your fly where you wish, but fish must not be scared. The higher an object is above the water, the more visible it becomes to a salmon.

You should therefore keep back from the bank, or kneel, or fish in thigh boots whilst wading below the bank. Not only that, you should keep your rod as low as possible and, as the line shoots out, it should do so close to the water

This rod is too long and the angler too visible.

surface. It goes without saying that a short rod is less likely to be seen than a long one. Avoid false casting. A line flashing across the water four or five times before alighting scares fish. This was brought home to me long ago whilst reservoir fishing. As 20 yd of line extended in the air over the water, a trout near the surface would, at times, splash in fright underneath the passing line. Salmon will not splash in alarm on the surface; they will melt away unseen close to the river bed. The foregoing is the reason behind the definition of a small river (see p. 8). In addition, the more time the fly spends in the air, the less time it is fishing in the water, and false casts may result in wind knots.

The roll cast

Imagine you are wading within a canopy of trees in a *narrow* river. The roll cast will enable you to fish with a short rod of 9 ft or 10 ft 6 in. The short rod is not only essential because of lack of space, it is also less visible than a long rod because, during the cast, the rod moves into the vertical position. It is

Stalk the fish; make a roll cast with a short rod.

easier to execute a roll cast when wading than from a position on the bank
above the water; this is fortunate because the lower the angler, the less likely
he or she is to be seen.

The roll cast is ideal when wading in a narrow river because casting is usually
downstream and little change of direction is required, or possible, if you can
almost touch the other bank with an outstretched rod. But it is not possible to
switch the fly from downstream of the angler to a point across a river of
medium width. In other words, the roll does not enable us to change direction
in a wide arc; for this we require the Spey casts.

The Spey casts

The single Spey is made facing downstream with the left hand up the rod if
fishing from the right bank, and the right hand up the rod if casting from the
left bank. The double Spey is made facing across the river with the right hand
up the rod if fishing from the right bank, and the left hand up the rod if
fishing from the left bank. To ascertain which are the right and left banks,
face downstream: the left bank is to your left and the right bank to your right.
This is so in all rivers.

The single Spey is used on most occasions, the double Spey in a downstream
wind. Most of the time in a narrow river you will use neither.

I am not an advocate of Spey casting in little rivers unless trees line the bank,
wide changes in direction are required and the angler is wading. The Spey is
all very well in major rivers, but creates disturbance on intimate waters.
If there is room, stick to a delicate, single overhead cast, ensuring that the
line and fly alight lightly on the water.

Cold water and the sinking fly line

Water temperature is a major factor in deciding whether we are to fish a
floating or a sinking fly line. Within 0.5°F, the temperature of the water is the
same as that of the fish. In cold water, i.e. up to the middle of April, or the
end of April in Scotland, salmon are cold and lethargic, stay close to the river
bed and are reluctant to rise to take a fly close to the water surface. In early
spring and late autumn, a sinking fly line is required if you do not wish, or are
not allowed, to spin.

The sinking fly line is less pleasurable to fish with than one which floats.
At which water temperature, as we progress through April, may the change
be made to a floating fly line? There can be no positive answer, no critical
'change-over' temperature to which one may adhere. The figure of 48°F is
bandied about as the magic level but factors in addition to water temperature
must be considered, such as clarity and depth of water. Even so, you are
likely to make the change within the band of 45–50°F, although I have taken
salmon on the floating fly line in water as cold as 40°F, but only when the air
was substantially warmer.

In the Introduction, Arthur Wood was saluted as 'ushering in the greased-line
era: *c.* 1920s'. In one of his letters, he wrote:

The lowest water temperature at which I fish greased line is about 39° or 40°, but if
there is a very cold wind I use a big fly and sink it.

In spring, if the air is colder than the water, it does not make a great deal of
difference whether we fish with a floating or sinking fly line, or take to a
spinning bait; we will not catch much. It is the same in trout fishing: warm
water, cold air, bad day.

The right day will arrive, possibly as early as March. I am ready to change at
any temperature above 45°F if the water is low and clear, and the air is
warmer than the water by at least 3°F. Thereafter, for a week or two, you may
alternate between the two lines, reverting to the sinker if the volume of water
increases and the clarity reduces. The time will come, usually in mid-April,
when you will decide to fish the floating line or a sink-tip for the remainder of the
season. If the river has a season extending into October or November, or even
December, it will almost certainly be necessary to revert to the sinking line.

I have recorded that a sink-tip line may appeal to the angler. Personally I do
not often carry one, but some fishermen swear by them. Watching these
anglers, and talking to others of the same persuasion, I find that they use the
sink-tip in warm water where the current is fast, to stop the fly skating on the
surface, and, when the river is dirty, to sink the fly some way towards the
depth at which salmon lie so that the fish can see it more easily. The sink-tip
helps to deal with these two problems. For myself, these factors are
overcome, when using a floating fly line, by fishing a slightly heavier and
slimmer fly in fast water, thereby creating less water resistance, or a larger

heavier fly in the turbid conditions of a spate. I have not noticed whether the sink-tip practitioners catch more salmon than I do. At the end of the day we may be equally rewarded, but I have noticed that they meet with greater success in deep pools, whilst I beat them in shallower waters.

Why do I seldom use a sink-tip line? There are two reasons: I find it quicker to change the fly than waste time changing reels; I do not like casting a sink-tip line. This dislike is due to the different densities of the two sections, which may cause the tip to splash onto the water. I also like to watch my fly line, right down to the line/leader junction, for the slightest check which may indicate a take; this cannot be seen if the tip is underwater. Furthermore, a fully floating line points out the position of the fly, which ought to be constantly watched.

Mending the fly line

When using a floating fly line and casting across a river, the speed at which the fly will return to hang downstream of the angler may be controlled by mending. The speed of traverse will be increased by a downstream mend of the fly line (uncommon) or slowed by an upstream mend (a common tactic). In fast water, when you wish to slow the passage of the fly across the main current or hold it in the mainstream, an upstream mend should be made as soon as the fly has hit the water on the far side. This is accomplished by lifting the rod point and the line up and over in an upstream curve; the final yard of line, and thus the fly, remain unmoved.

A downstream mend is accomplished by lifting the point of the rod up and over in a downstream direction. This forms an immediate and pronounced belly in the line, causing the fly to swim down for a yard or two and then whip around to hang below the angler. Such an action is useful in a restricted pool where there is insufficient length of bank to 'back-up', which we will consider next. Mending should be included in the lessons given by a professional instructor.

Backing-up

30 July 1990 Salmon 10½ lb. River showed its bones previous evening. A night of rain. Dustbin lid full of water at breakfast. 10 am. River high and thick brown. By 2.30 pm had cleared and fallen 4 in. Lara took the salmon in tail of Island Pool on 1½ in. Black Dart backed-up. A spate over-rides water temperature which would otherwise indicate small fly.

To 'back-up' means to start fishing at the tail of a pool, cast straight across the river at right angles, take two paces upstream, and strip in the line. These actions form a big, mid-river, downstream belly in the line, pulling the fly a yard or two downriver initially before it whips across the current in an upstream curve.

The fish, presented with so fleeting an opportunity, has to grab the fly or miss the chance – no time is given for sceptical inspection. This method may strike you as ham-fisted, and it is true that there is no fancy titillation of the fish – it is all or nothing for it. Caution is needed on the part of the angler, who must be aware that his rod and body may scare the quarry (when casting downstream in the conventional manner the angler is many yards away from the fish and is likely to be outside the vision window; when 'backing-up' his rod and body are adjacent to the salmon). Thus it is advisable to keep back from the river bank and make use of available cover.

The normal practice is to fish down a pool first in the conventional manner. If there is no response, or a salmon rises but does not take, change the fly at the tail of the pool and 'back-up' the new fly. It is surprising how often fish will rush at the lure from a pool which until then had seemed empty.

Warm water and the floating fly line

The essence of floating fly-line fishing is contained in an article published for me in the *Sunday Telegraph* on 26 August 1990. It is reproduced below and arose from this entry in my fishing diary:

31 August 1988   1 salmon 10 lb. 2 grilse, 5 lb and 6 lb. 1 ¼ in. Black Dart and 1 ¼ in. Hairy Mary. Fished from The Pines down to The Weir in heavy coloured water. Was about to give up when the 10 lb fish took as the fly swept across the top of The Weir at 9.15 am. At 9.30 am took 5 lb grilse in same place. At 10.00 am another grilse of 6 lb took 20 yd above The Weir in The Saucepan after it tried three times to catch the fly in rushing water. All netted.

The article, entitled 'Beguiled by Hairy Mary's lethal lure', is as follows:

It had been raining for hours when my wife gave me my orders at 10 pm. 'One salmon will be enough, but two grilse would be better'. She knew what she wanted all right: a 10 lb fish, or two of 5 lb each. There was to be a party, she had made the mayonnaise, it had just stopped raining, and now it was up to me.

The rain gave me a chance. The inverted dustbin lid on the lawn outside my study was full of water. The lid is my rain gauge. When full, it means the river will be running at the right level and salmon will be alert to grab my fly. Half a lidful is a meagre ration. A full measure is like half an avocado pear – just sufficient.

Soon after dawn I walked across the moors to the valley where the river wound black and snake-like in the soft light. Behind were the tracks of crushed wet grass left by my boots. Mine were the only prints. The 12 ft salmon rod was carried at the trail, point to the rear; a net was slung on my back. A heron lifted in alarm from the water's edge, uttering a harsh cry, then swept off to the marshes of the high moor. Frogs for the heron, salmon for me; when there is a need the river will provide. She has always been there, flowing down from mist-clad hills.

The rod swished through the air when I started to fish, casting the fly across each pool and stickle. The fly was given life by the moving water, which took hold of the orange bucktail lure, swirling it across the river until it hung in the current 12 yards downstream. In this manner a mile of river was covered with no response. Perhaps the rain had made the water acidic, sickening the fish. Perhaps my fly was too small, or the water too brown in colour. I tied on another fly, a Hairy Mary which had been resting in my pocket. She is a much abused fly, tatty, but irresistible. She has been gnashed by many teeth. And so it was again. The fish took the fly in one full-blooded rush. I set off down the bank in pursuit. In and out of the underwater rocks he swam; around and about the bankside bushes I followed. The nylon leader twanged on snags and was beaten by his tail, but the hook and nylon held. The net trapped him and scooped him out, a cock fish of 10 lb.

Perhaps, I thought, there might be another in that very place, and so it proved. No sooner had the fly hit the water than a black back slid over, a white-rimmed mouth opened, closed, and down went Hairy Mary, that enticing, irresistible seductress. This grilse would have nothing to do with me – she went downstream fast. Out of the tail of one pool and through the neck of the next. On we went. She didn't out-distance me to the extent that hope might be lost; from time to time she waited. In the end, I slyly scuttled by and enclosed her in my net.

The sun now lifted over the hill, but the rest of the world still stretched its arms and yawned. Seated on my rock, I took the flask from my game bag and drank coffee. The sun warmed my back. A dipper flew up the river. Midges came out, but were repelled by cream rubbed on my face, neck, wrists and hands.

I straightened my back, slid the two fish into the game bag and considered the state of play. Two fish were enough. She would be pleased. I could return with head held high. Triumphant homecomings are infrequent. But the river still flowed at a most inviting height; another dabble would do no harm. . . .

I set off up the bank to a whirling hole from which many victims have been plucked. There had been no response when the fly tracked across the bubbling current soon after dawn. Meanwhile, a grilse might have occupied the lie. It was worth a try. This time a nose came up, the mouth opened and down he went – without my fly! There is nothing restful, dreamy or tranquil about salmon fishing; one needs tranquillizers. My hands shook. I bit off the fly and tied on a black creation with silver tinsel ribbing. Salmon see the colour black when silhouetted stark against the sky. He responded to my offering, the fly was engulfed and I raised the rod as his tail sank from view. All was well and he joined the others in the bag.

The strap bit deep into my shoulder as I trudged up the hill. The sun had burned off the mist. There were two grilse for the party and a 10 lb salmon to smoke. The heron flew overhead and I doffed my cap, hoping his crop was full.

The story behind this account

Tackle

This consisted of a Hardy 12 ft carbon-fibre rod rated AFTM No. 9. The reel was a Perfect 3¾ in. on which was a light green Air Cel DT8F line, needle-knotted to 100 yd of 20 lb monofilament backing and, below that, some old plastic fly line to fill up the spool. This filling ensures that each turn of the reel recovers as much line as possible. It will be noted that, on the AFTM Scale, the line was one category lighter than that suggested for the rod.

The reasons for this reduction in weight were:

1 I like to fish as light a weight of line as possible to create less line shadow in bright weather.

2 The river to be fished was open, allowing a fair length, and thus weight, of fly line to be held outside the tip of the rod.

If a short length of line is to be cast, e.g. when wading whilst sea-trout fishing at night, the full AFTM rating for the rod, or one category heavier, should be used.

The leader was 20 lb Platil Strong; 9 ft straight off the spool. Today, I would use 15 lb Maxima Chameleon, Platil Strong being no longer on the market. In the top of the leader was tied a blood bight loop where the fly line, with a single-turn knot at the end, was attached by a double sheet bend. The tube-fly treble was attached by a four-turn tucked half blood.

In Chapter 6 I wrote about the conditions governing the choice of fly (p. 62). On that August morning I was fishing a spate river which was running full and coloured at a temperature which I know from experience would have been in the region of 60°F, a dip of the hand confirms. Of course, if you have fished for many years and know a river well, a glance at the water is sufficient to arrive at a decision on fly pattern and size. But the following factors flitted through my mind:

Coloured water – large fly
High water – large fly
Warm water – large fly

Leaving aside the smallest patterns suitable for the final hours of a spate as the water settles to low and clear, my choice of fly would have been made from:

a 1½ in. Black Dart tube fly.

b 1¼ in. Black Dart or Hairy Mary tube flies.

c 1 in. Copper Dart tube fly.

The decision would have depended on whether the water was:

a Cold, high and coloured.

b Warm, high and coloured.

b Warm, high and clear.

b Warm, low and coloured.

c Warm, low and clear.

The spate was falling and I knew from experience that the water would clear in a few hours. At that time of year the water is always warm. The correct choice was therefore the Black Dart, reducing to the Copper Dart in the afternoon as the water warmed further, cleared and dropped. In the event, the 1 in. tube was not required because three salmon taken by 10 am should satisfy any angler.

Finally, the net was a 24 in. Gye with the shaft end shortened by 6 in., enabling me to press through undergrowth, held on my back by a peel sling. A priest (a short length of iron pipe) was in my trouser pocket, with a loop of cord around my neck. I wore polarized spectacles and had applied midge cream and slung a game bag across my back to hold the expected catch.

Tactics

These were simple. I just cast down and across whilst working my way downriver. The first two salmon attached themselves as the fly crossed the current towards my side. The third fish had to be tempted by a change of fly and a little teasing – accomplished by drawing the fly a yard or so upstream two or three times and then letting it drop back, and by mending to keep the fly mid-river.

To net the first two, I descended into the river in my thigh boots, worked the fish upstream of my position and then hustled them back into the net. In they went, head-first, and I was able to climb back onto the bank, pull the priest out of my pocket and knock them on the head. After each netting, the treble hook was replaced with a new one – just in case it had been strained slightly out of shape. The third fish took in fast water in which it was possible to reduce some of its energy, but impossible to hold out the net against the current or persuade it to a position above my stand. This salmon was pulled downriver through some rapids, rod held high to prevent the nylon being trapped under a rock, to the place where the other fish were landed.

Hooking the risen fish

These comments refer to fishing with a floating fly line and do not include the salmon which rises and turns away without touching the fly. We will hook him later!

Many salmon attach themselves. The angler is surprised at a sudden pull, lifts the rod and pulls back in response. In these cases a good hook-hold is a matter of luck. The security of the hold, particularly if fishing a large single or double, *may* be improved by a sharp pull, achieved by lifting the rod on the first occasion that the fish swims away from you. This *may* drive the hook, or hooks, well home or cause them to slip into a more secure position in the scissors of the jaws. If the hook comes away, at least it is better to lose the fish early rather than after a protracted fight.

It is the salmon which rises into view and takes, or clearly wishes to take, the fly that requires the exercise of our skill.

The manner in which a fish may approach and take a fly, and the angler's response, is so varied that when instructing a beginner I advise: 'Do nothing.

left: Let go a loop of line when a salmon rises in a narrow place to give it time to take the fly and turn down.

right: Fishing with rod high and line drooping allows time for a salmon to turn down before the line straightens and pulls in the hook. Not advisable in a small river because the rod is high and visible.

Let him hook himself. You'll soon feel if he succeeds, then pull back.' If this advice is followed the salmon is likely to rise into view, take the fly, turn down, tighten the line and hook himself. Whilst all this is happening, it is by no means easy to control the desire to lift the rod to see whether the fish is 'on'; even the most practised angler is tempted. If the rod is raised as the salmon comes into view, the fly may be pulled away from the fish before it has reached the lure. It is the angler who has caught two or three salmon, who has seen the sequence of events, who may be helped into turning a likely hooking into a near certainty.

Timing is more important than anything else. A slow response is vital. The majority of salmon take in a fast curve, consisting of a visible rising surge, the fly being engulfed at the top of the surface bulging sweep, and the turn-down followed by the water closing over the tail. My response is to drop my rod point as soon as I see the fish take the fly and to leave the line slack until it has gone, or until there is a sliding away of the line/leader junction knot. Then I raise the rod and *feel* for it. If it has the fly, a good firm lift of the rod sets the hooks. If it has not taken the fly, your gentle *feeling* lift of the rod will not cause disturbance and it may be tried again.

Salmon risen in narrow fast runs are difficult to hook. They approach in two ways: the very fast, sharp taking turn and the porpoise roll, in which the salmon rises, takes the fly, and sinks back without turning. To deal with the first, which may take place 3 or 4 yd downstream of the angler, whose short line and low rod allow no slack line, I make my cast whilst holding a loop of spare line over the forefinger of the hand which is up the rod. The sequence is then as follow: lightning view of fish flank; line released; fish pulls out loop; and rod is raised and bent into the salmon. This fish could also be dealt with by fishing 'on the droop'. This requires the rod tip to be held high: the line droops in a curve to the river surface, the fish takes and the droop is sufficiently slack to give the salmon time to turn before pulling up tight. The disadvantage of this system in a little river is the high, visible rod tip.

The second 'porpoise' style of take in a narrow fast run is the salmon which rises, opens its mouth, closes on the fly and drops back without turning. You can always see its mouth open because of the white lips. It is not so easy to see whether it has the fly. I can only suggest that the correct course is to wait until it has put its head down and has sunk from view before raising the rod. Some of these fish are hooked under the snout, but the margin between success and failure is small. Others have the fly well back towards the throat, because they have approached from directly behind the dangling fly – they are always securely hooked. The cardinal rule with the visible rise is: Allow plenty of time before tightening.

The salmon which rises and misses

This may be a genuine failure to catch hold as the fly flicks about in the current; such fish usually have their mouths open, but the fly 'escapes'. These salmon usually come again and make sure of their prey.

The sceptical salmon is a different matter. This is the fish which rises and passes by 6 or 12 in. from the fly, giving your offering a baleful inspection as it passes. Such fish have to be tempted.

When a fish rises but does not take, I make no more than two further casts at it straight away. If there is no result, and the pool is long enough, I retreat 10 or 15 yd and fish down on it again. If there is insufficient length of pool for this, I rest the salmon for as long as it takes to eat an apple, then try it again with no more than three casts straight at the lie. In the absence of further response to the original fly, say a 1¼ in. Black Dart, I will try a 1¼ in. Hairy Mary, following this with the 1 in. Copper Dart. In general, it is accepted practice to change to a smaller fly, but a few anglers increase the size. My own experience is that, if you have caught a salmon or two on a 1 or 1½ in. fly, it is best to stick to that size with the reluctant fish, but change the pattern. If the salmon ignores all these wiles, I suggest you go away with the intention of trying the lie again after a break of 2 or 3 hours. It may have changed its mind by then, or been replaced by a more co-operative member of its tribe, for the fact that it is, or was, there means the lie is comfortable for fish at the prevailing water height.

In addition to pauses and fly changes, you may alter presentation. A 'backed-up' fly, or the short 'straight across' fly which is whipped around just downstream of the angler may spur a hesitant fish. To salmon, the most tantalizing of all minor movements is the fly which is drawn upstream a yard and then dropped back, all being in line with the current and repeated several times. Many a black head and white-rimmed mouth have set my heart pounding as the result of 'draw and release'.

On one occasion I came upon a friend seated beside the river on a boulder. We chatted, told each other tales, ate our lunch and drank a tin of beer. My friend rose with an effort, being plump, straightened his back, pointed to a narrow channel about 1 yd wide below a bush and said: 'There's a salmon in there. I've risen him. Now I'll take him home.'

He crept upstream to drop his fly on top of the indicated place, holding it there with a 13 ft rod which reached across the current. A head appeared and disappeared without touching the fly. He drew the fly upstream 1 yd, then let it wash back. The head came up again and I held my breath. But, no! On the third 'draw and wash down', the salmon was overcome by desire or irritation and took.

The dropper

My introduction to droppers took place on the Helmsdale in 1959.
The dropper is a second fly tied in one-third or half-way down the leader.
It is usually, but not always, smaller than the fly on the point.

To add a dropper to a 9 ft leader, cut the nylon 3 ft below the line/leader junction. Join the two ends thus created with a blood knot, but leave one end long, about 4 in., and cut off the other end as usual just outside the knot. The end to be left for the dropper should be the continuation of the top section of the leader nearest to the fly line. If a fish takes the dropper, there is then no chance of the fish being lost due to the knot coming undone.

The dropper is a summer, warm-water enterprise. A Shrimp Fly or Stoat's Tail is normally fished in this position, usually on a small double hook, or an Esmund Drury or Partridge X2B up-eyed treble hook.

The cast is made initially down and across, backed-up, or whipped around exactly as you would fish a single point fly, and many fish take when both flies are beneath the water surface. But, in addition, as the cast is fished out, the rod tip is raised to scuttle the dropper across the surface of the water to produce a wake. This action is most effective in rough, turbulent water at the neck of a pool, or when an upstream wind has created a ripple.

Some years after the Helmsdale initiation, I was reminded of the method in the south of England by two examples of the magnetic effect on salmon of a trickled fly breaking the water surface. On both occasions I was fishing one fly, a No. 1/0 Hairy Mary in a summer spate; a strong upstream wind caught the line, lifted it and dragged the fly pursued by a pair of open jaws, over the surface of the waves. They failed to catch up and close, but my interest was aroused.

All this is exciting stuff, heart stopping and hand trembling, but there is a problem! You may lose fish being played due to the free fly snagging. Do not be tempted to fish two flies in a river well endowed with snags or weeds, particularly weeds. A hooked salmon loves a weed bed. Many have been lost in past seasons in the *Ranunculus* at Broadlands on the River Test – mine among them – when the free fly has caught in those green stems!

When to fish

So many factors have to be considered: air and water temperatures, both individually and relative to each other; the tides and stage of the moon if near the sea; thunderstorms; rain; bird song; midges; the month; atmospheric pressure; and whether you are active or indolent! About the only certainty is the fact that 'the fly in the water' gives a chance. You never *know* with salmon but, after many years, you sense imminent productive moments. Let us study the indicators:

Air/water temperature

It is desirable in spring and late autumn for the air temperature to exceed the water temperature by several degrees. This holds good until a water temperature of about 60°F is reached; thereafter it is better if the air temperature is just a degree or two above that of the water. In other words, you hope for a warm day in spring and autumn, and do not venture forth on a hot day in summer. I have caught many salmon on a fly fished off a floating line with the water temperature not far below 70°F but not on hot days.

The tides and moon

Full and new moons result in high spring tides which bring in salmon from the sea. If your beat on a little river is within 7 or 8 miles of the tidal water, a spring tide may bring you a sea-liced fish, but tides and the moon do not signify much for higher beats.

The spate

A spate is caused by rain falling in the mountains, hills or other catchment area. The feeder streams fill and debouch into the main river, causing it to rise. A bulge of water then runs down the valley. This is the spate. Soon after rain stops, the feeder streams fall away and the upper, then the middle, and finally the lower river levels drop. It is possible to fish through a spate on the upper reaches of a short river for a day, find the water level the next morning too low for action, and jump into your car and catch up with the tail end of the bulge further down the valley close to the sea.

As the river rises and falls, when should you fish? On more occasions than it is possible to remember I have taken a salmon in the first 20 minutes of rising water. The beginner must realize that, at the start, the level will be low, as may have been the case for 2 or 3 weeks or even months, but rain has been falling for several hours in the catchment area. As he stands on the bank, he may notice the arrival of a brown tinge, just a stain in the water colour. Within an hour the level may have risen by 1, 6 or 12 in., depending on the amount of rain. Resident salmon are eager to take your fly during the first 20 minutes of the rise. Thereafter fish are more concerned with changing their positions or running upriver. The trick is to be in the right place, where you know there is a resident fish to take advantage of those few moments.

Anticipation is all!

A series of heavy showers may have the same effect. A slight rise in the level, or extra available oxygen due to the spattering of raindrops on the water surface, may trigger action.

22 June 1980 Run below Sycamore Hole. 8½ lb. 4 pm. 1 in. Black Dart tube fly. Went through The Saucepan, netted out in The Weir. River very low. Heavy showers raised water ½ in. during the afternoon. Fished 2.30 pm to 6.00 pm. Saw two fish in Rock Hole.

After the first few productive minutes of rising water your chances fall away with the arrival of the flood but, even then, you may take fish, but not by moving up and down the river. There is a saying, 'The man who moves his feet takes the fish', which means you should cover the whole of your beat in search of a 'taker'. This is not one of those times. At the height of a flood, go to the tail of a pool above a series of rapids and stay there, casting a large fly. Salmon pause in such places to catch their breath. You may be lucky.

29 July 1988 8 lb. 1¼ in. Black Dart. Opposite bushes at tail of The Flats. A very clean fish with large raw running mark. Must have come a long way up the river on the spate. 10.30 am.

That fish was taken above rapids in the tail of a long glide in high water. At no other water height does this place hold salmon. The 'running mark' is a raw red patch, about the size of a 5p coin. It is found under the chest of a salmon where it has rubbed off the skin against the bedrock whilst swimming up the river.

Following rain, the river rise and the full flow of several hours or perhaps days, comes the fall. Now the angler goes forth upon the business of catching salmon: not one, but two or three! As soon as a line of stranded flotsam is seen

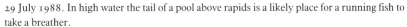

29 July 1988. In high water the tail of a pool above rapids is a likely place for a running fish to take a breather.

on the grassy slope beside the river, washed there by the now receding water, or twigs, leaves and bits of weed form a high tide mark on the sand or mud of a bay, you should set about catching fish. On the River Deveron in Scotland the down-turn of a spate is marked by washed-up whisky bottles! Be certain whether a river is rising or falling. On arrival at the river, mark the water height by a stick pressed into the sand, mud or gravel at water-lapping level.

The falling river brings the golden day: clearing water, the fly reducing in size as the colour of the flow changes from brown to green or a stain of whisky hue, and the torrent steadies. Fresh fish are in the pools! Two or three hours may suffice to take two or three fish – no more. Anyone who takes more in a single day should search his soul and hang his head. In later years, when you are over the top of the hill, a single salmon suffices – even then you wonder as it lies upon the grass. But three, there is nothing to be ashamed of in three, if fish are there a-plenty.

20 July 1980 7.15 am Bridge Pool   7 lb
                8.15 am Middle Stickle 9 lb
                9.15 am Sycamore Run 9 lb

The first two on a 1¼ in. Black Dart. The third fish rose to the same fly and missed. Rested him for 10 minutes. Tied on a 1¼ in. Hairy Mary which he took. All netted.

An early start led to the capture of these fish, and those which fell to my fly at breakfast time on 31 August 1988. These events lead us on to the correct timing of our visits to the river.

Time of day

As a spate falls away – fish all day. At other times it is well to consider which are the most productive hours of daylight. In March, warm air will warm cold water and cold fish as the day progresses. Thus, if the water temperature is 45°F and the air 55°F when you start to fish at 10 am, by lunchtime the water may be 46°F and 47°F by 3 pm, which is a peak taking-hour in that month. Thereafter, as the air cools, your chances reduce. Evidence of warming water, if you fail to carry a thermometer, is presented by a hatch of large spring olives at or after lunch. They are to be seen drifting by, like tiny parachutes, as you eat your sandwiches. A burst of bird song is another hopeful sign, and so are rising trout.

In April and May, the whole day is full of hope. During bright brassy weather in June, July and August, particularly in July, an early start soon after dawn may bring rewards, and so may the final hour of daylight.

September is the best month of the year for almost all game fishing. Don't waste an hour unless you are on a river where the main run of the year does not enter until November and December, in which case the afternoon may be better than the morning.

above left: Lara Bingham is visible mid-river; her cast is too high.

above right: Correct position tucked under the bank; low cast.

Take advantage of cover.

Thunderstorms, wind, rain, midges and the barometer

Reg Righyni (1973), a thoughtful salmon angler and author, wrote:

Unfavourable weather factors make for a *good drying day* for the washing, while the promising day is what the gardener recognizes as a *good growing day*.

So, smile as the rain runs down the back of your neck, particularly if a gale has robbed you of your hat! A wet, windy day is full of hope, particularly if the wind blows upstream against the current to create great waves. I lost my hat in the river on such a day and failed to retrieve it by casting a Black Dart, but that fly took three salmon in the next hour as the shirt became sodden around my neck.

A thunderstorm is different. Never fish with a carbon-fibre rod, or any other rod for that matter, when lightning flashes in the sky. You are holding a personal lightning conductor and risk electrocution. But, as soon as the storm has passed and the rumbles are beyond the hill, set about the business with determination because thunder stimulates salmon.

I love a midgey, drizzly day with overcast sky, a day when polarized spectacles and pullovers steam up and you are glad of a 'breathable' jacket.

On such a day in April I was teaching John Mills to fish. John had lost a salmon 2 years before but came back for revenge. I showed him where to fish and how, then left to walk up the river. When only 25 yd away he called that he had felt a touch. 'Touches' are unmistakable, alive and slightly soft, like a drifting leaf brushing against the fly. 'Start up here above the place. Fish down on him again. Salmon often drift back after touching the fly.'

Just 10 yd below the place of the touch, he hooked his fish:

16 April 1987 8½ lb. 1 in. Copper Dart. Air 58°. Water 51°. Floating line. River rose 4 in. in the day, but clear. John Mills first salmon in The Triangle. A warm drizzly day.

The barometer does not persuade me to fish or dissuade me from going to the river. I look at mine on my dressing table each morning, but only in the hope that a fall forecasts rain.

Stealth

I do not think it makes much difference to salmon if you wear clothes the colour of the Union Jack, but an angler so attired demonstrates a total lack of understanding of the way to catch salmon in a little river. Stand high on the bank of a small pool and the occupants will speed around in agitation before hiding under a rock or the roots of a washed-out bankside tree. Instead, hold back from the bank, or kneel down to make your cast, or wade below the bank. Fish with the sun in your face instead of letting it silhouette you from the rear. Cast from behind a bush or kneel in front. The bush will shield your outline against the sky. Don't thump about on metal-studded boots, jump down off a bank, or clatter with a metal-tipped wading staff. Fish pick up vibrations with the receptors along their lateral line. Above all – keep low. I know a man who catches many salmon on the fly in a little river. He fishes on his knees, his labrador lies beside his boots, his rod is short and he casts a long line – all outside the window of the quarry.

8 Spinning tackle

Spinning is considered by many to be less skilled than fishing a fly, to lack subtlety in the approach to the fish. But few consider that spinning is inferior when assessing the number of fish it places on the bank under certain river conditions. Perhaps that success is the reason for a certain jealousy amongst some fly fishers of their spinning brethren, the suspicion that these achievements are not the result of personal skill but of the ability of tackle manufacturers to turn out equipment which does the job without much assistance. 'Anyone can spin' is a common thought, if not an observation.

For myself I am pleased to spin when conditions lead me to the belief that the minnow or spoon bait give me a better chance than the fly. In other words, I take notice of experience and act according to my own judgement; this is quite different from preference. But I observe that all wish to catch a salmon on the fly, and, hour for hour, the fly provides me with greater pleasure.

It is true that a person may learn to *cast* a bait with modern tackle in a single hour, but he will not learn to *fish* with a spinning bait any more quickly than the fly fisher, who can already cast, will learn to *fish* his fly. In fact, he may take longer. The reason for this is that a salmon will assist the floating fly-line man by coming to his fly; the cold-water spinning angler has to go deep to find his fish and that requires a detailed knowledge of the river bed. The fly will rarely become snagged on underwater objects, but this happens regularly to the minnow of an angler learning a new piece of water.

To spin with success there are two essentials: acquisition of efficient tackle and the gathering of river knowledge and the habits of salmon. The second requirement takes longer than the first and much is only relevant to a particular piece of water. It is a mistake to visit different rivers each season in the hope of finding the rainbow's end. Instead, go year after year after year to the same place, learn the lies at different water heights, where to take advantage of an upstream wind which ruffles the water surface, and how two back turns of the reel will sink a Devon to the right level in a deep pot. But let us discuss tackle requirements first.

Rods

In March 1986, an article of mine on spring salmon fishing was published in *Countrysport*. The following is an extract:

I gave the name 'Droopy' to an angler who span opposite to me for two or three seasons on a salmon river in March. His bent neck resulted from peering at the water. A cigarette hung from his upper lip and his rod had a permanent downward set; the result of casting more lead than anyone else I have met.

When Droopy appeared, I stopped fishing and made ready, for he always became stuck on the bed rocks of the river. He did not pull from various angles, use an otter, or even haul and break – he used me. 'Cast your bait over my line and pull me off. There's a good chap.' I did this many times, as much for the chance to examine his bait as for good fellowship, for Droopy caught more salmon than anyone else.

'Any luck?' he would ask.

In reply I might mention that one springer had come my way so far that season.

'Had ten,' he would say, waggling the drooping fag.

A yard above his 2 in. Rapala, at the swivel joining the line to the trace, were two generous Hillman leads. Droopy scraped the bottom. He had no evil in him for he only behaved like this in cold full water when it was impossible to see fish and they were few and far between. Later in the season, when the water warmed up, he never appeared. Perhaps he did not have a fly rod.

Droopy knew how to catch salmon. It is true that his bait became stuck on the river bed from time to time, but he knew where the fish rested. He caught more than anyone else whilst using inexpensive tackle which had seen better days. Two or three carbon-fibre rods of different lengths and actions, expensive if need be, are necessary to meet various conditions when fishing the fly. To spin on a little river, a single 8 ft 6 in. rod of fibreglass will cover all situations. That rod must be of good quality, with well-placed rings of suitable size. The first spinning rod I possessed in the 1940s was of tubular steel, the 'Slapton' made by Accles & Pollock. Foolishly I shortened this rod by 1 ft to increase the power – subsequently losing salmon because it was too stiff and bent out my hooks when playing fish.

8 ft 6 in. Hardy Fibalite Spin with Hardy Elarex multiplying reel (discontinued) and braided Searanger line.

The second rod came in the 1960s, from the angler's Mecca, House of Hardy in Pall Mall, an 8 ft 6 in. metal-ferruled Glascona. This rod was a delight to use. It killed many salmon in conjunction with an Elarex multiplying reel, but was accidentally broken. Since then, well-rewarded trust has been placed in the Hardy 8 ft 6 in. Fibalite Spin. This rod will cast 1¼ oz, weighs 8½ oz and has a double handle, 22 in. long. The length of handle is important. The 9 ft 6 in. Fibalite Spin has a 28 in. handle which is awkward to shift from side to side across the tummy when casting. I am over 6 ft tall, with arms to match, but the manufacturers still imagine that my arms will extend if I buy a 9 ft 6 in rod to match the longer butt! The Fibalite weighs an unnoticeable 1 oz more than the same length in carbon fibre, the Favourite, which costs half as much again.

I doubt that Droopy would pay the extra or, if he did, that he would catch more. Fibreglass is not as hard as carbon fibre, but the only part of the rod likely to wear is the spigot on the butt section where it is thrust into the socket of the upper part. An ordinary candle rubbed over this spigot and smoothed off by warm fingers will protect the fibres. A further maintenance requirement: after each season examine the end ring at the tip of the rod for wear. The constant passing in and out of braided or monofilament line through this ring causes wear. The wear is in the form of grooves cut in the ring and line damage may result.

Spinning rods longer than 8 ft 6 in. enable a greater length of line to be kept out of the water because of their extra height. This enables a bait to be fished more slowly on the far side of a wide river, as the current is unable to take hold of a large belly of sub-surface line and pull the bait across at speed. This situation does not arise in a narrow river. The only need for a 10 ft or 10 ft 6 in. rod in a small water is that one may fish a worm, shrimp or prawn more effectively by dangling them in pools whilst keeping back from the bank. In this situation a long rod is an advantage, but the 12 ft or 12 ft 6 in. fly rod is available to fish the worm with a fly reel loaded with monofilament, although of course, there must be a little added weight.

Reels, lines and traces

Two types of spinning reel are available: the multiplier and the fixed spool. The multiplier casts heavy baits long distances. It is suited to wide rivers in early spring and late autumn, when cold water conditions lead us to fish deep with heavy baits. The reel requires plenty of room to swing the rod when casting and it is therefore difficult or impossible to use in restricted circumstances between trees. It is also unsuited to casting lightweight baits in summer; these have insufficient weight to overcome the inertia of the drum and keep it revolving. A good multiplier is expensive, finely engineered, good to look at and a splendid device for playing fish, but it does not fulfil all our varied requirements.

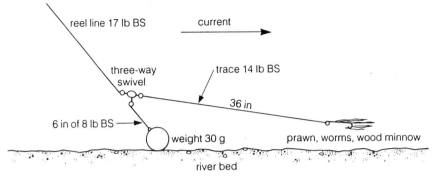

reel line 17 lb BS

current

three-way swivel

trace 14 lb BS

36 in

6 in of 8 lb BS

weight 30 g

prawn, worms, wood minnow

river bed

A paternoster, or ledger.

For the small river, a single fixed-spool reel will meet every situation. Two spools for the reel ought to be purchased, each to hold 100 yd of monofilament of different strengths. For heavy-water spinning at low temperatures, I suggest either 17 lb Platil Soft in 110 yd spools, or 17 lb Stren which is also available in 100 yd spools. Stren nylon is available in the fluorescent colours blue, white or gold. Both are supple and cast well, but the Platil is difficult for the angler to see against the water background when fishing. One might be persuaded that this makes it less likely to frighten fish. There may be some truth in this but, on the whole, a coloured nylon makes for easier positioning and control of the bait. On balance I suggest the coloured, because for many years I span with my Hardy Elarex multiplier and white braided line – this brought me as many salmon as the near-invisible monofilaments of my companions. For casting light baits in low warm water, the second spool should be loaded with 14 lb monofilament.

The trace is the length of nylon, about 3 ft long, between the swivel, or weight and swivel, at the end of the reel line, and the bait. It should be of 14 lb BS when using the 17 lb casting line, and of 12 lb when fishing the 14 lb line.

There is a wide choice of fixed-spool reels on the market. You cannot try them all. My own experience has been largely with Mitchell; the long-established and respected, metal Model 300 and the lighter, less expensive, carbon-bodied Model 1160G.

The Mitchell 300

I have half-a-dozen Model 300 reels in my fishing school. Some have been in use for 15 years. Not one has worn out or broken down other than through misuse. The Model 300 is left-hand wind whilst Model 301 is wound on the right; on neither can the handle be switched from one side to the other. Two spools of large and small capacity come with the reel. The small-capacity spool is insufficiently deep to hold the required 14 lb nylon, therefore a second, deep spool must be purchased. Drag is set by a simple adjustment on the front of the spool and there is a small anti-reverse level at the rear. The reel weighs 18 oz. A small oil can should be carried and a single drop of oil applied daily at each of the points suggested in the instructions. Whilst the Model 300 is a reliable 'founder member' of the fixed spool tribe, Mitchell have recently produced a number of more modern fixed-spool reels. Their Excellence and Performance series are ambidextrous, have rear-drag adjustment and a convenient anti-reverse control operated by the thumb.

Loading the line

It is convenient to mount the reel on the butt section of the rod. Attach the nylon to the spool as shown in the reel instructions, and click over the bail arm to the winding position by turning the handle of the reel. The spool of nylon to be loaded must not be placed upon a pencil and wound onto the reel, as you would do when loading a fly line. Instead, to avoid twists, one of the flat sides of the line spool must face the reel spool and the line must be pulled off the line spool over its edge. The line must come *off* the line spool in the same direction as it is wound *on* the reel spool. If the incorrect side of the line spool faces the reel, spool twists will accumulate and the mistake will be obvious. The line should be wound on under slight pressure – running the line through a handkerchief squeezed between thumb and forefinger is a simple method. The spool should be filled to within $\frac{8}{100}$ in. (2 mm) of the front lip. If filled to capacity (overfilled), loose coils will come off as the angler casts, and tangles will result. If the spool is underfilled, long casts will be impossible because of the loss of energy as the line has to lift itself up and over the spool lip.

During the course of several days' fishing, some length of nylon may be lost, the line will no longer come within $\frac{8}{100}$ in. (2 mm) of the spool lip and casting will be impaired. You must then add additional nylon beneath the line or fit a new line. The cost of 100 yd of monofilament is about £5. It is much better to go to this expense than attach extra nylon with a blood knot, because this might jam under the angle of the bail arm or between the angle of a snake ring and the body of the rod.

On the first outing with a new line, it is well to take out any twists before starting to fish. To do this, feed the line as usual through the rod rings and

8 ft 6 in. Hardy Fibalite Spin with Mitchell 300 fixed-spool reel and monofilament line.

then take a 17 g (approx. ⅝ oz) Wye weight. Tie the end of the line to the *swivel* of the Wye and cast out two or three times into the river; any twists will be released. (The swivel is the end opposite to the end where the line would be attached when actually fishing).

Baits, weights and swivels

The original Farlow-Sharpe ball-bearing swivel, known as the 'BB', is more efficient than a box or barrel swivel. The BB has ten stainless-steel balls inside, is rustless and offers almost no resistance to the spinning bait, which will revolve freely. These easy revolutions allow the bait to be fished more slowly, if this is desired. No more than one BB swivel is needed for a trace.

You will find that some baits do not need additional weight at the line/trace junction, in which case a BB swivel must be used to join the two nylons. When additional weight is needed, I use the lead-free Wye in weights of 8, 11 and 17 g (approximately ¼, ⅜ and ⅝ oz). The Wye has a brass loop at one end and a barrel swivel at the other; *always* tie the trace to the swivel so that the bait may spin against the 'stop' of the weight. If you see a made-up spinning rod on the rod-room racks of a fishing hotel and the reel line is tied to the swivel, you will know that the owner is a novice. You also know that his morning will be twistingly frustrated.

The other weight I find useful is the Hillman favoured by Droopy – he who scraped the bottom! This must be used in conjunction with a BB swivel at the line/trace junction. The Hillman attachment wire should be passed through the top loop of the swivel, which may then revolve freely to match the bait. Hillmans are available in various sizes and are easily changed when more, or less, weight is required.

Spinning baits

In the discourse on salmon flies, the proposition was put forward that salmon will have a go at almost anything if in the mood. The suggested range of flies was thus small in order to avoid the angler being labelled a 'tackle fiddler'. There is an unlimited choice of artificial baits in both type and colour. Amongst these lures is the popular Toby, which I do not include in the small selection carried in my pocket. The reason is contained in the following diary entry:

13 September 1989 One salmon 9 lb. 4 sea trout. Total weight of fish 17 lb 12 oz. No. 4 U/S Mepps. With Brian and Tony. Very thick water clearing in pm after first spate for 4½ months. Low water. Brian lost a fish on 2½ in. U/S Toby – jumped and came unstuck. Salmon and sea trout taken on No. 4 gold Mepps thrown upstream.

Brian's fish was a grilse which he hooked whilst I was watching. It leaped once and the treble came away. The Toby is a good attractor, but a higher percentage of salmon and grilse come unstuck than is the case with minnows and Mepps. This lack of hooking and holding power is probably due to the

13 September 1989. One salmon of 9 lb and four sea trout, total 17 lb 12 oz No. 4 U/S (upstream) Mepps.

length of the body, which may prevent initial hooking and often levers out the hooks. Hooking and holding may be improved by re-fitting the treble to the end of a short wire trace attached to the swivel at the head of the bait.

The hook hangs just behind the body, held there by a twist of fuse wire passed through the hook eye and the hole at the end of the body. When a fish takes, this wire breaks and the body cannot interfere with the flying treble. I sketch this possibility because the bait is popular, but the alteration takes time and trouble and other baits are more reliable.

The Devon minnow

This is an excellent bait for hooking and landing fish, but one must examine purchased hook mounts. These should be protected against rust by plastic-coated wire, and the wire should pass through the eye of the treble, be turned back and crimped in a sleeve. Some mounts on sale have spade-end trebles; plain wire is passed along the shank and turned over between the hooks. This wire is then held in place by a plastic sleeve or whipped in position by silk. This is not secure and, if the binding is of varnished silk, it may rot and/or be cut by the teeth along the edge of the lower jaw of a salmon. The best mounts

Materials to make a Devon minnow mount.

I have seen come in the plastic Spey minnows from Fog Fishing Tackle of Ross-on-Wye. I emphasize *in* their Spey minnows – spare mounts may be of the plastic-sleeve type. If in doubt, make your own mounts. All you require is a spool of Berkley 30 lb Steelon wire, No. 4 sleeves, No. 7 barrel swivels, red plastic tulip beads and No. 4 or No. 6 Partridge x1 outbend trebles.

The body of a Devon may be of metal, weighted plastic, or wood, with or without a copper tube insert. I prefer metal and weighted plastic: both are durable and their weight makes them ideal for deep fishing in cold water. You do need to know the river bed when using a heavy Devon, or the bait may snag and be lost. Fewer wooden Devons will snag on the bottom when fished in conjunction with a Wye weight because the minnow will swim above the weight. Set against this advantage is the delicacy of their plastic fins, which tend to break, and the fact that the paint tends to flake off the body.

A friend of mine, Derek Myhill, catches many salmon on wooden Devons that he makes himself from dried hazel branches. He cuts these to the required lengths, drills them, shapes them by hand with a knife and fits plastic fins. The minnow is then given two coats of aluminium paint, over which the desired colours are applied. His minnows are called WHORGs and REWHORGs (WH=white, OR=orange, G=gold, RE=red). The minnow is shaped unevenly and the hole drilled down the middle of the body is slightly on a slant. These malformations cause the minnow to wobble as it spins and this, judging from the number of fish Derek catches, must make it irresistible! The WHORGs are fished in conjunction with a Wye weight. The trace is plain nylon passed directly through the body of the minnow which sits on a red tulip bead. A black Partridge outbend treble is pressed into the bead. When a salmon is hooked, the wooden body floats up the trace out of the way and, having watched him from the far side of the river, I can vouch for the fact that the salmon is landed!

Standard Devons are available in many colour combinations. My choice is:

1   Yellow Belly for heavily coloured water, particularly in early spring

2   Black & Gold when the water is merely stained

3   Blue & Silver in a clear flow.
Devons are available in lengths of 1 to 3 in. I limit my burden to 2 and 2½ in.

The Devon fishes well in fast water and may be reeled back to the angler with no unpleasant resistance against the flow after completing the fishing of the cast. When a river falls, the speed reduces and the temperature rises, you should, if persisting with a Devon, reduce the minnow size, but I prefer to change my bait to a Mepps or a Rapala.

The Mepps

There are many models: Aglia, Aglia Decorée with black or red spots, Aglia fly (mouche) with a red or black feather or wool dressing on the treble,

2 April 1985. Andrew Livingstone with a 19 lb spring fish taken with a 2 in.
Black & Gold Devon minnow.

Aglia Longue and Longue Rainbo, and more besides!

You will not go wrong if you confine yourself to the original Aglia, which has
been in use for 50 years. It is available in silver, copper and gold. Buy sizes
No. 1 and No. 2 in gold for downstream casting when the water has fallen
below a level at which you would choose a 2 in. Devon. The No. 4 revolves
too fast for downstream spinning, but is ideal for the upstream cast in
summer. Beware the treble hook on the small sizes. This may be of too light a
wire to cope with salmon. I know, for I lost a good fish years ago when the
hook bent out, but landed one of 14 lb when the hook had been replaced with
something more substantial. Cut off the treble, fit a Mustad No. 1 oval split
ring and a No. 6 round-eyed bronze Partridge x1 outbend treble. (The
colours black and silver are also available).

The Aglia Longue in the copper shade is an attractive bait that revolves more
slowly than the Aglia. It could be used downstream in fast water in place of
the Devon minnow, but the No. 4 is unsuited to the upstream cast because it
does not revolve well when moving with the current. The small Aglia spun
downstream will almost always need additional weight at the line/trace
junction. When casting the Aglia No. 4 upstream an 8 g (¼ oz) Wye should
be added.

The Rapala

Every salmon angler should have a plug in his pocket if he is fishing artificial bait. Until recently I carried the red rubber Flopy which is made in France, but recently I have found them unobtainable. Lt. Col. S. H. Crow, who managed the Somerley water on the Hampshire Avon in the 1960s, favoured the Heddon River Runt; Bernard Aldrich of Broadlands went for a pink or green Flopy and Hugh Falkus was 'looked after very well' by the River Runt.

Jock Scott, author of *Spinning Up to Date* (1950), experimented with plugs in conjunction with Mr L. R. Hardy. Following the American practice, they called the baits 'wigglers'. Wigglers were small but led to the production of the 3¾ in. Heddon River Runt Spook, which took salmon in a full river. This long plug suffered leverage problems on hook-hold by the three trebles under the belly.

Droopy used the Rapala, and I suggest you give it a swim in a little river. The great advantage of a plug is that it starts to dive and wriggle as soon as it hits the water – no 'start-up' room of wasted river width is needed before it commences its attractive antics. The most popular colour combination is the black back and silver belly; in dirty water a fluorescent red back and gold belly is favoured.

The Rapala is available as a single body or jointed in the middle. When fishing the single body, lengths of 5 and 7 cm (2 and 2¾ in.) are sufficient to cover needs. The smallest jointed Rapala is 7 cm (2¾ in.) and if this size and the 9 cm (3½ in.) are carried in addition to the singles, you may cope with all water conditions. Rapalas of these descriptions are made to float or sink; be sure to purchase the sinking type.

This bait does not spin and thus a swivel is not incorporated in the head. The nylon trace should be attached direct to the built-in wire loop at the head with a tucked half blood knot; a BB swivel or Wye weight should join the line to the trace.

The Flying 'C'

This recently introduced Mepps lure has a silver or gold Mepp spinning blade at the head, and a long body sheathed in red, brown or yellow rubber with two tails. It is available in weights of 10, 15 and 25 g (approximately ⅜, ½ and ⅞ oz). The 15 g has produced a number of fish for pupils I have been teaching, and is probably the most successful bait available today. My diary reads:

10 September 1991 The Manse pool. Grilse 7 lb. Having fished up the pool with a Toby cast by Stephen, Hilary followed with 10 g red Flying 'C' and took this fish by casting across the river.

29 September 1993 The Manse pool. Grilse 6 lb 6 oz. John took this fish on a 15 g red Flying 'C' cast downstream after we saw it splash on arrival at the pool.

9 Fishing the artificial bait

Casting

When teaching people to cast with a fixed-spool reel I like them to commence with a 17 g (⅝ oz) Wye and no bait. Whilst they are learning, the weight is attached by the swivel to the line. My reason for this is that the beginner, having cast into the river, spends a few seconds dithering before remembering that his first action should be to turn the handle. The retrieve is thus delayed and a hooked bait sinks to the river bed and snags. A Wye, having no hooks, is unlikely to catch on an underwater obstruction. When you are fishing a bait, the Wye is tied by the metal loop to the reel line but, when you are learning to cast, attaching it to the swivel prevents twists in the line.

There are two methods of casting: overhead and the side swing. I always teach beginners to cast sideways. The overhead cast, in which the line rises high above the water and then falls, may drop through the branches of a tree on the far bank – a dangerous situation (see p. 98). The sideways, horizontal cast, with near flat trajectory, will pass underneath branches which overhang the water.

Proceed as follows. Allow the weight to hang 3 ft below the rod tip and turn sideways to the river with the rod tip at right angles to the river. Pick up the line with the right forefinger and turn over the bail arm with the left hand, which then returns to hold the butt button against the caster's stomach throughout the cast. The right hand now punches the rod forward. The path of the rod tip should be scooped, being lower at the centre than at the beginning and end of the throw. (If the trace is longer than 3 ft the rod will have to be held too high and the cast cannot be scooped.) The right moment to let go of the line will only come with practice, but if one consistently casts too far to the left or right, re-position the feet to counteract this tendency. Learning to cast with a spinning rod is easier than with a fly rod. Even so, an hour with a professional instructor will set the novice on the right path. A whole day will be too little to teach him to *fish* with the spinning rod!

Setting up the tackle

Having passed the line under the bail arm, run it up through the rod rings and tie it to the wire loop of a Wye weight with a tucked half blood knot.

If the Wye has a spring clip attached to the swivel, remove and discard this clip; it might bend open when playing a salmon. The clip is placed there by the manufacturers to enable the rapid attachment of an extra swivel. Now, tie one end of a 3 ft trace to the bait and the other to the Wye swivel, in each case with the tucked half blood. If an additional swivel is required, the trace should be cut in the centre and a BB added in that position.

If the angler prefers a Hillman weight, a BB swivel should join the line to the trace. The Hillman wire should be passed through the top ring of the swivel. As previously mentioned, the trace nylon should have a 2 or 3 lb BS less than the reel line.

It is now necessary to set the slipping clutch so that line will be released at an ideal pressure when pulled by a salmon. Hook the bait to the base of a fence, stump or other fixed object, not the tail of your instructor's dog; back away for a few yards with the bail arm open, turn the reel handle to close the bail arm and raise the rod. Set the clutch adjustment so that the reel gives line when the rod is well bent when held at an angle of about 45 degrees.

When playing a salmon, the clutch setting may be altered as found necessary. Do not wind continuously with a slipping clutch whilst playing a salmon. This does not recover line and each turn of the bail arm puts one twist in the line if the clutch slips. In this event, tighten the clutch and pump the salmon towards you by raising the rod almost to the vertical; then wind in line as the rod is dropped to 45 degrees.

Releasing snagged baits

Releasing a minnow stuck in a tree, or in any position above the water, is a potentially dangerous operation. This is particularly so of baits tangled in the end of a branch. Nylon is elastic, the branch bends and a giant catapult has been set up. The weight and bait are the projectiles and you are the target! If the bait is on the far side of the river, you may have to pull and break. The risk of being hit by a flying projectile can be minimized. Wrap a handkerchief around your hand, or pull on a glove, take two or three turns of the reel nylon around your hand, turn your back put down your head and walk away with the hand held out from the body until the trace snaps. The weight will fly across the river and probably bury itself in the bank. I have a repaired hole in the back of my Barbour made by a Wye. Always wind the nylon around your protected hand; do not tighten the clutch and pull from the reel. This latter action may cause the tightened line to cut down into the coils of nylon on the spool, resulting in a tangle.

When casting downstream, the bait snagged underwater should not be pulled. Instead, open the bail arm and let 20 or 30 yd of line form a loop downstream of the bait. Close the bail arm and strike sharply with the rod. If you are lucky, the bail will be pulled off from below. Other than this, you should jiggle and pull from various directions, generally from downstream of the bait if you are casting downstream. If casting upstream pull from above the snag. If release proves impossible, there may be no alternative but to pull until the trace snaps; use the handkerchief and proceed as described.

I cannot be bothered to use an 'otter' when trying to release a snagged bait. The 'otter' disturbs the water and much time may be lost. However, I appreciate that Rapalas cost in the region of £5 each and therefore some anglers will use a homemade 'otter' from a piece of wood or stick found on the riverbank and a piece of string.

It is not sensible to climb trees to release baits or flies. I came across an angler who had climbed, slipped and fallen, all for a 75p bait. He cracked three ribs!

Spinning in cold water

There are those who *fish* with a spinning outfit and others who are *turners of reel handles*. Salmon will not be caught consistently by those who cast out and automatically retrieve the bait without thinking about the depth of its passage, the speed at which it is travelling and where fish are likely to be resting. Many times in early spring I have seen anglers chuck the bait to the far side of the river, click over the bail arm and start winding the reel handle. Through polarized spectacles the bait is visible speeding back across the river just below the surface. These operators do not have a hope! To fish and succeed in taking salmon in cold water requires knowledge of the river bed and a thoughtful assessment of where a salmon is likely to be found. A bait of correct size and pattern must then be presented at the right depth and speed, and the angler must *will* the salmon to take. I try to project myself down the line, to be with my bait, feeling its way as it follows the rises and dips of the river bed.

The water is generally cold from the latter part of October or early November until the middle of April. It is accepted practice, confirmed by my own experience that large baits fished slowly, close to the river bed, provide the best chance of a fish in those months of the year. Devon minnows of 2 or 2½ in., preferably Yellow Bellies, and the larger Rapalas are suited to the full, fast water of early spring and the colour at which it runs when in spate. Almost always additional weight, perhaps 11 g (3/8 oz), will be needed to keep the bait close to the bed of the river against the lift of the current. This weight will need to be increased or reduced in different pools. If too much weight is used, the bait will have to be retrieved faster than is desirable; if too little, the bait will swim too high. Rapalas and minnows will fish deep in fast water because they are slim, but they are less suited to the wider splay at the tail of a pool. In these wider places where the current may be slower and the depth a little less the No. 2 Mepps Aglia with an 11 g (3/8 oz) Wye has killed many salmon at water temperatures of 40°F and above.

It is clear that, from the throat of a pool to the run-off, changes of weight and bait may be required if all areas are to be fished correctly. In a little river, the pools are short and a change may not be needed if the pool is almost uniform throughout its length. Holding the rod at different heights and slightly altering the speed of retrieve may be sufficient. Extra depth may be achieved initially, as soon as the bait hits the water, by a single back-turn of the reel handle. To accomplish this, close the bail arm as soon as the bait hits the water in order to establish contact, then unwind by one or two turns of the reel handle; the bait will sink sharply. The anti-reverse lever must be in the off position for this to be accomplished.

When fishing a pool, the position of the rod tip is important. If the pool is wide, and you wish to fish the far side slowly, the tip should be high. This keeps the centre of the line out of the water; preventing the formation of a downstream belly, which would sweep the bait towards the bank where you are standing. The near side may be fished with the rod at 45 degrees when the bait hits the river mid-stream. It may then be lowered almost to touch the river as the bait swings to the near side and hangs below the bank.

It is said, when fishing at this time of year, that the weight or the bait should occasionally bump on the river bed. This is correct for the angler learning a new beat; he must be willing to lose some ammunition in the interest of gathering information on the river contours. The angler who knows the river well, and fishes a wooden minnow which swims above the weight, will lose very few minnows – his weight ought to bump the bed from time to time. On the whole, provided that the bait is fishing close to the river bed, the less weight the better because the fishing may be slower without snagging.

The decision to use a particular bait must be based upon the condition and volume of the water. According to these, my choice would be:

1 Water: temperature 40°F; full flow; coloured.
Choice: 2½ in. metal Yellow Belly Devon minnow, 7 or 9 cm (2¾ or 3½ in.) jointed Rapala in fluorescent red, black and gold belly

2 Water: temperature 44°F; medium flow; coloured.
Choice: 2 in. Spey Yellow Belly Devon or 7 cm (2¾ in.) Black & Silver Rapala (not jointed).

3 Water: temperature 44°F; medium flow; little colour.
Choice: 2 in. Spey Black & Gold Devon; 5 cm (2 in.) Black & Silver Rapala.

4 Water: temperature 44°F; medium flow; clear.
Choice: 2 in. Spey Blue & Silver Devon. 5 cm (2 in.) Black & Silver Rapala. In pool tail No. 2 Mepps Aglia, gold.

5 Water: temperature 46–50°F.
Choice: 2 in. Spey Devons. 5 cm (2 in.) Rapala. Colour choice depending on water clarity. No. 2 Mepps Aglia fished more widely as water level falls in April.

Some illustrations of correct choice appear in my diary:

22 March 1979 8 lb. No. 2 Mepps Aglia. Rookery Pool. Walter Reid's first salmon, a bright clean fish. Air 52°. Water 46°.

He was lucky to land that salmon. I inspected the treble – one of the hooks had opened. The taking-place in Rookery Pool is in the middle of the tail, a smooth, settled shallow piece of water where the salmon took the bait.

5 April 1970 Uncle Kiff's water. River clear but high. Air 44°. Water 42°. 10 lb. 10.15 am. 2 in. Blue & Silver metal Devon. Cold and sunny. Gave fish to Uncle Kiff.

That salmon was taken from the Welsh Dee, at a stage when I meticulously took water and air temperatures with my thermometer. Having worked it all out, the 2 in. Blue & Silver was attached. The thermometer was of glass, protected by a sturdy brass case with a window to see the scale. House of Hardy still make them and I still have mine!

Up to mid-April in early spring my first action on reaching the river at about 10.00 am is to mark the water height with a stick and have a good look at the colour of the flow. The second is to take the air and water temperatures. I then choose a bait as the result of this assessment and, taking into account water depth and rate of flow, a weight. At lunch-time, on returning to base, I check the water level against the stick and increase or reduce the bait size if the river has risen or fallen. Clarity will also be taken into account half-way through the day, for spate rivers clear and fall rapidly. An unfishable highly coloured river, offering little hope after breakfast, may be inviting at tea-time; whether there is hope or not will depend upon my boots. If I wade in up to my knees and can see my feet there is a chance.

I also check the temperature of the water at lunch-time; a 1°F rise is to be expected, and 2°F by 3.00 pm if the air is 6 or 7°F higher than the water. As I wrote in Chapter 7, a mid-day hatch of large spring olives is an encouraging sign, indicating that the water temperature has risen – if there is a bitter wind the nymphs keep their noses down and salmon do the same. But if there is a hatch, the temperature rise may continue through the afternoon until about 4.00 pm. At 4.00 pm, the chance is slipping away; the peak occurs within an hour of 3.00 pm.

The paternoster or ledger

This system enables slow, deep fishing. Tie the reel line to a three-way swivel and a wooden minnow to the 1 yd trace. To the third eye of the swivel, which is at right angles to the barrel, attach about 6 in. of 8 lb nylon, to the end of which is tied a 30 g (1 oz) shaped lead weight. Lead is legal in weights of 30 g (1 oz) and above. The lead will rest on the river bed whilst the minnow streams in the current, swaying a few inches above the bottom of the river.

It is unlikely that any part of this outfit, other than the weight, will become snagged. This would be lost if snagged due to the fine nylon, whilst the bait will be retrieved. The system may also be used to fish a worm or prawn.

Spinning in warm water

After the middle of April, two options are open to us: to spin downstream as described, or to cast the bait upriver. The second option becomes available because the water temperature will be above 50°F and salmon will rise from the river bed to take a bait, chase it downstream, and sometimes intercept!

Once these two options are available, I rarely take advantage of the first. Why spin with a downriver cast if there is the pleasurable alternative of fishing a fly off a floating line? I would need to be forced to spin by too little room to cast a fly, and not many such situations arise if you have a short fly rod. Even so, let them be considered. Later in this book, we shall walk up the narrow, wooded valley of the River Teign. Much of the water there is unfishable, other than with a short spinning rod and fixed-spool reel to flick out a natural or artificial bait. So, in a spate, take your alternative spool of 14 lb nylon, an 8 g (¼ oz) Wye, a 12 lb trace and a 5 cm (2 in.) Rapala or small Mepps. Flick out the bait between the trees and let it swing across the river. In addition cast a No. 2 Mepps straight upstream, or at 45 degrees upstream and across, and retrieve quickly.

Smaller baits will normally be fished than in the cold water of spring and less weight will be needed, for it is likely that, even in a spate, the depth of water will have reduced. It is not always necessary to add weight.

If the water is stained with peat, tie in a BB swivel at the line/trace junction and fish a No. 1 Mepps Aglia Longue in the copper colour. This bait weighs a little more than the No. 1 Mepps Aglia and fishes deeper due to its slower revolutions.

The upstream cast will take fish in low water. Salmon, grilse and sea trout all go for a bait thrown upstream and reeled back a trifle faster than the current. There need not be a spate, or even the freshener of a shower, although both of these excitements increase your chances. To achieve a long upstream cast, it is no use fishing with the 17 lb spool. Fit the 14 lb nylon to the reel and make sure the spool is filled to within 7/100 in. (2 mm) of the spool lip.

My preference now is for a Mepps Aglia No. 4 in gold, fished with a small Wye. Baits should be large: many use a gold, copper or silver Toby, but the risk of losing a fish is considerable. Cast upstream well beyond the lie; when the bait has hit the water, let it sink for a second or two to achieve a depth of about 1 ft and then reel back with the rod high if the water is shallow, or closer to the surface if it is deep.

It has been written that upstream casting with a large bait is 'not the done thing' if it is allowed to sink, because of the chance of foul-hooking salmon.

I was taught the upstream method by the Broadlands head keeper, Bernard Aldrich. I never saw him foul-hook a salmon and neither has this happened to me. I have foul-hooked three salmon over the years, all in spates on the fly! One weighed 18 lb, 'took' a No. 6 Low Water Hairy Mary close to the tail, and was landed after a struggle on 10 lb Fog Camouflage nylon. One does not have to be an expert to use the U/S No. 4 Mepps. This fish came to a beginner.

4 September 1988 U/S No. 4 Mepps. First salmon to Bob South in tail of AM Pool. Very bright fish. Plenty of water.

And to show that a Toby sometimes lands a fish:

10 September 1989 Grilse 6 lb. 2½ in. U/S Toby. Tail of AM Pool. Brian Parker, the Bossington head keeper.

As evidence that a No. 4 Mepps is not always good:

17 July 1987 Sea trout 5. Black Lure and Alexandra tube at night. With Brian and Tony. 4 in tail of AM Pool 1 in tail of CT Pool. Lost two or three, including one being played in the dark by Tony whilst I photographed. Removed the tail of a stoat killed on way over moor, amputation by pocket knife, will make good peal tube flies. On way home saw first roe deer I have seen at night on Dartmoor – jumped out of road, over wall and into prison farm fields. Many bats about on river in warm cloudy night. Brian lost a grilse in morning on a No. 4 U/S Mepps. Sea trout caught 10.30 pm to 12.30 am.

I rarely take a salmon on a metal Devon minnow cast upstream, because the Mepps is my favourite, but the upstream minnow has a long history. Read *The Science of Spinning for Salmon & Trout* by Alexander Wanless (1930). This was the bible of the practice then known as 'threadline spinning'. Tackle for this method was developed in conjunction with Mr L. R. Hardy, who was quoted in Wanless' book:

Upstream spinning for salmon with Heavy-weight and other Devons, is a method of spinning particularly adapted to clear and clear-low water conditions. Be it well noted that it is only possible to catch fish in this way so far as I know when the water becomes reasonably warm. I have never known it do any good before the end of March, but it goes on right through the season after that. Perhaps April and May are the best months. My experiences and those of some friends of mine are the same, so we may conclude that the method I am about to describe is what we might call standardized.

'Commence at the end of March or the beginning of April with the first clear waters, when the ordinary catsmeat slinging fails. The outfit comprises a Hardy-Wanless rod 7 to 8 lb or 9 to 10 lb calibre, a Number 2 Altex reel and a Hardy Nylon line, 8.5 lb breaking strain, the bait being a 1¾ in. Hardy-Pennell Devon. Various colours will doubtless suit various waters better than others. I find blue and silver and brown and gold to be the best. Later, if the water gets warmer still and lower, reduce the size of the bait. It can come down to as small as 1 inch.'

The method still works as I found to my pleasure:

2 May 1978 CT Pool. 8 lb. 4.00 pm after a good spate day before. 1½ in. Brown & Gold Devon (metal). Had sea lice on with tails. Also another followed.

You will have more 'follows' than 'takes', but sooner or later will come a 'tug'.

10 Natural baits

I have never doubted that, of the three natural baits, worm, shrimp and prawn, the worm is the real killer. It is no longer fished on the lower Test in order to conserve stocks of salmon, whilst prawn and shrimp continue to be used. Of the latter baits, I have not known the shrimp to frighten salmon whilst, on occasion, the prawn scares them out of their wits.

If it became absolutely necessary to catch a salmon, in high or low water, with no regard being paid to pleasure or conscience, I would pull three lobworms from my pocket and place them in a little box containing a special lotion:

And now I shall tell you that which may be called a secret. I have been a-fishing with old Oliver Henly, now with God, a noted fisher both for Trout and Salmon; and have observed, that he would usually take three or four worms out of his bag, and put them into a little box in his pocket, where he would usually let them continue half an hour or more, before he would bait his hook with them. I have asked him his reason, and he has replied, 'He did but pick the best out to be in readiness against he baited his hook the next time': but he has been observed, both by others and myself, to catch more fish than I, or any other body that has ever gone a-fishing with him, could do, and especially Salmons. And I have been told lately, by one of his most intimate and secret friends, that the box in which he had put those worms was anointed with a drop, or two or three, of the oil of ivy berries, made by expression or infusion; and told, that by the worms remaining in that box an hour, or a like time, they had incorporated a kind of smell that was irresistibly attractive, enough to force any fish within the smell of them to bite. (Izaak Walton, 1676)

Well, there you are. Failure may be a thing of the past. It was rare with Oliver, friend of Izaak Walton (1593–1683), and there may be more in this than meets the humorous eye. Before setting a mole trap, mounting a prawn or shrimp, or threading worms on to a hook – *rub your hands in earth*. I cannot vouch for this practice, neither can anyone gainsay me, but it is possible that salmon scent the smell of the human hand, particularly the male hand, and reject the bait. I can say with truth that I catch both moles and salmon. Anyone wishing to study the subject in depth should read the section on salmon taste and smell by Professor Peter Behan in *Salmon and Women* (Paterson & Behan, 1990).

I do not think it is entirely necessary to rub the hands in earth before attaching a fly or spinning bait because these lures are taken at speed, but a fish has the time to scent a worm or prawn. Behan finds support for the fact that women anglers catch more large male fish than their menfolk – so, take a woman fishing and ask her to tie on the lure, natural or artificial.

The worm

You will find good advice on fishing this bait, by those who use it more than myself, in Chapters 12, 15 and 16. All the same, I will tell you of my simple methods, rarely used but entirely reliable.

If you already possess spinning tackle, the only items you need to purchase are hooks on which to mount the worms. Choose Mustad, Code 92641, in sizes No. 2 and No. 4. This is a beak hook with reversed hollow point. Bronze in colour, the shank has two slices (small cuts) which point up towards the eye. These stop a threaded lobworm from sliding down to the bend of the hook.

A spinning rod with fixed-spool reel is more versatile than the fly rod, for you are able to flick out the worms from tree-restricted places. Use the spool holding 14 lb nylon. Attach a barrel swivel to the end of the line and then a trace of 12 lb monofilament. The hook may be tied to the end of the trace with a tucked half blood knot.

You may, or may not, according to depth and speed of water, need some additional weight, despite the natural ability of the worms to sink. This may be provided by the paternoster system as described on p. 101, but only 6 or 8 g (about ¼ oz) weight will be needed for worming. If a three-way swivel is not available, attach 6 in. of nylon to the top eye of the swivel, tie a thumb knot (a single turn) at the end of this piece as a 'stop', and squeeze on one, two, three or more lead-free SSG Thamesley Sure-Shot with a pair of pliers. A Wye or Hillman weight may be used if preferred.

Lobworm should be dug up or collected on wet nights in summer from your lawn. Follow the plough – but go for active fellows, long, tough and squirmy. The closer in size to a young grass snake the better! Kept in wet moss for a few days, they will harden and be less inclined to fly off the hook when cast. I like to mount three, threading the first up the hook shank onto the nylon trace. The hook is passed in and out in two places through the next two worms, just above the tail and just below the head; in this manner head and tail hang free. Be certain that the hook point is enclosed and thus is invisible within the body of the worm. The first worm is then slid down to cover the eye of the hook. You should aim to have three heads and three tails hanging free, giving the appearance of a squid.

You may be able to see the salmon that you are stalking lying there, grey and inert, but desirable. If so, make sure it does not see you. Plop in the worms a few yards upstream, let them sink and then curl on the current just ahead of its nose. If it does not take the first time, give it another chance. If it is still reluctant, leave the worms resting on the river bed 1 ft in front of its jaws. Suppose it picks them up. What then? Do nothing, absolutely nothing for at least 20 seconds; count them – then strike. If you strike as soon as the salmon takes the bait, it may blow out the bunch of worms without being hooked – it may suck them in again, I have seen it happen, but this is uncertain.

If the water is murky, hiding all fish, touch is the only indication that a fish has taken the bait. Of course, those trembles transmitted up the line to your fingers may be the work of a trout or an eel, for they also love a worm. Interference by other fish is a regular annoyance. Many are the disappointments of the worm angler. But, when there is something there, out of sight, jiggling, allow plenty of time, do not let the line tighten: feed nylon to the fish with the bail arm open or 'free-runner' in action – then, when the salmon has had time to swallow, strike.

The methods described entail casting across the river to let the worm swing back to your side on the current, or else rest stationary on the paternoster system. In low water, the worm may be cast upstream and allowed to trot down past the angler. The rod tip must be held high for this operation to prevent snagging and little, if any, additional weight is required.

The worm may rescue you from desperate situations even though you go unprepared. Imagine that you have gone to Scotland to fish the fly. On your arrival, the sun shines, the river is low and it is doubtful if it will ever rain again – certainly not during your week or fortnight. Each evening your wife asks the dreaded yet hopeful question: 'Any luck?' If salmon are in the river do not lose heart. Take a No. 4 single-hooked salmon fly from your box, strip off the dressing with a knife and tie the hook to an untapered length of 10 lb monofilament. At the river, turn over boulders, pull up clumps of heather or grass, or kick over dried-up cowpats until you find a couple of worms.

The casting by fly rod has to be in the manner of a gentle swing or the worms will fly off the hook. Generally, even in a spate in a small river, worms will sink without additional weight. If extra weight is needed, cut a sliver of lead from roof flashing, an old lead pipe or the covering from the neck of a wine bottle. It is some years since I last went after a salmon with a worm, and there are amongst anglers those who feel the practice should be banned. I am not within their ranks. But this I must say: fish the worm if other methods are hopeless. Take one fish if you need to and if you are allowed, and then desist.

The prawn and the shrimp

15 July 1973 Test. Longbridge. Rose a fish to No. 4 Thunder & Lightning, No. 2 Mepps, and took it on a prawn. 8½ lb.

The response of salmon to a prawn is unpredictable. Sometimes they become savage, taking the bait between hard jaws, crushing it, shaking their heads and even, somehow, sliding it up the nylon away from the hooks. On other occasions when a prawn is trotted down just outside a fish lying under a hollow bank, the salmon will dash away in alarm. They may take gently, tweaking and plucking out of sight in deep water. Often you are hard-put to decide not only when to strike but what is nosing at the bait: salmon, eel or a large trout. An eel is very fond of half a prawn left on the river bed and armed with a single hook – a method worth trying at lunch-time. As was shown on 15 July, a prawn can hook a reluctant but interested fish, one which has risen to, but failed to take other baits.

For 6 years, once a fortnight, I had the opportunity to fish the prawn at Broadlands on the Test. During those visits 12 salmon fell to my fly, four to an upstream Mepps, one to a Yellow Belly Devon in early spring and 11 on prawn and shrimp. From the prawn victims, I learned much about salmon behaviour. Visualize the long grey shadow of a salmon resting on the light chalk of the river bed: its tail waves slightly, and the white rims of its jaws are visible from time to time as it yawns. Do salmon yawn? Perhaps. Maybe they need to obtain extra oxygen from an increased flow through the gills, but certainly they open and close their mouths at intervals.

Above some lies on the Test were climbable trees. Up I used to go, squirrel-like, pressed against the blind side of the trunk until a supportive fork of a branch was reached. Down went the prawn on a paternoster, sometimes a Wye weight was used, but the purpose was the same – to sway the prawn or shrimp in front of its nose. It might take at once, in which case I always struck as soon as the bait was engulfed because salmon are able to blow out a prawn in a split second. Sometimes the prawn drifted on to its nose, in which case, if it did not take, it would sway to one side out of the way. At other times, the bait might rest on the river bed to its front for 10 minutes, the fish apparently lacking interest; then it might awake, move forward and take. But never, whatever you do, allow the prawn to drift down its flank to swim beside its tail. A prawn in the region of the adipose, anal or caudal fins is in the salmon's blind spot; to a fish this is intolerable. Let your prawn once drift to the rear of a resting fish and it will dash away across the pool. When this happens do not despair. Stay in the tree. It will return, perhaps in 5 minutes, seldom more than half an hour.

Of course, the water is not always clear and then salmon have to be sought using the knowledge of their lies and the tickle of their jaws on the bait. In such situations a 10 ft rod provides extra length, enabling the prawn to be manoeuvred between weed beds or slowly passed downstream just beyond the end of a wooden groyne. A fixed-spool reel is better than a multiplier, and monofilament better than braided line. The fixed spool enables the bait to be swung out with an underarm cast, and the thin nylon is less water-obstructive and more sensitive between the fingers. The only messages to be received from the bait will pass up the line. Touch is all. Flick out, the prawn and weight sink from view and the first message is the bump of the weight on the river bed. Now feel the line, hold it with delicacy in the fingers of the hand which operates the reel. Raise the rod tip slightly, lifting the weight off the river bed to allow the prawn to drift on the current, then bump the weight again. Raise, drift, bump; raise, drift, bump. Feel the prawn searching each irregularity in the bottom. Imagine it swaying beside the washed-out roots of a bankside tree, tempting the salmon you suspect is there. Then a tweak comes up the line. Tweaks are different from thumps and bumps and the touch of an inert boot. You cannot mistake a tweak. Next time, count two, tighten your fingers on the line, and strike.

On wide pools, where the bait is to be swept across the width of the river, the paternoster is not ideal. In those places tie in a Wye weight of about 14 g (½ oz) at the line/trace junction, cast across and let the prawn drift around on the current. If the bait skids on the sand or gravel of the river bed, so much the better. All the time your fingers should be on the line, seeking information.

My order of preference in salmon fishing is: fly, spinning, worm, shrimp and, last of all, the prawn. But the prawn has its moments: situations when water levels are low, the worm is not allowed, and shrimps cannot be obtained. A red cock salmon, fit to be smoked, will go with anger at a prawn in the autumn.

30 September 1976 Test. Lee Park. Rose 2 fish under left bank at top of Oak Tree, second one took a prawn behind lst groyne. 10 lb. A red cock fish which ran downstream and was netted by Bernard in Kendle's Corner. Tony lost a fish on prawn – weeded in tail of Black Dog. This was the season of the Great Drought when there was insufficient water to fish a fly. There were very few fish: the Broadlands total for the season was about 68 compared with 350 the previous year. Tony and I took 6 fish each.

Prawn and shrimp mounts

The prawn may be spun on a purchased mount incorporating a swivel and two celluloid fins, a central pin to insert down the prawn from the tail, and two trebles. The end treble of the mount is placed in the whiskers of the prawn; the mid-treble has one hook straightened and this is thrust into the body of the prawn. The vanes of the mount are at the tail and the whole is wrapped about with a few turns of fine copper wire. Spun prawns catch salmon, but it is not a method which appeals to me, firstly because it seems unnatural for a prawn to revolve and secondly because you have to purchase a complicated piece of equipment which may not match your prawn in size.

If you are fishing the prawn and, after experiencing an unsuccessful take, inspect the bait, you may find that it is crushed in the centre of the body. This is caused by salmon gripping the bait across their mouths. To hook a salmon in these circumstances, my fishing partner, Tony Allen, devised a mount with two trebles. One is positioned in the whiskers and the other in the middle of the body amongst the legs. Some prawns are short and others are long; in his mount the central treble may be moved to the required place by

Tony Allen's prawn mount, shrimp and prawn pins and sliced worm hook.

Alan Dodd's shrimp mount from the River Coquet.

sliding it along a wire, as in the illustration above. The whole is then bound with fine wire unravelled from an electric cable.

A well-thought out device on the same principle, illustrated above, using two, small double hooks for the smaller shrimp, was shown to me on the River Coquet in Northumberland by Alan Dodd. The simplest method of mounting a prawn is to thrust an eyed Partridge T2 prawn pin inside the body from the tail to hold the prawn straight. The nylon trace is then passed through the eye of the pin and tied to a treble, one hook of which is pressed into the head of the bait amongst the whiskers. The nylon is then run back between the legs to the tail and the whole is wrapped with fine red wire, which is not allowed to interfere with the natural positioning of the legs. The two tail flaps are then broken off to prevent the prawn twirling in the current. It is advisable to snap off the spear of the prawn; this sharp serrated spike might deter a fish from gripping the head of the prawn so that it fails to be caught on the treble in the whiskers.

Preparing the prawn

Prawns of Scandinavian origin from the fishmonger are usually too large, overcooked, smelly and, being soft, break up when fished. British are best. Catch your own or purchase some from a local fishing boat, or place an order with a school boy with his net. Now is your opportunity to lay in a stock of tough, small specimens. Proceed as follows. Boil them in a little water until they are just pink, then remove them at once. They must not soften.
A magenta dye may be added to the saucepan if a dark prawn is desired.
Now drain them, place them on a rough towel and fan them with a hair dryer. Package in half-dozens of matching size and freeze. You now have a season's supply; the large specimens for spring and autumn, and the small ones for the low, warm water of summer.

I do not like shrimp to be cooked. They retain toughness and appeal in their natural grey colour. Partridge T2 pins are available in four lengths: 25, 38, 50 and 64 mm (1, 1½, 2 and 2½ in.). The short pin is right for the shrimp. Press it up the body from below the tail with care (shrimp are delicate) and then feed the nylon trace through the eye of the pin. A single Partridge bronze Code X1 treble in size No. 12 or No. 14 should be pressed into the head, the nylon fed back between the legs and the whole bound with fine wire or silk. Some weight will be needed. This may be provided by lead wire twisted around the reel line above the swivel; the 0.37 mm (¹⁄₁₀₀₀ in.) supplied by E. Veniard Ltd of Croydon is suitable and is the lead wire with which I weight my Black Dart and Hairy Mary tube flies.

Both shrimp and prawn may be fished beneath a float. If you are on holiday and have already used the lead wrapping from the neck of the wine bottle to weight your worm outfit, you can press the cork into service to fish the shrimp. The reel line may be held against the cork by an elastic band and the trace weighted with a split SSG shot or sliver of lead. The mounted shrimp is then fished on a length of nylon, below the cork, greater than the depth of the river. This extra length is needed because the nylon under the float will not descend directly at 90 degrees to the river bed, but will flow at about 45 degrees. The shrimp should search the river as close to the bed as may be arranged, whilst you watch the float for any indication of a 'take'. At the first bob or tremble – strike. The fish I have taken on shrimp have all been in the clear water of chalk streams. It seems unlikely that catches would be made in heavy water where the worm and prawn are more likely to yield a dividend.

11 General information

Single-bank fishing

No problems arise when fishing a wide river. Consideration of the pleasure of an angler fishing the opposite bank in a small river is a matter of courtesy. Certain principles are involved.

I expect those fishing from the opposite bank to cover the whole width of the river, and for them to welcome the same action on my part, but we should not fish opposite each other at the same time.

When fly fishing and spinning, which are mobile methods, should I arrive at a river to find an angler fishing a pool from the other bank by the same method that I intend to use, I wait until he has finished before starting to fish. If the pool or run is long, I would follow him down, but not press upon him, allowing a gap of at least 50 yd between our rods. It is incumbent upon him not to dally, and to continue down the river having reached the tail of the pool. He should not 'back-up', unless by agreement. If he wishes to fish the water down a second time, he should follow me.

Problems arise if one angler is spinning downriver and another is spinning his way upstream. If I were the upstream caster, I would allow the downstream fisher to pass through without interrupting his progress. This may not be rational, but fewer anglers cast upstream than down, and the arrival of the upstream angler will be unexpected.

The fly should take preference over the spinning bait in 'first down the pool', and the spinner over the worm or prawn. Because worm, prawn and shrimp anglers fish by more static methods than fly and artificial bait anglers, they should wave them through.

The canoe

I do not think that the passage of one or two canoes a day through a beat makes much difference to the fishing. Salmon soon settle down, and I have often caught sea trout as soon as the light has gone and after a canoe has passed at dusk. After all, salmon beats are fished from boats on wide rivers, and these boats pass over the lies a number of times during the day.

Nevertheless, I make every effort to discourage canoeists on my stretch of water. If allowed to pass uninterrupted, they tell their friends 'We know a

29 September 1984. 1¼ in. Black Dart tube fly. First salmon (10 lb) on the fly to Lara Bingham (aged 16 years). Single-bank fishing in such narrow places requires courtesy.

good place'. In addition to my wish to deter them they may have no legal right of navigation, and that is the case on my river. This is recognized by the British Canoe Union who have a representative in our area of Devonshire. It is agreed with them that certain sections of the river may be used by their members in the off-season; in return, they desist during the angling months.

It is the non-members who cause trouble. They set out to cover several miles of water, leaving a car at each end of their route. I always ask them to pull into my side of the river and have not so far been disregarded because they are unsure of their position and wish to hear what I have to say, even if they have no intention of agreeing! My explanation then follows that they have no right of passage and that we own the river. The response to this is usually: 'Nobody owns a river'. I explain that they do not actually *know* that to be the case and that, if they return, I shall take the registration number of their car and practise my casting in their garden. It is also sensible to make clear that they have contributed nothing financially to the river and that the angler has paid rent to an owner, rates to the local authority and has spent much time and money keeping the waterway clear of washed-down trees. I then allow them to proceed, having asked them not to return, and only once have I had a second visit from the same persons. There were two of them and I pursued them across Dartmoor for 15 miles in my car until, in desperation, they drove into the yard of the prison. Perhaps they 'knew a good place'. I followed onto Her Majesty's property to say my piece.

Loop the cord around the wrist of the tail and through the mouth and one gill to form a handle.

The wading staff

Even on small rivers there are places where a staff enables you to wade in order to fish lies otherwise out of reach. I do not normally carry a staff on my river because I know the bed thoroughly, but I am always glad of a length of driftwood when crossing the river in spate. To this end, a few trimmed branches are placed at fordable sites, and there they remain unless washed away. The ability to cross may make all the difference, enabling you to return home with a salmon which would otherwise have remained in the water. I remember taking a 7 lb fish in June 1960: it rose three times to a No. 6 single Low Water Hairy Mary. Between each roll at the fly I changed banks.

A staff is a blessing in a strange river. There is no need to purchase one. Cut a straight length of stout ash with a 'Y' thumb grip at the top from an overgrown hedge. Trim off the side growths, shorten to a length of 50 in, then store it upright for a year in a cupboard to allow the wood to harden and dry. Take a piece of lead pipe 2 in. long with the standard 'old country house' bore of 1⅛ in. This length will weigh 12 oz, will hold the end of the staff down against the flow of the river and, being a soft metal, will not clatter on underwater rocks. Now, and this is essential, soak the bottom 6 in. of the staff overnight in hot wood-preserving liquid, and then fit the lead. If the wood is not treated in this way, it will rot inside the pipe. When wading the Derwent with Con Waldron, the heavy brass spike at the end of her staff broke away from the rotted wood.

Approximately 6 in. below the 'Y', bind on a clip of the type found on landing-net handles, or the clip from a dog lead. The staff may now be clipped to a metal ring on a lanyard, which can be passed over your head to hang beneath the left armpit. This is the ideal position if you are casting single-handed with the right hand, or 'right hand up' using a double-handed rod. The staff may be detached when you are walking or playing salmon.

Carrying, cleaning and freezing salmon

In my pocket, there is a length of stout baler twine. To carry a salmon, form a loop in the centre of the twine and settle this around the wrist of the tail (see illustration on p. 114). Pass one end through one gill and out of the mouth and tie the two ends together to form a handle.

The twine should be of ample length, so that, when the second and third fish of the day are caught, and you are still travelling along the river, the twine may be undone to add the additional fish.

On returning home, clean all salmon at once unless you are sending them to the fish-smoker. The head and tail of grilse should be left on the fish, but the gill filaments, gut and the blood along the backbone should be removed and the fish washed. Wrap it in a polythene bag, sealed tightly to exclude air and labelled with the date, weight, where it was caught and condition, and freeze it flat on the base of the deep freeze.

Salmon should have their heads, tails, guts and blood removed. They should then be cut into two or three pieces and packed individually into polythene bags, all of which should be placed in a single carrier bag and frozen. If a salmon of 10 lb is not cut up before freezing, and only a portion is needed for a meal, the frozen fish has to be cut with a hacksaw – a lengthy, greasy and hand-chilling task!

Washing-off a 14 lb spring salmon.

Salmon should be cleaned before being frozen.

Frozen salmon will keep for months. I once swapped a grilse for four mallard shot on a Cotswold farm – the grilse stayed in the farm deep-freeze for 3 years before it was remembered and eaten – the family are all alive today! The practice of our household is to finish eating the fish of one season before the grilse run of the following year.

The gillie

I like to fish alone, tie on the fly I have chosen, make my own decisions and land my fish myself. My reasons for salmon fishing are to divorce myself from conversation, stretch my eyes to the hills, stalk and catch fish. These pleasures are achievable if you know the river.

On a strange water, engage a gillie and take his advice in all matters. He knows his river: the lies which will be occupied at the water height at which you are fishing; how long it will take rain in the hills to raise the level in the beat and where to await the arrival of the first lift. Such facts are crucial to success and are only known by a local. Tie on the fly he offers – yourself! If your knot comes undone, he will be cross; if his knot is faulty, you will be cross and he will be embarrassed. At the end of the first 2 days, mutual respect and friendship will have been established. You may then try out one or two of your own methods.

Don't offer the gillie whiskey all through the day, just at lunch and when packing up. A helpful gillie should be tipped generously, not after each fish, but at the end of the week or period of employment, whether or not salmon have been caught.

Where to fish

The advertisement pages of the magazines *Trout & Salmon*, *The Field*, *Salmon, Trout and Sea-Trout*, and the Yearbook of the Salmon and Trout Association (Fishmonger's Hall, London EC4R 9EL) offer a wide selection of beats and hotels which have fishing. Which to choose? Purchase a copy of *Where to Fish*, edited by D. A. Orton and published by Thomas Harmsworth; the book is updated biennially, supplies detailed information, and provides a map of the rivers of the British Isles. An interesting source of available fishing and tactics on the river bank is *Salmon & Trout* (Astley House, 33 Notting Hill Gate, Notting Hill, London W11 3JQ).

Regional offices of the National Rivers Authority publish angling guides and leaflets of game and other fisheries in their areas. The sporting departments of national firms of estate agents regularly mail lists of fishing lodges to let by the week, particularly in Scotland. Their particulars usually include the average seasonal salmon catch over the previous 5 years. Choose the right weeks – they will almost certainly be the most expensive!

Part 2
Small rivers

12 River Dovey
(Afon Dyfi), Powys

About 7 miles north of Mallwyd, at just under 3000 ft above sea level, the Dovey rises in the mountains at Llyn Craiglyn to the west of the hamlet of Pennant. The fall is steep, 1700 ft in the first 16 miles of the 32 miles to the sea at Aberdovey. Along its course, it is joined by tributaries more numerous than the veins rising in the fingers and surfacing on the back of an old man's hand. There are 400 miles of streamlets, or *nants* as they are called, which, together with the main river, provide 300 miles of water suitable for the spawning of migratory fish. The Dovey may be long but, unless in full spate on the lower river, it comes into the small-river category. At Mallwyd, at reaches lower down the valley, and certainly upstream, the water may be covered with a 10 ft 6 in. fly rod without false casting.

Stand on the bank at Mallwyd, 200 ft above sea level, at the junction of the Dovey and Cleifion rivers, and lift your eyes to the hills; they rear 2000 ft or more, their outlines sharp against the sky. The scenery is awe-inspiring and so are the fish. Nowhere else have I come across a river holding sea trout of a size that matched the grandeur of the scenery. Salmon too, and more of them than 20 years ago. It is a river whose contrasts match the hills, the valleys and the lower plains. Shallow runs, clear, and thigh- or gum-boot-deep in times of drought, link deep gulleys where broadleaved trees cut out the light, making the pots, holes and waterfalls dark and mysterious. This river of moods and changes reminds me at once of the intimacy of the streams of a rock-lined Cornish combe where the worm and prawn hold sway, and the wide-open sweep of a Scottish moorland river where the fly is all one needs.

I make no apology for including sea trout (*sewin* as they are called in Wales) in this chapter on the Dovey. Sea trout are present in most of the salmon rivers of the British Isles, but on the Dovey both fish go hand in hand, and one cannot forecast which will take the fly or worm. On the Brigands Inn water at Mallwyd, the first two fish taken in 1990 were an 8 lb sewin on 24 April and an 8 lb salmon on the 29 April, both falling to a worm. I was fortunate to meet two men who know the river well and to record my conversations with them.

Emyr Lewis 11 September 1990

Emyr is 48 years old. Stocky, tough and bright of eye he is a 'no nonsense' bailiff who has the river at his fingertips.

'I started fishing at a very early age, mostly for trout. When I reached 16 I began fishing for salmon and sea trout, mostly on the Dovey. Fishing always interested me, always. Then, at the age of 24 years, I took over the job of water bailiff for the Dovey Catchment on the river and the tributaries.'

Since 1985, Emyr has represented Wales in the Home International fly-fishing competitions against England, Ireland and Scotland. Fourteen anglers are selected from each country and, in 1990, Emyr had the honour of being the Welsh captain.

I asked him about alterations which had taken place in the river during his time, and whether he had problems with silting in the 300 miles of spawning tributaries in his area.

'My problem is afforestation and the drainage this entails, which results in flash floods down the valley. When I was younger, a heavy rainfall would run off slowly; fishing could continue for 10 days or a fortnight. Today a spate is gone in a torrent in 2 or 3 days. In between spates, in summer, some spawning tributaries dry out with the consequent 100 per cent mortality of game fish fry.

'Although we lose fry in this way, we compensate by rearing salmon and sea trout in our hatchery. We micro-tag the smolts, clip the adipose fin for identification, and thus know what is coming back into the river. Although afforestation has caused much damage, we have no dams and reservoirs, and that is a good thing.'

I asked whether there had been any alteration in the timing of salmon runs, and whether there are now more or less spring fish or grilse.

'The runs have got later. At one time we looked to the end of July for the start of the grilse run; now they come at the end of August and in September. There are more grilse than in the past. Two-sea-winter salmon arrive at that time as well, and both continue until the end of the season on 17 October. Spring fish were common in April years ago; they are now fewer in number, although we did a little better this year. In total I think grilse runs are increasing. Even with these changes you can still catch a sea-liced salmon on the Brigands Inn water in April; very often the first fish of the season on the river is caught there. There are no obstructions that fish will not jump in the cold water of spring. The first falls are at Pen-y-Bont on the Brigands Water.'

On fish of outstanding size, Emyr had this to say:

'Big sea trout of 18 lb and 20 lb come in during April and May. Our best sea trout this year was 24½ lb, taken in the nets. Last year their best was 22½ lb. The largest sea trout caught on fly weighed 20¾ lb, being taken in 1958 by Arthur Humphreys. One angler in 1990 took two sea trout of 13½ lb in one week on fly, but this was broken two weeks ago by another angler who took one of 14 lb 7 oz, again on a fly.'

When fishing at night Emyr uses 12 or 14 lb nylon, a straight length off the spool.

'On the point I like a good-sized tube, with a No. 6 or No. 8 Haslam double as a dropper. The tube could be 2 or 2½ in. long, of black, orange, silver, a combination of these, and jungle-cock cheeks. A black body ribbed with silver, a black squirrel wing and two jungle-cock cheeks make a fine fly which may be improved still further if it has a bit of orange hackle. I like an Esmund Drury treble as the hook, or a Partridge outbend. All these good things come in our own fly, the Dovey Black and Orange.'

Haslam

Tag: Flat silver tinsel
Butt: White wool or floss silk
Tail: Small golden pheasant crest
Body: Flat silver tinsel
Rib: Oval silver tinsel
Throat hackle: Blue jay, or guinea fowl dyed blue
Wing: From hen pheasant tail, tied slim
Horns: Blue/yellow macaw tied in so that they curve along the sides of the wings and
    so that the tips cross over each other above the tail
Head: Black varnish
Hook: No. 4 to 10, single or double

Dovey Black & Orange

Tail: Red swan
Rib: Silver thread
Body: Black floss silk
Hackle: Orange hen
Wing: Black squirrel
Cheeks: Jungle cock
Hook: No. 4 to 8, double
Head: Black varnish

'The Hairy Mary is a good fly. One autumn afternoon in 1974 or 1975 I joined Elfyn Wigley on the middle beat at a pool called Sywllyn. He took four salmon on that fly, a single No. 6, when the water was dropping after a flood. I also remember a gentleman on the Brigands Inn in 1972 or 1973 taking three salmon to 15 lb on a Shrimp fly in the run just upstream of the Bathing Pool. I think his name was Sylvester.'

It is rare for anglers to fish two flies at once for salmon on the Dovey: a point fly and dropper. At times grilse take little flies when anglers are fishing for small sea trout by day. It is not unusual for a grilse to be landed on a No. 14 double. Daylight sea-trout fishing takes place in low, clear water if there is a strong, upstream wind to produce a well-rippled surface. Then a team of three flies may be cast upstream on a floating line and ripped back fast. This method is a waste of time in calm water. The upstream cast is the Welsh equivalent of the Scottish 'backed-up' cast for salmon.

Not the place for a 12 ft 6 in. fly rod, or the overhead cast right hand up.

The majority of the anglers on the lower water use a 10 or 11 ft carbon-fibre rod and an AFTM No. 8 or No. 9 floating line to which they splice their own sink-tips. Various tips are used: fast-, medium- and slow-sinking. That is for the sewin. For salmon, a 12 ft rod is about right, usually double-handed, although some anglers use their single-handed, sea-trout rod. By day, salmon floating fly lines are usually the mahogany-coloured Air-Cel Supreme. John Garside of Brigands Inn uses a white floating fly line for salmon. Wet-Cel 2 fast-sinking fly lines, which are dark in colour, are favoured.

Fish may be beached on most sections of the river but nets are also carried. Emyr uses his hand on most occasions, even for grilse.

On worm fishing Emyr had this to say. 'The New Dovey Fishery Association (1929) Ltd controls the major length of the river. Tickets may be obtained. When the water is high and coloured, the head keeper of the Association puts out yellow flags; people may then worm and spin. At other times, the 20 miles of the Association water is fly only. This prevents the foul hooking of salmon in low water.'

He went on to discuss worming methods. 'There are three sorts of worm, but some anglers only fish with brandlings, which are small with a striped tail. You find them in manure heaps and where the council dump grass cuttings and leaves. There are also two kinds of lobworm: the red head, which is a soft worm, and the blue and grey heads, which are tougher. The blue head is best. We collect them early in the season when digging the garden, and keep them for weeks and weeks in moss, and in other ways. We feed them – dried milk is good – then we have enough to last the season. We also catch them at night with a torch, but they are very quick. If you show your hand in front of one you'll never catch him, he's back in the hole so quickly. You must come up from behind. John says they flash back in the hole as soon as they feel the heat of your hand. It is not a bad idea to put a red filter on the torch. Golf courses are productive hunting grounds. '

Emyr told me that old Dovey anglers used to mount their worms on a long-shanked spade ended hook to which they whipped 15 lb nylon with thread and cobbler's wax. They did not use a bristle whipped to the shank to stop the worm sliding down. Three lobworms were mounted: the first two were threaded up the hook onto the nylon and the last one covered the hook; the upper two were then drawn down. Today, anglers use eyed hooks for salmon, in sizes No. 2, No. 4 or No. 6. For sea trout, they may use something smaller.

When hooking fish on the worm, Emyr gives a salmon plenty of time, letting the line slide away. With sea trout, he favours a quick response. Eels sometimes take the worm, as recorded in the Brigands Inn fishing diary:

2 August 1990 Name: A. Weldon. River: Dovey. Pool: the wet one. Species: the long slim fish (eel). Weight: 4 lb. Length: don't know. Fly: about 60 around me. Bait: worm.

Some Dovey fishermen use a long carp rod to fish the worm. Others favour a 9 ft rod which enables them to change to spinning at a moment's notice. Both mount a fixed-spool reel with 100 yd of 15 lb nylon, one or two pierced-bullet weights and then, beyond a swivel, 18 in of lighter nylon as a trace to the worm.

Spinning on the Dovey

In general, the Toby is favoured more than the Mepps. It is normally fished with the standard single treble at the tail and it is unusual for a flying treble to be added. The Toby is thrown straight across the river, the current carries it around and then the final travel is curved upstream by a few turns on the handle of the reel. This spoon is large in cold water, 2½ in. or 3 in., depending on the colour of the flow which, if clear, warrants a smaller bait. Devon minnows and Mepps are also used but are not so popular. In warm, low water, these baits are also thrown up and across, followed by a fast retrieve, but this may only be done on the upper reaches because spinning is not allowed in low water on the New Dovey sections of the river.

Netting

Emyr has a photograph of an 18 lb salmon with a 13 lb sea trout. In the same net was a sea trout of 24 lb, all three fish being caught together.

The nets start operations about the first week in May, by which time there are already quite a few fish in the river. The netsmen then fish heavily in May, June and July before ceasing, except for the occasional draw in August.

This early cessation favours autumn-running fish, which thus have an uninterrupted passage up the river.

To conclude our meeting, I asked about the prizes given to the captains of the four national teams at the 1990 fly-fishing contest. After the other three captains had been rewarded, there was nothing left for Emyr but a substantial wooden spoon. Having lost his bailiff's truncheon he was delighted: 'Any poacher knocked over with that will give no further trouble.'

John Garside, proprietor, Brigands Inn, Mallwyd, Powys   10 September 1990

The Brigands Inn has been a fishing hotel for over 100 years, and has 2½ miles of the River Dovey and River Cleifion. The dramatic Pen-y-Bont Falls, the first obstruction to a travelling fish since leaving the sea, are within easy walking distance of the hotel. The Falls are part of the hotel fishings and it was to this beautiful place that John took me as soon as I arrived. We sat above the Falls over which clear water gushed in two channels to run down the valley between high sides of rock. Trees lined the river: beech, oak, Scots pine, silver birch and rhododendrons. Behind us, a single, isolated stone cottage overlooked the scene. In 1976, the lane behind this cottage was awash in a heavy spate which carried away a bridge 5 miles (8 km) downstream at Aberangell.

John told me: 'I hooked a fish in the falls early this morning. He took a worm but came off, probably a sea trout. They start to arrive here in May and then continue to run into our water until the end of the season on 17 October. Salmon run at the same time. We had one here this year on 29 April just above the Falls in low water on a worm. That fish weighed 8 lb, and I had an 8 lb sea trout below the Falls on 24 April. If they run up here quickly they still carry sea lice. Grilse start to arrive in June. Our main run of salmon and grilse takes place in September and October, and most of the fish are of two sea winters'.

We then went to the Junction Pool (Aber Dwy Afon) where the Cleifion, flowing from the east, joins the Dovey. Both banks are fished by Brigands Inn, the Pool being fished from the open left bank. The Junction fishes best in high water, but sea trout may be taken even in the low-water conditions which prevailed during my visit. In spate, the Cleifion carries much dark peat, whilst the Dovey runs a milky colour. Salmon lie where the colours start to mingle, which is also the deepest part of the pool. An inch or more of rain in the hills would cause the water to rise at Brigands Inn by 1 or 2 ft within 4 or 5 hours. A full spate might then give 5 or 6 days of good fishing before the level dropped back completely.

According to John: 'The fishing is best for salmon and sea trout as a spate runs off. Even so, one needs settled conditions for sewin, which continue to run in low water. Salmon like to lie in front of rocks, just above the lip of a

River Dovey (looking downstream). A typical lie on any river is just below, and out from, a line of rock or a man-made wooden groyne.

waterfall and just in front of the place where the water shallows out at the tail of a run. Sea trout are different; they lie behind rocks. If you are upstream spinning, and can curve your Mepps around behind a rock, you're in with a good chance.'

On methods for salmon he had this to say. 'We tend to spin and fish the worm in the early season for both salmon and sea trout. Shrimps are used and also the prawn, which anglers bring with them. Personally, I don't fish the prawn. To mount them, the locals buy a packet of cheap sea hooks, straighten them, and pass them up the inside of the prawn's body. The nylon is fed through the hook eye under the tail and is then carried forward and tied to a treble in the whiskers.'

He continued with the system for worms. 'We fish worms all through the season, even in cold water. I like to mount them on a single carp hook, a large or small one depending on the water. In low water, I'll use a wide gape No. 10 on 6 lb nylon; in a flood a No. 4 on 15 lb nylon. We often take salmon on 6 lb nylon, sinking the bait with a pierced shot or bullet. Some say: "If you want a bit more weight, put on an extra worm". We cast the worm upstream in the runs and let it trundle down using a spinning rod and fixed spool reel. Some use a fly rod and centre-pin reel – that's really skilled. In low water a couple of small brandlings is better than a lobworm.'

In April, their water temperature will be about 50°F and the fly, fished off a floating line, comes to the fore. Sinking fly lines are rarely used because of the shallowness of the pools, but have a place in high water with a large fly between the Junction and Bend Pools. Water conditions alter rapidly in the valley and the angler must be prepared to change the size of his fly, or even switch to bait, or vice versa, within the time span of a morning. Most of John's fly fishing, for both salmon and sea trout, is done with a 10 ft 6 in rod, an AFTM No. 6 floating line and an untapered cast of nylon straight off the spool. For salmon 10 or 12 lb nylon is best – and 8 or 10 lb for sea trout at night.

'I wouldn't like to go lighter than that as most of us catch one or two sewin of 8 lb or 9 lb each season. My favourite fly is a Black Pennell on a 1 in. tube, or a double Thunder Stoat (a Stoat's Tail with jungle-cock cheeks). For salmon, I like a Haslam or an orange-and-black fly dressed in the Waddington manner, for which I take a paper clip, straighten it, twist a loop at each end, one of which goes through the eye of the treble, and dress my fly on the shank between the loops. For tube flies, I pull the wire out of an electric cable.

'When playing a salmon, I never drop my rod point when a fish leaps. To stop them running out of the tail of a pool, I slacken the line. They then turn and settle on the bottom before swimming upstream. To slacken takes a lot of nerve. I carry a Gye net when fishing the deep pools but, in the open, I beach them on the shingle banks. I beach all my sea trout.'

John is of the opinion that early morning and late evening are the best times for taking a salmon on a worm in low water. His experience coincides with my own, namely that the afternoon is best in the cold water of early spring, and that a hatch of large, dark olives at lunch-time in April is a good sign, indicating that the water is becoming a trifle warmer. At that time of year,

Small trebles from tube flies sometimes have to be cut free with a knife.

spinning would be with a large Mepps or Toby. In summer, an upstream cast with a No. 2 Mepps on 10 lb nylon, with a pierced-bullet weight, is a useful method for both salmon and sea trout.

Later, we went back to the water above Pen-y-Bont Falls where John told me of an incident which is recorded as follows in the Brigands Inn fishing diary:

23 July 1988 I was just about to move down to the landing point and as I turned I fell into the Falls, so lost the rod with the fish on. One hour later, my wife snagged my rod with her line, retrieved it with the fish still on, played the fish and landed it. Sewin 3 lb.

John recalled the incident of a guest who caught a small sea trout of 1 lb 4 oz, which he put in the hotel refrigerator, intending to take it home. One of the staff cooked the fish for another guest by mistake. 'I phoned Emyr Lewis who quickly brought me a sewin of 1 lb 12 oz which I wrapped up in many layers of newspaper. The guest took it home. I never heard a thing thereafter.'

As I have already described, the scenery in the Dovey valley is awe-inspiring. This is matched by the bird population which includes kites, goshawks, peregrines and buzzards amongst the raptors. A few grouse are in the hills, and woodcock arrive in winter.

13 River Coquet,
Northumberland

The wind blaws saftly fra the west, the dew hings on the lea,
The speckled lark aboon my head sings a' its sangs to me;
The glint o' Coquet's lovely charms, my heart can ne'er withstand,
So with my trusty rod ance mair, I'll try my eager hand.

'The Coquet', John Harbottle

The Coquet has its source in the Cheviot hills amongst wild open moorland.
For much of its upper course the river meanders slowly through boggy
moorland with only the bleat of sheep, or the call of curlew or snipe breaking
the solitude of the hills. On passing through the Wedder leap, and joined by
the hill streams Alwine and Usway, its character begins to change. Pools and
streams of better size appear, where trout and parr abound. Useful salmon
pools begin to form as the river reaches the town of Hepple. The river now
widens through fertile land from which, in time of spate, much soil is carried
into the water and the worm rewards the angler.

At Thropton, the river is joined by the Wreigh and from here to the sea are
many salmon pools. Much of the water can be covered from either bank, but
Spey casting may be necessary with the fly rod.

River Coquet. Head bailiff, Alan Bagnall, at Acklington dam.

Alan views the fish pass around Acklington dam.

Salmon enter the river in a mild season during January and, by 1 February, the opening day of the salmon-rod season, are to be found in the lower pools just off the tideway. The run continues through March and April, with fish taking the Acklington Dam fish-pass to move into the lower beats. Grilse begin to run in June, in spate conditions, and are joined by sea trout. The main autumn run of salmon comes into the river, if there is high water, in late September and October.

Most of the local rods use artificial or natural bait, but the river is suited to the fly, either on floating line in warm water or well sunk in early spring or late autumn. Much of the best fishing on Coquet is available to any visiting angler. By courtesy of the Duke of Northumberland, many miles are controlled by the Northumbrian Anglers' Federation, and licences may be obtained from the head bailiff, Alan Bagnall.

The Northumbrian Anglers' Federation was formed in March 1897. In 1957, the Duke of Northumberland contributed the following foreword to the Federation's *Handbook*:

Alnwick Castle
Northumberland

I am very glad to contribute this short foreword to the Handbook of the Northumbrian Anglers' Federation. This year the Federation celebrates its 60th Anniversary and, since its inception, my family has had a long and happy association with Northumbrian anglers. This excellently produced Handbook indicates the many miles of our sporting Northumbrian rivers – running through some of the most beautiful scenery in Great Britain – upon which the Federation can provide sport for fishermen.

In our rivers and in our scenery we in the north are fortunate – for it is surely not only the excitement of the rise and of the tug that tells that the hook has hold, and of the

Con Waldron. River Derwent, Cumbria.

River Coquet, Northumberland.

Fingle Bridge, River Teign, Devon.

Pen-y-Bont Falls, River Dovey, Powys.

Nicholas Peppiatt's first salmon of 9lb, 14 July 1988.

The River Coquet, Northumberland.

Opposite above: A salmon leaps at dusk on the spawning beds of Dartmoor in December.

Opposite below: Try every little pot and stickle.

River Camel. Tony Powell: 'We've just put one back; 8lb it was, but too red.'

Opposite: 'Those who would fish the narrow waters and stalk their salmon in secret hidden valleys.' River Dovey, Powys.

Ray Burrows fishing the River Camel in December.

The River Camel.

playing of the fish to the bank, but also the anticipation of these thrills, and the happiness of a few hours' recreation and relaxation to be spent in the open air along the rivers, each stretch of which has its own characteristic and life – whether they run between the wooded valleys of the lowlands, or along the open country of the hills, that gives us so much pleasure and happiness.

All true anglers cherish and appreciate these things, along with their memories of great days when skill and patience have been rewarded – as also the days of disappointment and of the big one that got away. I hope the Federation may long be able to provide water where good sport may be had and fairly practised, and I wish my fellow anglers happy days on the rivers, and tight lines.

Northumberland

Today, the *Handbook* is available from the head bailiff, Alan Bagnall, Thirston Mill, West Thirston, Felton, Morpeth, Northumberland, NE65 9EH. The book contains eight maps of the Federation's Coquet waters, the rules of the fishery, a list of distributors of permits and their cost, and a record of holders of the River Coquet Trophy.

The Trophy is awarded annually to the Federation angler who catches the first salmon of the season. His name is engraved upon it and he receives a replica and a free season permit, valid for 3 years. John Foster won the Trophy in 1986 and 1987, and thus fished without paying for his permit for six seasons. His fish were taken on 5 February – of 17 lb on a Black & Yellow Devon minnow, and on 4 February – of 7 lb 7 oz on a Sand Eel. The salmon itself is taken by the angler, James Hardy and Alan Bagnall to Alnwick Castle, where it is presented to the Duke.

The *Handbook* is compiled and edited by the Federation Chairman, James L. Hardy, with whom I talked.

James L. Hardy 9 October 1990

James welcomed Alan Bagnall and myself in his office at the House of Hardy in Alnwick. He handed me a number of historical documents, including a list of the 1903 permit charges of the Federation for '12 miles of the finest fishing' demised by His Grace the Duke of Northumberland KG. The season licence at that time was 1 guinea (£1.05)! There was also a copy of the 1916 Rod Licence of L. R. Hardy, issued on 5 February for the Fishery District of the River Coquet by the Clerk, Charles Percy. The name 'Hardy' is closely connected with angling on the river. As James wrote to me on 13 September 1990: 'My family have fished Coquet for more than a century', and thus it is not out of place to include a short history of the House of Hardy.

The business was started in 1872 by two engineers, William and John James Hardy. From manufacturing the best guns in the north of England, they soon started making the best fishing tackle, not only in the north of England but internationally. Their favourite hobby became their profession and the foundations of the great Hardy tradition were laid. The firm grew and grew, taking in further members of the family. Foster and Robert Henry Hardy joined the firm at the turn of the century and were shortly followed by Laurence and William II, both being sons of the founder William. Frances A. Hardy, sister of William and John James, was the firm's secretary.

In 1881 the Hardys won their first exhibition medal with the Palakona cane-built rods. John James became the World Champion Fly Caster.

On the retirement of William I in 1914, Laurence, referred to as 'L. R.', became co-managing director with his uncle, John James. L. R. could often be seen leaving the Alnwick shop with rods, net and bag for the Coquet 'to try out some new gear'.

The connection of the firm with the Royal Family is of long duration. Ten Royal Warrants of Appointment, including those of the late king George V and the last three Princes of Wales have been awarded to Hardy during the twentieth century.

In 1928, on the death of William II, two more brothers of L. R. joined the firm: Fred and Alan Hardy. Just prior to World War 2, William III joined and became managing director in 1958, on the death of L. R. After the war, James Hardy, son of William II, joined the company and at the time of our 1990 meeting was group commercial director. This Hardy is the 'Mr Jim' to whom I spoke. In 1983, William III retired and John B. Holland became managing director of the company which, in 1967, had become a subsidiary of the Harris & Sheldon group. In 1986, the company received the Queen's Award for Export Achievement and, in the following year, HRH The Princess Margaret opened the Hardy Museum at the Alnwick headquarters.

I spent a full hour in the museum, finding the wall charts of particular interest. These show, for rods and reels, the years of introduction and production and, if production was terminated, the final year. I picked out my Elarex spinning reel, my 3⅞ in. Perfect and the St George of my father-in-law. My 8 ft 6 in. CC de France split-cane trout rod and 12 ft A. H. E. Wood No. 2 split-cane salmon rod were also shown. Silex, St John and Uniqua reels; Farnborough, Jet, Fibalite, Palakona and Graphite rods – all were recorded.

Seated behind his office desk, Jim answered questions and reminisced. 'When did you start to fish the Coquet?'

'It was in the Easter holidays of 1940. My first fly rod came on my seventh birthday; a 7 ft greenheart CC de France and an old Sunbeam reel. I used to go and fish the Aln. Then, as I said, one day in 1940 I got onto Coquet. The family always had a stretch. Up to the age of 21, I used a fly rod. In my 21st year I started working at Hardy's and obtained a greenheart spinning rod. With that rod I caught my first salmon on The Bend at Acklington in about 1952. That fish weighed 20 lb. A great struggle took place to get it out. In the afternoon, just in time, the girl who eventually became my wife joined me at the river during the fight. I gave her the rod, waded in, got my arms under the fish and hoiked it out. I was about 22 or 23 years old at the time. The bait was probably a Yellow Belly, and the rod was a small one of 7 ft in length.'

'How often do you fish today?'

'Well, not often in the last couple of years, due to the drought and low water. Normally I fish the Coquet every Sunday. Last Sunday I went down because there was a spate. I might have stayed if I had had a can of worms. Perhaps next Sunday will be good. I fish according to the conditions: fly, spin, worm, prawn, shrimp.'

'Do you have a favourite fly for salmon?'

'I like the General Practitioner. Also the Shrimp Fly dressed on a No. 4 or No. 6 double hook. It was with Esmond Drury that I first used the General Practitioner – an excellent fly. Stoat's Tails and little tubes are good. The leader straight off the spool; 10 lb or 15 lb according to the size of fly.'

'How do you land your salmon?'

'Tail them by hand. Grilse I beach. If a beach is not available for grilse I wrap a handkerchief around my hand or wipe my palm in the sand.'

Alan broke in. 'The hand is best. That's what I do. In the spring when I'm asked to land large fish for anglers they offer me a tailer. You should see their faces when I go in bare-handed. They're grey-faced and terrified. I've never lost one. It is no problem at all.'

I asked Jim to describe his ideal day on the Coquet.

'The time of year must be early May. Life is coming to the river, the trees, the flowers, and things are starting to come through. A cloudy day with the clouds drifting spasmodically across the sky and shafts of sunlight. A gentle breeze. I would start at Acklington dam on the right bank, just below the fish pass. I always fish that bank because the Duke of Northumberland lets me have it on that day. A 12½ ft fly rod suits that water due to the trees behind. A floating line and maybe a little Shrimp Fly, or a Stoat's Tail or Hairy Mary. I would stay below the fish pass for some time. It is a good place with the Federation Rock out in the middle. Fish lie on the other side and often take as the fly swirls by the Rock.

'I would then move down to the Duchess Stream, named after one of the late Duchesses. There is a handy beach there for landing salmon. Then one comes to The Gullet, which has a rocky face on my side and goes steep down; a narrow place where fish lie close to the rock face. If you hook a fish there in heavy water you are in some difficulty for they try to go down through some rapids and it is hard to follow due to trees. Two years ago I had a fish on in that place in rising water. It insisted on going down and down and down, until I couldn't go any further. I might have gone in when younger, but I'm getting on a bit. I thought of tying a stick to my line and finding it later lower down the river. By the time I'd thought all this out, bang, the fish had gone. That's my sort of day: May, with a bit of excitement.'

I asked for an amusing incident.

'If I had been a cartoonist I would have loved to have drawn the look on the face of a salmon I saw being played up at Grantown on the Spey. It was on the Association water, many years ago. Jack Martin was spinning and hooked a fish. This salmon played in a peculiar manner and came in tail-first. What had happened was that the fish had been caught originally on a bunch of worms, but the line had broken. The snood had gone through the fish and emerged, trailing, at the vent. At the end of the snood was a loop in the nylon in which Jack's minnow had become entangled. I don't know what the fish thought, but it must have felt very undignified.'

Alan Bagnall, head bailiff, Northumbrian Anglers' Federation 9 October 1990

Alan has been head bailiff to the Federation since 1979. Before then, he worked part-time on the river. He has 12 assistant bailiffs and, in addition, can make rapid contact with the wardens of the National River Authority whose vans are equipped with radios.

Alan is 48 years old and started to fish when 4 years old with an army tank aerial. Being born close to Rothbury, on the upper reaches of the river, his first fishing on the Coquet was for trout. He served for 12 years in the Royal Air Force, being demobilized in 1972. In 1974, he caught his first salmon. He was fishing for trout with a tiny natural minnow on 30 September, the last day of the trout season. The minnow was mounted on a tackle with 'swing-in' metal gills, which were pressed into the head of the bait; a metal spike went down the inside of the fishlet and there were two trebles, one hook of each being straightened into a spike pressed into the flank of the bait. The total length was 1½ in.

'I was after a big trout. He must have been 4 lb. There are many large trout in the Coquet. I went there early in the morning and crept across the grass on my stomach for I knew exactly where he lay. I cast across. There was a swirl and I found I had hooked a salmon. I was fishing 3x nylon on a tiny spinning rod. That fish went round and round and round and, man, he never jumped. Eventually I tired him out in the pool. I landed him. He was a cock fish, slightly red, but I didn't care in the slightest. I looked around, bonked him, and fled in the car. I went straight away to Alnwick and bought a salmon licence for the season – with only one month to go! Then I started showing him to everybody.'

I asked Alan when runs of fish enter the river, and the average weights of the salmon.

River Coquet below Rothbury. In high water, salmon lie in front of this causeway.

'We have what we call "hitty missy" years. Some seasons the springers are all about the 8, 9 or 10 lb mark, with the occasional 12 and 14 lb fish. Other years, we don't get so many, but they are larger. In those springs, the fish are of 14, 15 and 16 lb. But the greatest change sometimes comes at Easter, or thereabouts, at intervals of 3 or 4 years, with the entry of what we call "the little Norwegian fish". They are lovely little fish with tiny heads, all running at the 7 or 8 lb mark. Unfortunately, the guys who are fishing tend to have on too large a hook. They lose them. That is on the tidal water where, most of the time, they are spinning.

'They also fish eels' tails. That is the sand eel, which they dig up on the sea shore. He's silvery, with a mouth, and about 6 in. (15 cm) long. They cut off the head and mount two trebles, one at the tail and the other half-way along. Sometimes they dye the eel to a yellow shade with acriflavine. Well, as soon as they realize it is a Norwegian year and reduce the size of their trebles, they start to land them. They mount the eels' tails with spinning vanes at the head, a 3 ft trace, and then a weight. The thing is to spin the tail parallel to the bed of the river.'

'Do you use the prawn?'

'Yes, prawn is used, but the shrimp is the main bait. Worms too after 1 June, but they are not allowed on the tidal section.'

Sea trout start to come in during April. Alan describes them as 'little ones of 3 or 4 lb', although some reach 16 and 17 lb. Then, depending on the season and whether there have been good falls of snow in the hills to keep the river up in May, runs of salmon continue. Grilse arrive in June; sea trout as well. By the first 2 weeks of July, sea trout can be right up at Alwanton not far from the source of the river.

'The farmers at Alwanton usually have their freezers filled by the end of July. They have peculiar ways of fishing!'

'Licences?'

'Perhaps. Mind you they only "fish" for the pot, and salmon don't go that far.'

I asked Alan whether there had been an alteration over the years in the weights of salmon.

'We get a few very big fish. A lot of my family in the old days were poachers. I remember my grandfather used to transport his salmon in a pram. They used to boil them for the hens. Big fish they were – we never see them now. Grandfather was a blacksmith. In the winter, when there were fewer horses to shoe, he made cleeks and tar burners. The cleek is a hook to pull fish out of the river at night when illuminated by the tar burner. This burner had a hardwood handle; at the top of this was a bundle of twigs dipped in pitch.'

Salmon fly rods on the upper river may be of 10 or 10 ft 6 in. long. Lower down at Warkworth, and on the tidal water, double-handed rods of 14 and 15 ft are favoured.

Alan commented: 'I'm not very happy about those long rods. Not happy at all. Heavy flies are used, which sink to the bottom and rest there. After 10 minutes, if a salmon rubs along the sunk line, that line seems to twitch. I call it "the Warkworth Twitch". It is a joy to see a genuine fly fisher down there.'

The salmon and sea-trout flies used are as one might expect on any spate river: for salmon, the Stoat's Tail and, if there is peat stain in the water, a red or orange fly; sea trout regularly fall to a Teal & Silver Blue.

Spinning rods are usually 9 ft long and stiff. 18 lb monofilament is used for heavy springers, particularly at Warkworth, where there are many rocks in the river. In the early weeks of the season, Yellow Belly Devon minnows are popular, and eels' tails. A Silver & Grey Devon is favoured in snow water, or a light blue Devon with silver belly. Red and brown minnows also suit the water. Shrimps are mounted with a shrimp pin and worms on a single hook.

'How do you catch your worms? At night with a torch?'

'I'm not too keen on seeing torches at night. Poachers use them. In the seventeenth century, the Bishop of Durham came up here at Michaelmas to collect his rents. The farmers used to say: "We can't pay you yet because the rent is in the river." They meant that salmon had not yet reached the spawning area and thus could not be poached to pay the rent.'

Alan told me that in 1989 the catch on the Federation stretches of the Coquet were: sea trout – 324; salmon – 175. Notable catch returns by individual anglers are shown in the following tables.

John Foster: 1989 catches on the Coquet

Date	Place	Fish	Weight in lb
28 Feb.	Stream Foot	Salmon	6
5 Apr.	Swans Neck	Salmon	8½
22 Apr.	Swans Neck	Salmon	6½
6 May	Swans Neck	Salmon	9½
20 May	Houndean Burn	Salmon	10½
7 June	Swans Neck	Salmon	9
10 July	Swans Neck	Salmon	8
7 Sept.	Houndean Burn	Sea trout	5
22 Sept.	Castle Pool	Sea trout	18
25 Sept.	Castle Pool	Sea trout	3
26 Sept.	Stream Foot	Salmon	13
26 Sept.	Houndean Burn	Salmon	11
26 Sept.	Stream Foot	Salmon	6
17 Oct.	Hermitage	Sea trout	8
20 Oct.	Betts Pool	Sea trout	4

David Allen: 1989 catches on the Coquet

Date	Place	Fish	Weight in lb
4 March	Houndine	Salmon	16½
1 July	Tidal	Salmon	10
16 July	Swans Neck	Salmon	9½
17 July	Brewery Stream	Sea trout	4
17 July	Brewery Stream	Sea trout	3
20 July	Hermitage	Salmon	13
31 July	Brewery Stream	Salmon	3½
31 July	Brewery Stream	Sea trout	3½
6 Aug.	Stream Foot	Salmon	10
6 Aug.	Warkworth Bog	Salmon	8½
8 Aug.	Warkworth Bog	Salmon	10
10 Aug.	Black Bog	Salmon	7
13 Aug.	Warkworth Bog	Salmon	10½
24 Aug.	Brotherwick Quarry	Salmon	9
24 Aug.	Brotherwick Quarry	Salmon	5½
26 Aug.	Warkworth Bog	Salmon	18½
26 Aug.	Warkworth Bog	Salmon	9½
28 Aug.	Grandstand ·	Salmon	8½
30 Aug.	Grandstand	Salmon	8
23 Sept.	Brewery Stream	Sea trout	3
23 Sept.	Brewery Stream	Sea trout	1½
25 Sept.	Brewery Stream	Sea trout	5
25 Sept.	Brewery Stream	Sea trout	2
15 Oct.	Warkworth Bog	Salmon	12½

River Coquet. Bob Foster has fished Stream Foot for 55 years. He is seen here with an 8 lb sea trout taken on a No. 2 Mepps.

We then left Alan's house for the river, and the first fishable water above the tide – Stream Foot. There we found four or five anglers, two of whom had caught large sea trout. I spoke to Bob Foster who had landed a sea trout of about 8 lb on a silver No. 2 Mepps Aglia. Bob is 70 years old and has fished Stream Foot since he was 15 years of age. As well as the Mepps, he favours a Toby with the single treble at the tail; he does not add a flying treble. He likes to fish the worm, gathering lobs at night in the rain from a rose garden by the light of a torch. Bob does not fish the fly. Many salmon have fallen to his rod from Coquet, including two of 20 lb each.

Alan Dodd then showed me a sea trout of about 8 lb which he, too, had taken on a silver No. 2 Mepps Aglia. This fish had been attacked by a seal, which had left tooth scars above the tail. Alan does not like the worm. He concentrates on spinning and fishing shrimps on a mount of his own invention. This incorporates a shrimp pin inserted under the tail and two No. 8 doubles whipped to a bent galvanized wire, which is thrust into the body underneath the head. One of the doubles lies under the head of the shrimp and the other between the legs. His shrimps are fine, undamaged specimens, each with two feelers, which he catches himself in the sea. He does not bind the hooks to the body of the shrimp, they are held in place by the pull of the nylon trace upwards through the eye of the pin beneath the tail. Alan observed:

'If you look at a salmon's mouth you will see that it is narrow, not more than 2 in. across. Now measure my shrimp and you will find it is the same length. As the hooks are within the 2 in. overall length of the bait the salmon must have them in his mouth if he grips the shrimp at right angles.'

Alan told me a tale. I think he likes tales! This one was true.

'I cast in this afternoon and the line tightened. I struck and the fish took off, but I could see the spinner on the flank. When I landed the fish it was lassoed with the line around the body and hooked onto the treble. The harder the fish pulled, the tighter became the noose. I hand-tailed it and unwrapped the line from behind the dorsal fin. That fish weighed 7 lb, there wasn't a mark on it, and I let it go.'

I conclude this account of Coquet fishing with the bailiff's report to the Northumbrian Anglers' Federation for the 1989 season.

Fishing

For the second year running, the season got off to a slow start in low water conditions. The first fish was taken at 7½ lb on 7 February on a Gold Devon. Eleven days later the next fish was taken of 6½ lb above the dam.

Towards the end of the month a good flood occurred with the level up 6 ft. This produced a small run and six more fish were grassed, the largest being 16½ lb.

Stocking took place in early March with top-quality fish being put in the Rivers Tyne and Coquet. It is a much better system having the fish go in at this time of the year and has proved very popular with the anglers. They now have a chance of catching a few decent fish and can see some return for their money.

Fishing continued through March with not a lot of salmon being taken, but some very good brown trout were caught in the first few days of the season. Water conditions remained low into May, but plenty of salmon were being caught, mostly on shrimp and most of these above the dam. By the middle of May there were plenty of sea trout in the 3–5 lb range to be seen in the woods above the dam, also some good salmon. River levels remained low and weed started to grow quickly.

June saw bait fishing start with a flourish. Early morning anglers caught some well-conditioned brown trout up to 2½ lb. Weed growth caused difficulty for those who span. Salmon and sea trout continued to be taken on the lower reaches of the river during June and July – mostly on shrimp. Brown trout were in good condition, but the upper river was quiet due to weed and low water.

July and August were very slow, with low water and much weed. Few fish were taken in the heat of the day. September came – and still no water. Sea trout were moving slowly into the upper reaches of the river, but many were dark in colour. Towards the end of the month a lot more fish came in, but due to the low water conditions they tended to remain on the tidal sections of the Coquet. The last 6 weeks of the season saw so many fish lying in the tidal water that it was impossible to count them. Odd fish made their way up the river, and when a little fresh water came in the last week of October a few days of good sport resulted from High Bank to Pauperhaugh Bridge. Most of these fish were dark in colour.

Early November has seen one small flood with a rise of 1 ft. This brought up some fish, and the first redds were seen at Pauperhaugh Bridge.

Disease

There has not been a lot of disease on the river this year, and the late fish look good.

Notice boards and repairs

Boards have been replaced and new ones are to be put up at Lady's Bridge, Felton and Thrum Mill.

Permits

Permit sales went well again this year, and although there was no large increase I feel we may have reached a stable level. The tidal numbers are down as anglers are waiting to see the effect of the new fish pass.

General

A fairly good year with those anglers who can spend a lot of time on the water getting good returns. The low water was always a problem as far as attracting visitors, so I expect these numbers to be down. We had to have a constant presence on the tidal water towards the end of the season as there were so many fish that it was almost impossible to cast and not foul hook one. A few years ago these conditions would have resulted in a slaughter of fish, but as we have now got rid of most of the bad anglers things went quite well.

The removal of the 'fly only' stretch at Felton proved very popular and we had a lot more elderly and disabled anglers using the water. No problems or complaints were passed, and I would recommend that it continues in 1990.

Our part-time bailiffs again did a good job and are on top of most problems as soon as they occur. We are looking for a good back-end spawning on the rivers and a successful year in 1990.

Yours faithfully
Alan Bagnall
Head Bailiff

Open seasons for the Coquet are:

Salmon: 1 February to 31 October
Sea trout: 4 April to 31 October
Trout: 22 March to 30 September

14 River Derwent,
Cumbria

The River Derwent, rising high in the fells, flows north through the Borrowdale Valley, Derwent Water and Bassenthwaite Lake before swinging to the west to pass through the town of Cockermouth, where it is joined by its tributary, the Cocker, on its way to the sea at Workington.

The Derwent is the widest of the English rivers covered in this book; it is also prolific. The average *recorded* salmon rod catch for the years 1980 to 1989 inclusive, and the National Rivers Authority in Warrington doubts that all were recorded, was 733 fish. In the wet summer of 1988, the *recorded* catch was 1449 fish and, in the following dry season, 941 salmon were taken. To these figures may be added an annual take of about 25 fish from the River Cocker.

The salmon season commences on 1 February and closes on 31 October. The river is best described by those who fish her regularly.

John Nolan Cockermouth, 11 October 1990

John has fished for salmon since he was 11 years old, an angling span of 29 years, 16 of which have been spent on the Derwent. He landed his first salmon when he was 12 years old from the River Ehen, a small Cumbrian river with an average salmon-rod catch, over the 10 years to 1989, of 107 fish, and a good sea-trout run.

'I took him on a worm on a cheap little fibreglass rod, an old spinning reel and some nylon I'd found somewhere.'

Since then John has assisted in the production of a number of angling videotapes for Silverstream Films. On 14 October 1990, he took over the management of the The Fitz water on the Derwent for Alan Addison, who completed the purchase of the beat during the month. This water runs from just below Cockermouth Bridge for about 2 miles, 1½ miles of which is double bank. A number of rods will be let in the 1991 season, including some day rods.

I asked John to describe salmon and grilse runs on the Derwent.

'The river used to have greater spring runs and some of my early records show fish in March. The numbers of these spring entrants have reduced. Early in 1989 they were netting Derwent Water for pike and took two

River Derwent. The lie at Fitz Mill Pool is the smooth water above this blown-up dam. The old fish pass is out of sight to the right.

springers of 9 lb each. Not many people fish persistently until July, when the main bulk of fish start to arrive. Mind you, there is a small run of grilse as early as May, but they are only taken by locals who know when and where to go.

'In late June and early July, sea trout start to enter. Some of these are large; the majority are herling – smolts of the same season returning after a few months in the sea. Other than herling, sea trout run between 1½ and 2½ lb with some of a much higher weight.

'Summer salmon of 10 and 12 lb come in during July and August if there is good water. This run, including some large fish, continues until the end of the season. I have not noticed an increase in grilse at the expense of two-sea-winter fish; in fact it may be that the number of large fish is increasing. There is always the chance of a fish of over 20 lb, and one of 30 lb is a possibility. Looking back at the old *Fishing Gazettes* of the 1950s, when the Derwent was reported, I see that there were no exceptionally large salmon. There were one or two of 20, 22 and 23 lb, but no 30 lb specimens. Today there are quite a few in the 30 lb bracket and some exceed that category. Perhaps a few kelts are going out and recovering. Some fish must be staying at sea an extra year and coming back as three- or four-sea-winter fish.'

I asked John to describe an outstanding day.

'Two of us were on a private stretch just below Cockermouth in mid-September. We had fished all day without result. Deciding to give it another half-hour, Colin went in and took a salmon of 21 lb. We rested the pool for a couple of minutes, went back in and took another of 19½ lb. We had six fish that day and not one was smaller than the second salmon. Just before we finished, I had a final throw with an Irish Lane minnow; grey and brown in colour. That minnow has lead thrust down the plastic body, and the wire mount is wrapped about the treble and painted red. The red colour of the mount is important. Anyway, a heavy salmon took hold. After 10 minutes I realized that it was a monster. It came into the bank and I gave the tailer to Colin. He went down, looked, came back pale and shaking and dropped the tailer at my feet. "There's no way I'm going to tackle that. You can have it." That salmon had a tail like a shovel and he didn't want the responsibility. It was a difficult situation. A recess had been washed out under the bank. The salmon could put his nose in, down, and stay there. I leaned back perilously on the rod, down went his nose, up came his tail and I made Colin take the risk. We had him out, a cock fish of 31 lb.'

'You've never had a day like that again?'

'Not really. I've had days of 9, 10 or 12, all on fly. Beautiful fresh fish of between 8 lb and 12 lb.'

John told me that the prawn is banned and the shrimp is likely to be prohibited. In low water, few people fish for sea trout other than at night.

In dry weeks, John sometimes takes dour, resident salmon on small doubles: No. 12 and No. 14 being favourite sizes. Spinning and worming are not allowed on most stretches other than in high water. He has taken salmon in low water by casting a dry floating Yellow Dolly upstream and stripping it back. In this manner he has attracted stale fish.

'Sometimes, when a salmon has been static in a lie for many days I take him on the Yellow Dolly. I use a 10 ft fly rod and am able to hold a long length of a double-tapered No. 6 line in the air. The leader is of 8 lb breaking strain, straight off the spool. I spray the fly with floatant, but make the cast sink with Permasink, except for the final few inches closest to the fly; these I grease. Then, starting at the bottom of a pool, I cast up under bushes where a salmon is likely to lie, and flick back fast to make the fly skate. Sometimes they take straight away, or else move down and attack the fly on a subsequent cast. It is the speed of retrieve that counts and early evening is the best time, when they move out of the pools into the streams to get some oxygen.'

John considers the Derwent to be a moody river. With the gauge at 3 ft at Cockermouth Bridge, one would expect great things, but 'It can break your heart'. Fly size is critical: more so than pattern. In July, with the water at 3 ft on the gauge, a Low Water No. 8 Wilson double is about right. The pattern is: black hair wing, silver body, blue or black throat hackle and jungle-cock cheeks. This fly serves well for the remainder of the season.

The Thunder & Lightning brings results, particularly if squirrel tail dyed brown, or natural brown bucktail, is used instead of mallard flank feathers for the wing. Heavier water requires a larger fly on a No. 6 Partridge CS12 up-eyed treble. At the head of the treble shank, he ties in brown bucktail to extend beyond the hook to twice the length of the shank, making a total of at least 2 in. The waving hair of this lure is at its best in streamy water. From the gleam which came into John's eye, there is no doubt that his favourite for summer fish on a sunny day is a derivative of the Thunder & Lightning. He dresses this magnetic attractor on a No. 10 Partridge X2B treble, substituting copper Lurex for the normal black floss silk body ribbed with silver tinsel.

'One morning in spring, we went down to a beat and went through it with a No. 8 fly. The river was perfect and fish were heaving themselves out of the water. They wouldn't look at the fly, and turned their noses up at a No. 10. I came out of the pool, sat down and watched. Sea trout were coming up like trout to take natural fly on top of the water. So, I thought, I'll go for these sea trout and put on a No. 14 double. The water was quite high. I went back in. First cast – salmon 8 lb. Andy came up and netted it for me. He said "I'll take it down to the beat hut and put it in a bass". He only got half-way and I was into a second. Six salmon came in 2 hours on those No. 14 doubles: Badger & Silver, little black Stoat's, anything small. It was a unique day. I've never seen sea trout feeding like that. That's what made me go small.'

He went on: 'In the final week of the season, 5 years ago, in low water, I took 13 salmon in one day and lost one of over 35 lb. They all took these tiny doubles. The pool they came from was very deep, but they had moved into the shelter of some trees because it was sunny. I was using a soft 13 ft Bruce rod, a DT7F/s line with a 8 lb leader. Five of these fish came in the morning. I then had to go to the funeral of my wife's elderly aunt, but returned in the evening to take eight more fish. That fish of about 35 lb – I had him on for three-quarters of an hour, but couldn't handle him on 8 lb nylon and the soft Bruce. He took me down to the next pool, a distance of several hundred yards and I had to cross the river, which was low. He came back up and I crossed again. At one time, he was belly up but unreachable, even in my chest waders. He then went upstream, threw himself out and fell back over an overhanging branch. Twang – gone.'

We changed fish.

'Sturgeon used to run the Derwent. Julian Shaw, of John Norris of Penrith, showed me an old book which recorded a sturgeon in the last century. The most recent experience happened about 5 years ago when a Dane had a fish on for about 5 hours. It hardly moved and he never saw it. We all thought it must have been a sturgeon.'

John's favourite rod is a 15 ft Universal Hexagraph. This Spey casts well with a floating line and has the power to fish a sunk line in a deep pool. At one time, he used a 14 ft Walker but found this too powerful when fishing small flies. Ideal in low water is a 10 ft 3 in. rod. Chest waders are always worn. To land salmon he carries a 30 in. Gye net, or 24 in. Falkus net, or a tailer, but prefers to beach and use his hand. The gaff is prohibited on the river.

I asked John if he had had any amusing experiences on the river.

'I don't know about amusing, but I've often been frightened at night. There is a beat about 5 miles from here called Camerton which is right beside a graveyard. I fish there at night for sea trout, and I can tell you that the hair rises on the back of my neck as I stand in the river. One night I had to go through the yard in the dark, the wind was howling in the trees and I picked up my feet and ran – straight into an open newly dug grave.'

John spins with a 10 ft rod, a fixed-spool reel and 15 or 18 lb Maxima. In heavy water in the back-end of the season, he may increase to 20 lb. At the end of the reel line is a swivel, followed by a trace of 15 lb. No weight is added, reliance being placed on the weight of the bait, which might be a Toby, a Derwent spoon or an Irish Lane minnow. A favoured minnow is in the Devon style, of wood with a copper tube in the centre, and coloured Ox Blood & Gold, or Black & Gold. When using a 2½ in. wooden Devon, he carries three traces with varying amounts of lead wire wound around these mounts, which pass through the body of the minnow. If using a Toby, he removes the hook, and fits an extra link and a Partridge outpoint treble. This arrangement moves the treble away from the fins of the Toby on which, in standard form, they tend to catch. He considers the Toby loses fish because the barb of the hook is too far back from the point; the Partridge barb is well forward. He does not favour Wye weights because these have to be large when made of non-lead metals.

Mrs Con Waldron near Bassenthwaite Lake, 12 October 1990

Drive out of the gate of Con's house, follow a lane for 500 yards, park the car, cross two fields and you are on the Brock Hole section of the Higham Estate water of the Derwent, which Con fishes on Fridays. We went together to the beat hut.

'How long have you been fishing for salmon?'

'About 24 years, if not more, and in all of those years I have fished the Derwent. I started as a Cockermouth Angler. In those days it cost £30 a year. When I also got onto the National Trust water I had to give up my membership. You had to be a resident of Cockermouth in those days. Then the Cockermouth Castle Estate released extra water to the Anglers who took in a few outside rods to help pay the rent. I was able to make someone from Skipton a member. Sometimes the Castle lets a day or two to outsiders.'

I asked about the timing of salmon runs into the river.

'Occasionally I have had a fish or two in March, but generally not much happens until June, when both salmon and sea trout start to arrive. This year, being very dry, I caught my first salmon on 13 August. It was a hen of 14½ lb, taken on 8 lb nylon and a double No. 10 Blue Doctor. I don't think there are more small fish than there used to be. We find large fish come in towards the end of the season. I had another salmon in August – he weighed 18 lb.'

'How many fish have you had so far this season?'

'Ten have fallen to my rod, of which I caught eight, all of them on fly except two. I don't like spinning.'

'Are the men jealous of your success?'

The question delighted Con who burst into torrents of laughter. 'They hate it!'

In spring, she prefers to fish in the afternoon, when natural flies start to hatch, showing that the water is a little warmer. As the season progresses, she fishes later, when the light has gone off the water. Sometimes she rises early to fish for trout in May and June, rarely bothering with salmon until July.

Con loves to fish the fly, her favourite being a Shrimp on a double hook. Her rod is a 12 ft Lakeland carbon-fibre with which she casts a sink-tip line, rarely using a sinking line. Sometimes she uses 8 lb nylon with small flies, but, in the summer of 1990, she had such a struggle with the 18-pounder that she has increased the nylon strength to 10 or 15 lb. The fight with this fish was particularly worrying because she had tied in a dropper – not her common practice.

'I kept saying to myself "please don't let the free fly get caught", but when I had the salmon on the bank I found it had both flies inside its mouth.'

'How do you land your fish?'

'I carry a tailer and play them out. Sometimes I use my hand and then I really play them to a standstill. I tried to use my hand this summer with a fish of 15 lb but couldn't manage it. He was too heavy for me.'

Con's fishing diary recorded 11 salmon in 1989 and, up to the day of my visit on 12 October, 10 for 1990.

Date	Place	Fly	Sex	Weight in lb
13 Aug.	Brock Hole	No. 10 Blue Doctor	Hen	14½
24 Aug.	Brock Hole	No. 10 Blue Doctor	Cock	18½
31 Aug.	Brock Hole	No. 12 Blue Doctor	Cock	15
31 Aug.	Brock Hole	No. 12 Blue Doctor	Cock	10
1 Sept.	Brock Hole	No. 12 Blue Doctor	Cock	10
*8 Sept.	Brock Hole	No. 10 Shrimp Fly	Hen	8½
*8 Sept.	Brock Hole	No. 10 Shrimp Fly	Cock	22½
21 Sept.	Brock Hole	Black & Gold Toby	Hen	14½
21 Sept.	Eel Settings	Small Shrimp Fly	Hen	8
4 Oct.	Dunthwaite	Black & Gold Toby	Hen	12

*Caught by Ronnie Wise fishing Con's rod.

'Finally, tell me of any highlight in your angling life.'

'About 10 years ago I caught a salmon of 12½ lb on fly. That was when I was a Cockermouth Angler. I took it into the shop to be weighed. Unknown to me, they entered it in the Association competition for the heaviest fish caught on fly that season. It won the cup. In addition, because it was the heaviest, and taking my age into account, it also won the cup for the heaviest fish caught on fly by an old-age pensioner, male or female. I think I was the only woman in the Association at that time. I had to leave – it made the men very cross!'

'Do you have your own special method of fishing?'

'Yes. I cast out at an angle of about 45 degrees, and then let the line and fly swing. When the line has straightened the fly is allowed to hang for a moment or two. That's when they take.'

I walked across the meadows to my car, leaving Con and her dog beside the water which she loves.

Charley Bateman Cockermouth, 12 October 1990

Charley was 70 years old at the time of our meeting. Two or three weeks before my visit he had broken his femur. I called at his house and he came into the sitting-room with the aid of a walking-frame, sat down and looked out of the window. Without being there I know that is what he will always do – look out of the window. Outside is the Derwent. There is nothing other than a sheet of glass between him and the river which has been at the centre of his leisure hours, and the bank is 20 ft away. He has fished there since 1928, when he was 8 years old, his father having fished before him since the final years of the nineteenth century.

He looked out of the window. 'When I was a boy I collected birds' eggs. The best I had was a corncrake. Every year, they nested over there in the meadow beyond the river, in the corner by the bridge. They make a funny noise, just like a garden rake.'

Recently Charley purchased four houses backing onto the river and built his own behind them. At the same time, mysteriously, a concrete block appeared in the river outside the window by which we sat; salmon pause there, it is a good lie; Charley sees them.

'At one time there were dams and mills all along the river; every village from the Lake down had one. Then they blew the dams and that helped the fishing. Cockermouth Mill was for tweed; they also made fishing lines from flax. Fitz Mill dam was blown and others down to Workington. On the Cocker there was a bobbin mill, one for wood turning, making kitchen-chairlegs and such like, and others provided power and electricity for farms. Fish can now go through unchecked. You see, in the old days, there would be a sluice inside the mill, a sort of by-pass. When fish were running, the mill employees opened this sluice, salmon would then enter the channel, the men shut the sluice and waited at the downstream end with nets for the fish to turn back to regain the river. All this took place inside the building where no one could be seen. They didn't get much for the fish because there were so many of them; fish I mean, and fridges and freezers were unknown.'

Charley told me a little of the history of Cockermouth Anglers. 'At one time we had many leases from farmers on the Derwent and Cocker. About 40 or 50 years ago Tommy Rook, the Castle manager, decided that if the Castle took over all the leases they would then always be able to provide fishing to the Anglers at a reasonable price. This happened, and we had inexpensive fishing. We still have inexpensive fishing. Recently our rent trebled but we have been given more water. To keep the cost low to ourselves we let 12 rods to anglers outside the county at a higher figure. We are happy and they are pleased to pay. A member can invite a guest for 6 days fishing. The member has to live within the Cockermouth postal area. There are 35 of us on the Derwent and some more on the Cocker.'

The earliest Charley has had a fish was 18 April – this salmon weighed 18½ lb. 'One day I had four, on the worm. If you take four you stop if you've any conscience. If I'd carried on I could have had a dozen, but I stopped. Last week there were three rods fishing together. Jack didn't get anything and neither did Jack Wood, but the chap between had eight, the greedy devil! Then he said: "I can't bear the thought of Charley sitting up there with a broken leg, and he as crazy as he is on fishing, so I'll send up 3 salmon". It was very good of him. I felt better. We've cooked them and they're in the freezer.'

'What are the rules governing when one may spin and fish the worm?'

'Every morning I read the water level at Cockermouth Bridge and telephone the Castle. They can spin at 2 ft 6 in., and worm at 4 ft if the water is dirty, and at that height there is always some colour.'

'How did you catch and keep your worms?'

'When I've cut the lawn, I go out on a damp night with a torch. You mustn't shine the torch on the worm, but keep the light to one side. You can then grab them and drop them into a jar or bucket. I used to keep three buckets in my shed with wet earth, moss and farmyard manure in the bottom. Worms keep for months if you give them something to eat, such as cabbage and lettuce leaves. They come up to the surface and eat the leaves. We don't use brandlings, just large lobworms.'

'How do you mount them?'

'Three at a time on a No. 12 hook. Come down about one-third of the length of the worm from the head with a single hook. Put it through and bring it out one-third from the tail before pushing the worm up the nylon. Do the same with the second worm. Put on the third and draw the others down. In the water it looks like a small squid with six tentacles. I like to use the hooks from old gut-eyed flies to mount my worms. They have a flat end and serrations on the shank to which I bind my nylon.'

Whilst we were talking, Charley was sorting through tackle boxes which his wife had placed on his knees. Out came a vast No. 2/o double-hooked fly of a blue-grey colour. I commented: 'That's got some weight. That'll swim well'.

'Aarrh,' said Charley, a delightful sound which brought out the full savour of his appreciation of the fly. 'I sat here one evening and looked at the water which was rather lower than it is now. [It was about 5 ft on the gauge as we spoke.] I have a sixth sense of when to fish. I said to Jack, who was here, "Would you do me a favour in the morning?" He said: "Yes". I said: "Drop me off at Cherry Tree". That is about half a mile upstream. I had a big Yellow Torrish, about the same size as that fly. Cherry Tree is my favourite pool. I took my son-in-law up there and he caught his first salmon. Every time he went there last season he had two fish, which rather spoiled him, if you know what I mean. Well, I was sure that next morning I would have a salmon if I could get there. Everything worked out perfectly. I came down to the big stone and I had a take. It was a fish of about 18 lb and I played and played and played it, walking backwards downstream all the time. Then it swam up onto the gravel, I dropped the rod to go and grab it, but it swam off again. I snatched up the rod and held on, but it broke me at the knot. You get these hunches. I sit here and I can visualize it all. I'm actually fishing the river when I'm in this chair.'

We were joined by Jack Abernethy, who had introduced me to Charley, his father-in-law, in the first place. During the previous week, he had been fishing one morning with two friends by the iron bridge. One of the trio, David Hackley, caught six salmon on the worm. Even though he assisted the other two, and they fished in the same places and in the same manner, they caught nothing. They discussed the matter, but could reach no explanation.

Charley's favourite fly is a single Silver Wilkinson. He also likes the Thunder & Lightning, both on No. 4 hooks, but considers that, as the years pass, salmon flies fall in and then out of fashion. In recent seasons, a small Stoat's Tail on an Esmond Drury treble has done well. The Garry is gaining popularity. His line is level and of neutral density for he finds this swings evenly across the river. He is averse to sink-tip lines for a convincing reason: he finds, when casting across the width of a river, that the floating section bellies downstream faster than the sinking tip which is then dragged across at speed. His level lines come from McHardy's of Carlisle who cut off 25 yd lengths.

He uses three fly rods: 15 ft in heavy water; 12 ft 6 in. in the summer and 10 ft for the sea-trout fishing. Nylon is drawn straight off the spool and is never less than 10 lb BS. He carries a tailer but prefers to beach his fish.

The 15 ft fly rod is used for worming, with 50 lb monofilament on a fly reel.

The fixed-spool reel enables baits to be flicked out between trees.

The trace to the hook is of 25 lb monofilament. On an even, gravelly river bed, he casts out as with a fly but adds a little weight. The worms then drift across, trundling seductively over the gravel and small stones.

Spinning equipment consists of a 10 ft rod and 100 yd of 18 lb monofilament on a fixed-spool reel. The baits are large brass spoons. He gave one to me which measured 3 in. long and 1½ in. wide; at the tail was a large single treble hook. Extra weight is not required, but a swivel is tied in about 2 ft above the spoon, where the line meets the trace. This is by no means the largest spoon in use; he once caught nine salmon on one 5 in. long. The colour should be dull, or copper-coloured inside and silver on the outside. To get the desired dull shades, he hangs up new spoons outside to weather. Sometimes he cuts off and throws away the handle of a tablespoon, drills a hole at each end of the spoon itself and fits a swivel and treble hook. But best of all is the slim brass or copper Derwent spoon which is stamped on the outside with scale-like depressions, which protrude as pimples on the inside. In the autumn, a metal Red & Gold Devon finds a place in his armoury.

Where the river is wide, Charley fishes first down the side of the river nearest to his bank, just casting half-way across and retrieving with the rod held low. He then transfers his attention to the far half, casting right across but holding the rod high during the retrieve. A high rod keeps most of the line out of the water, consequently the current cannot take hold of the nylon to put a belly in the line which would drag the minnow too rapidly across the width of the river.

One of the advantages of his long fly rod is the ability to cast a small spoon of 1 in. long into the necks of pools. He always carries such a spoon when fly fishing. It will be tried if the gauge rises to 30 in. during the day, particularly if a strong wind roughens the water surface.

Charley is certain that the seasons have changed from the time of his youth and the fishing years of his father.

'Borrowdale used to be the wettest place in England. When snow fell and blocked the valleys in the hills, the farms were cut off – they only had a pony and trap in those days. They stored food for the winter by salting down salmon and pigs. Today it is different. There is less rain, the bogs have been drained, and Thames Board, who make chipboard, have planted thousands of pine trees. Each tree sucks up 40 gallons of water a day in summer, so the river doesn't keep up as well as it did in father's time.'

The River Derwent and River Cocker long ago

What changes in angling on these rivers have taken place over the last 130 years? John Fleming of Cockermouth vividly recalls scenes in his 1927 booklet *Reminiscences of a Local Angler, 60 years ago*. The 60 years to which he refers were, of course, prior to 1927; in fact the first date of which he is certain is 1862. It is beyond the scope of my book to include his brown-trout and sea-trout fishing memories but the following extracts will carry us to the banks of the Derwent and Cocker. He concluded the story of his angling life:

And now, having fished for an hour in the river of memory, I have put up my rod and emptied my creel for the readers inspection.

These are extracts:

At that time the fish coops were fished with two coops and there was no free pass. The concrete barrier or weir across the river was studded with iron bars, bent to prevent the salmon jumping over, and it was really impossible for fish to get beyond the weir until after the 10 October, and as the season closed on 1 November there was, in those days, very little salmon fishing to be had. The iron bars were eventually knocked down by some Cockermouth anglers, and never replaced. The fishing season then commenced on 1 February and there was some rare fun kipper fishing, and you can bet they did not all go back into the river. It was quite a common sight to see three or four fishermen playing a fish at the same time, especially in pools like Stoddart Pot, Crossar and Whinnah Dub, and often a man could land half a dozen in an afternoon. This state of things continued many years, and the watchers were never very strict.

Charles Lawes fishes The Fitz water on the Derwent where spoons are popular.

After 1862 (that is the first season I can really fix on) tickets were 2/6d each for lads, and 5/- for men . . . . In those days the Cockermouth Angling Association paid on an average only £80 a year for watchers, and in 1867–8–9 there were 119 prosecutions in the Cockermouth Court alone.

In those days the streams at spawning time were a sight to see, especially Crossar, Bromfield Stream, Battling Dub, above Derwent Bridge, and Cass Bay on the Cocker near the old dog kennels. One afternoon, I think in 1867, I slipped out of the shop, through the Croft, by John Pearson's Woollen Mill to Cass Bay, and I counted up to 35 salmon on the 'redds'. Kipper, that winter, could be bought for 3d a pound, or even less. It was quite a common occurrence for a company to have 20 to 30 fish to divide after a good night's 'kippering'. Many of the female fish were taken merely for the roe, which, when cured, brought from 7s 6d to 10s a pound. In those days it must be remembered, no salmon could ascend the river before October 10.

In those days we lads fished with a hazel rod, with line wound crossways on a stick put through the butt, as reels were then very dear. I was down the river on one occasion in 1901 or 1902 with a water bailiff who pointed out a pool where he and another, twice through with a net, took 165 fish – first time through 130, and second time 35 fish.

I have seen some rare sport salmon fishing. I think it was in 1868 when the first attempts at 'snatching' were made, in a very primitive way. There was a big run of fish that year, and we lads were watching the salmon trying to run the Fitz stakes, whilst some of the old hands tried snatching them in the water at the foot of the weir. One man, Ben _ by name, did eventually get fast to a fish which immediately went with a rush downstream. Ben took to the water at the wall-end up to the waist, another fisherman holding his rod until he got past the bye-fall; then up the steps he came and along the wall as far as the lavatory, then in again and right down to the Fitz Banking. Here Ben again came onto the grass, but the fish made another rush, and encouraged by his admirers with 'Go it, Ben, it's a whale.' Ben again took to the water and followed it down to opposite The Burrough, where it was at last gaffed, and you can imagine our surprise when we saw a small fish of 8 lb. Ben's face was a picture of disappointment.

Another day I went down to the same place (Lamb's Scaur). John Graham was on the opposite side of the river, and he called across there was a big fish rising just off the rail end. I tried it several times without any success when Sam Stephenson came along, and we sat down beside the wall to compare flies. Sam showed me a new cast he had made which he swore would hold a whale. After a while he started to fish a few yards above the rails and immediately he hooked. Away went the fish down almost to the streamtop, then turned and made up the river under the shadow of the Scaur. John Denwood was on that side of the river, and Sam called to him to gaff the fish. John, in his quiet way, said it was ten yards from the bank, and Sam began wailing he would lose his fish as his greyhound pups had been playing with the cast, and he wanted a fish as a present to John Hall of Stanwix for the use of a small field he allowed him to have. We cheered him up, and the fish at last settled down stream into Crossar Pool. Sam got back about ten yards into the field, and put a good pressure on the fish, whilst I lay flat on the bank with gaff ready. The surface of the water was fully two feet below me and the pool very deep. However, the fish was close in the side, and I struck the gaff home just under the dead fin. It was a good lift, but I rose at the same time, and landed it safely on the grass, a splendid male fish of 27 lb.

On another occasion he caught a man in the act during the day. John (water bailiff) said he would have to summons, but the man begged to be let off, as he could not afford to pay a fine. John noticed that the man had on a pair of strong shoes that were better than his own, and he agreed to let the man off if the shoes fit him and he would swap. The shoes fitted alright and each went their respective ways (wearing each other's shoes) as if nothing had happened.

Job Moses, brother to John, did a little salmon fishing with a spoon. He had a very big spoon made from a pale yellow table spoon, which was christened 'Bulger' and he killed some very big fish with it.

One of the earliest anglers I can remember was Edmund Ashton, a shoemaker who lived in Horsman Street. Every Monday during the season he fished worm, clear water, in the Cocker, and always made a good fishing. At times his pannier was full, and tackle in those days was coarser than it is now.

Of recent years there has been much discussion regarding the scarcity of salmon. In my opinion it is not due to the destruction of fry, as in years gone by thousands were killed compared with what are killed now. Years ago when the tinplate works were in full swing at Barepot, thousands descended the race into the reservoir, and settled down near the grating. They were taken out in bucketsful, and potted smelts was a favourite dish with the workmen. I was the means of having a grating fixed in the race in 1920, so the fish could not get into the reservoir, and by lifting the sluice a few inches they were all turned again into the river.

In those days we lads spent some delightful times on the gravel bed at Toad Beck. The stream was a grand place for smelt fishing. I caught the fish. Jake Hewitson got the potatoes from his father's shop, Joe Bolton was cook, and Adam Gray stoked the fire. Fuel was plentiful in the wood. The fish were cooked on flat stones made hot, the potatoes roasted in their skins, and we had many a glorious repast. No one ever said anything to us, go where we would – a free roving commission. But, alas, all 'the old familiar faces' are now gone. Once, I remember, we had an amusing encounter with the late Mr Fisher of Wood Hall. We were bird-nesting up the Mickle Brows path. Goodwin Young was with us on this occasion. Goodwin was lame, and his crutch was very useful for giving a push up any big trees. This time we were attempting to scale a tree, when Mr Fisher suddenly appeared beside us, and wished to know what we were after. Joe Bolton said we were looking for the road to Cockermouth. 'Then you'll hardly find it up that tree,' replied the old gentleman, when we suddenly remembered it and made off.

So I will to the wilds away

The living beauty of the fields,
The music of the streams,
To me a richer pleasure yields
Than poet's wildest dreams.
There's peace that money cannot buy
Among the purple ling,
And heart-rest by the tumbling burn
Where white-throat dippers sing.

E. R. Denwood, Cockermouth, 1927

15 River Camel,
Cornwall

The River Camel rises on Hendraburnick Down, about 5 miles north-east of Camelford, the first town through which the river flows in a southward direction. Two miles south of Camelford, at Trecarne, it is joined from the east by the Stannon Stream, which flows from Crowdy Reservoir and Rough Tor Moors.

Four miles south of Trecarne, and ½ mile below Poley's Bridge, the De Lank River runs in from Rough Tor Marsh and the hill known as Brown Willy, which are situated to the east of Bodmin Moor, the main catchment area. The rapid rises and falls of the moorland streams, some of which may be only 2 or 3 ft wide, impart to the Camel the characteristics of the true spate river.

After being joined on the left bank by the Clarkenwater Stream, the Camel takes a wide curve in a north-westerly direction above Bodmin town, and is then joined by the Ruthern River flowing up from the south. This north-westerly valley continues until the river becomes tidal in the region of Polbrock Bridge. Below this bridge, fishing is confined to the hours of low tide. The Camel then flows out through Wadebridge, having been joined from the north by the River Allen, past Padstow to the sea. The distance from source to mouth is in the region of 30 miles.

Ray Burrows, Hon. Sec. Bodmin Anglers' Association
29 November 1990

I met Ray in his house in Bodmin town and asked him to describe the waters of the Association, which has approximately 10 miles of the river. Some sections are double bank but, in others, rights are limited to single bank. Much of the Camel valley is overgrown and wooded, which leads to a predominance of spinning and natural bait fishing; there is little room to cast a fly. At the same time the valley is both wild and beautiful; during my visit, I saw by the river Britain's smallest bird, the goldcrest, which is just 3½ in. long.

Ray told me about the waters. 'The river above Camelford is very small; you could catch salmon there but you are really on the spawning beds. In my view it is not right to fish for them in that area; they should be left to do their business. Our fishing starts at Keningstock and goes down to Trecarne, then Penrose to Wenfordbridge, and some more from below the clayworks at

Ray Burrows fishing the Bodmin Angler's water on the River Camel.

Poley's Bridge to the junction with the De Lank River. We miss out some private water at Tresarrett before entering Shell Woods, where there is free fishing for ½ mile. Between Shell Woods and Dunmere we rent water, and some we have purchased. Below Dunmere there is private water for ½ mile, and then we rent a number of short stretches down to Boscarne. Below this the river is private to the Ruthern Stream, downstream of which we have sections of the river as far as Polbrock Bridge.

'Ours is a true spate river, flowing off the moor. If it rained for 24 hours the water would come down very acid and dirty from the peat. This acidity keeps insect life at a low level, trout food is scarce and these fish are small. Lack of food slows the development of salmon parr which take at least 2 years to smolt.'

The timing of salmon runs

The river has a small run of salmon weighing between 6 and 8 lb in April and May. These fish tend to stay in deep pools in the lower river throughout the summer. If there is a series of spates they may move upstream but, in general, they do not run up the river until September and October. The eggs of these fish on entry are very small, like pin-heads; the sacs in their bellies being only 2 or 3 in. in length. Ray mentioned that he had caught a red cock fish of about 6 lb the day before our meeting. This salmon was ready to spawn, had clearly spent some months in the lower reaches and would now move upstream to spawn. He returned this fish to the river.

The next entrants are grilse. Their rather sparse run commences in June, but many stay in the estuary and may not run the river until the autumn. In fact some come in during November and swim straight up to spawn in the headwaters. As we spoke, Ray told me that he knew of grilse already spawning above Camelford.

The main entry of salmon takes place in November and December. At this time the other major Cornish river, the Fowey, also has its main run. These fish weigh in the region of 10 lb, are fresh from the sea, silver-flanked, hard-fleshed and heavily sea-liced. The roe of the hen fish is only half-developed, but the eggs ripen rapidly in time for spawning in January. As kelts, having laid their eggs, they are thin but in good condition because they have been in the river for so short a period. The majority return to sea, and all are gone by the end of March. There are few mortalities, although some are lost to ulcerative dermal necrosis (UDN, the salmon disease), which is still present. Ray believes that a few of these kelts return as second spawners.

Some heavy fish may be of three sea-winters. In the last 2 years salmon of 22 and 23 lb have been taken, and one of 19 lb 8 oz to date in the 1990 season. When Ray was 12 years old, 50 years ago, he saw a salmon of 39 lb. One ancient netsman told Ray that, many seasons back, he took 17 salmon in one net, but he was doing 'naughty things'. The largest salmon which this man had netted weighed 45 lb.

Lack of information on sea years and spawning runs will soon be rectified. The National Rivers Authority are issuing small envelopes to anglers to hold scales from the flank of each fish. Scale readings will be made and life histories ascertained. Many years back, the Cornwall River Board took scale readings which revealed an appreciable percentage of second-spawning salmon. In 1988, a sea trout of 13 lb 8 oz was caught on a fly at night where the river runs through Outlands Wood near Bodmin. The scales of this peal revealed that it had made three spawning runs.

At one time, when the fishing season opened in mid-March, and closed 30 November, kelts were caught in the first 2 weeks. It was then decided to open 2 weeks later, on 1 April, by which date all kelts had gone back to the Atlantic. In recompense, the season was extended from 30 November to 15 December to take account of the entry of fresh-run winter salmon which continues after the closure of the season. Sea trout start to arrive in May, peak in August, and are sometimes accompanied by grilse which weigh in the region of 5 lb but can be as small as 3 lb 8 oz.

Ray reminisced. 'As a boy I lived in a village up the river. If we wanted a salmon to eat, not to sell you understand, we would take a rod and go out and get one by the usual method, if you know what I mean. In those days, the old men told me, there was a March run of fresh dumpy-shaped salmon of about 6 lb. They had a blue sheen and were called "blue poles". The old timers talked about these salmon, but they died out along with the old men.'

For a moment or two we digressed to sea trout, of which Ray has seen a steady decline over the five decades he has fished the river.

'Twenty years ago the runs of sea trout in the Camel were incredible. I mean incredible. You could stand on Polbrock Bridge and it would take minutes for a shoal of fish to pass. They covered the whole width of the river. Up they went and dispersed in the pools. In any decent-sized pool it was nothing to see 200 or 300 sea trout. In some cases they would be one on top of another, and if disturbed the whole river bed seemed to move. Over the years, starting when UDN arrived, there has been a decline. That disease hit sea trout as well as salmon. I think pollution: silage, slurry, nitrates and so on killed off much of the river food chain. During the war and immediately thereafter there were no slurry pits; the farmer mucked out the yard onto a dung heap and then spread it on the land. I don't blame the farmers; they followed advice to install these pits, and were told to make silage in wet regions instead of hay. Today the farmers are responsible people and are putting matters right.'

Before leaving the subject of salmon runs into the Camel I give below the monthly rod catches for the river.

Year	Apr.	May	June	July	Aug.	Sept.	Oct.	Nov.	Dec.	Total
1985	2	6	6	8	18	24	39	29	21	153
1986	0	0	8	11	27	26	36	63	51	222
1987	0	1	0	10	8	4	33	79	63	198
1988	0	3	2	41	78	92	122	109	108	555
1989	0	3	7	8	13	46	50	79	38	244
1990	0	1	8	15	9	30	48	115	72	298
1991	0	3	12	7	10	16	18	40	15	121
1992	0	0	5	11	22	32	33	61		164

Fishing methods

There are no water-height restrictions on fishing methods, but, in certain sections of the Association waters, worm and prawn are not allowed. The worm is totally prohibited in the month of April. In addition, some areas are set aside for fly fishers at particular times of the year. The gaff is legal from 1 April until the end of August, but Ray has not seen anyone use a gaff on the river for a very long time. He carries a tailer which he uses with the noose curled in the upward position: 'I find it whips over more quickly from above than if the loop is hanging down. I move the noose over the tail to just behind the dorsal fin and then pull in an upward direction.' For grilse: 'I wait until he is on his side, then lift the gill flap with my finger nail and get a finger in that way to pull him out.'

Hold the rod high to fish the far side slowly.   Always walk with the rod tip to the rear.

He does little fly fishing for salmon because of the physically restrictive nature of the river banks.

To spin he uses glass and split-cane rods. 'I've never progressed to carbon. They're nice rods, a bit expensive, but if you've got an old rod with which you are happy, why change? It is not the rod which catches the fish, it is the angler. I have some fly rods for sea trout, but not for salmon. In some places, if you poke a fly rod through the trees, you can almost touch the other bank. A few people fish the fly, but their rods are not longer than 10 ft. I have known one or two visitors who have come down, persevered in a particular pool, and caught a salmon on a fly.'

Ray thought it likely that 99.99 per cent of salmon caught by his members were taken on artificial or natural bait.

Spinning

Most of the members use rods of 8 ft or 8 ft 6 in. in any of the three materials: glass, split cane or carbon fibre. Due to lack of room to swing a rod fitted with a multiplying reel, almost all anglers cast underhanded with a fixed-spool reel. This low-level throw suits the situation, projecting the bait out underneath overhanging branches which are left to provide cover for salmon in shallow sections of the river.

'We say: "Don't cut the trees, improve your casting". When you can cast your bait onto a plate on the grass you can put a minnow where you wish. If you make big movements, as in fly casting, fish will be diving everywhere. With the fixed-spool reel you can creep up behind a bush and just flick out the spinner. With a multiplier casting overhead, or to the side, your bait would be in the trees most of the time.'

When spinning for summer grilse, a 10 lb monofilament line is sufficiently strong. Ray puts his trust in an unpainted brass minnow, 2 in. long, turned for him on a lathe by a friend who then solders in the fins. In coloured water,

this Devon is fished in the unpolished colour of naturally oxidized brass. As
the flow clears, Ray lights two matches which, when held under the minnow,
change it to a smoky black shade. If he wants it to gleam again, he rubs the
metal with a pinch of sand from the bed of the river, and, like the genie with
the lamp, the minnow flickers in the darkest places. But 'If I go down and the
river is really dirty I knot on a silver Devon'. Additional weight with a metal
minnow is unnecessary, just a *small* swivel being used to attach a 3 ft trace of
8 lb nylon to the reel line. The mount of his minnow is also home-made of
heavy nylon, with two trebles, tied one behind the other, and a hook size of
No. 4 or No. 6. The eye of the front treble slides up into the body of the
minnow, the tail of which rests against the bend of the hooks – neither a glass
bead nor a plastic tulip bead is fitted. It has been noticed that salmon often
take a bait across the body, gripping it in the middle. I have seen a salmon
grip a long tube fly in this manner, with the hook and head protruding on
either side of the mouth. With Ray's mount, the hook points of the front
treble are closer to the minnow centre than if held away from the tail by a
bead. If a salmon takes from behind it will almost certainly be hooked by the
rear treble.

A *small* swivel on the mount protrudes slightly from the head of the Devon.
Two swivels are thus present. Ray's reason for using the small No. 8 swivel
is: 'These metal minnows sometimes stick on the river bed. If you go
downstream below the snagged bait, stick your rod point deep in the water
and jiggle it about, the minnow will often slide back over the swivels to your
position. You can recover the bait and thus only lose the trace and hook
mount if you have to break.'

Some members carry a round plastic otter to release baits; another method is
to cut a short forked stick from a tree, the stick slides down the line to float
out on the water and pull from below the bait. The stick should be in the
rough form of a shepherd's crook; the handle being about 18–24 in. long and
the crook in the region of 6 in.

For heavy winter fish, a strong line of at least 18 lb with a 15 lb trace is
needed. Many anglers use 20 lb line or even 25 lb. Robust monofilament is
needed. Not only is there the chance of meeting a great fish, but bankside
trees stop the angler following a salmon making a hard run down the river.
The fisherman has to stay where he is and fight the fish to a standstill:
strength of tackle makes a more crucial contribution than guile!

Other popular baits are wooden Devon minnows, Mepps Aglia, and the
floating Rapala which dives only when retrieved. Orange-coloured Rapalas
are popular, also blue, but Ray does not think the colour is very important.
'He'll take anything if he's in the mood, even a banana skin.' He is not
impressed with the hooks on the Rapala. 'They are too small. Fish are lost.
You must fit larger trebles.' The wooden Devon has its adherents, but when
cast with a weight 18 in. (45 cm) above the minnow: 'The weight goes

through the air in advance of the lightweight minnow; it will hit the target if the wooden minnow, whirling about in the air, doesn't catch in a tree.'

The Mepps has many advocates who praise the slow attraction of its swim across the wide slow tail of a pool. 'I like a Mepps. You can fish them very slowly. The slower you fish for salmon downstream the more likely he is to take. If you are going to cast upstream in our shallow river a metal Devon is no good – you get stuck on the bottom. But an upstream Mepps takes fish if reeled back fast.'

The worm

'The ordinary worm that you dig out of the garden, we call them blackheads, is the one we use. Two on a No. 6 hook is normal, and some people these days fish them with a float.'

It was clear from our conversation that the methods of fishing worms were many and varied. Some cast light tackle upstream. Others cast across the river, with a small weight at the line/trace junction. This combination then trundles back across the river, bouncing on the bottom, until the bait hangs below the angler.

Others, in a somnolent post-prandial state, weight the line/trace junction sufficiently to maintain a static position on the bottom, with the worms swaying in the current at the end of the trace. It is surprising how attractive this is to resident salmon, which may regard their lunch for 20 minutes, then swim forward and take. The float method is tantalizing. Anyone who has fished for grayling in this manner will already be addicted to the sight of a red-topped cork. First there is the tremble, then the bob which sends out a circular wave the size of the palm of your hand, then the sliding away followed by submersion. But you must not strike – yet! Wait, count to 20 blow your nose softly, polish your spectacles – then lift the rod and tighten.

Some members collect their worms from the lawn at night by torchlight. 'Others take a bar of iron 2 ft or 3 ft long, go out into a field, drive the bar into the earth for 1 ft and rattle it about. After two or three minutes all the worms within a radius of 1 yd will come out.'

'You're joking.'

'No I've seen the boys do it. Another thing. Water the grass with detergent and the worms pop out their heads.'

Prawn and shrimp

Bodmin anglers do not normally net their own prawns in the estuary. The baits are purchased from the fishmonger, or bought in packets from tackle shops. A prawn pin is used with a single treble in the whiskers, the whole bound around with thin wire or silk.

'Not many of us fish the shrimp, and only a few more rely on prawns. The major methods in our river are worming and spinning. I don't want you to think we are against fly fishing, it is just that the method is not suitable for salmon in our river. When going for sea trout in summer in low water it is different – we can wade. When mid-river your back cast extends upstream and the pool tails may be swept by the fly.'

Salmon lies

Ray considers that salmon like plenty of cover. They feel secure in deep water, under the washed-out roots of bankside trees, of which there are many, and where the water has cut under the bank. A favourite place is where water on the surface rushes downstream, but underneath the current is slow, perhaps with a back eddy and a depression in the bed.

'He feels safe under that turbulence, and you've got a job to see him. If there are big rocks, salmon will lie alongside; they also take advantage of a rock ledge. A single boulder in the stream is not so attractive, even so, he may lie 1 yd to one side and a little below. They don't like lying behind these obstructions.'

Ray's history

'I was born in Bodmin, but when I was 2 years old we moved to St Breward. My father was a naval man and he didn't fish. I taught myself. There were few anglers on the river in those years. I could fish all day and not see a soul. I started young at 6 or 7 years old in the little streams that ran into the river. All I had was a bent pin and a worm. If I caught an eel I ran home with it dangling to be taken off. Then I went for the sea trout. After, at 15 or 16 years of age, I caught my first salmon. I was spinning in Rock Pool with a lead minnow. I cast those minnows myself from melted scrap lead poured into a mould. I left school at 14 years old and went to work in the granite quarries where I polished the stone which was set in plaster of Paris. A mould could be made from this plaster in the shape of a minnow. Before pouring in the molten lead I put a greased nail up the middle to form the central hole for the mount. Cast like this the bait was rough but could be shaped as required with a pocket knife and a file. Not many people do that now because it is easier to go and buy one.'

Ray had a friend who lived at Lanivet many years ago. 'He used to go to the Tamar near Launceston. Early morning was his time, before the gentry and hotel guests came out. He knew when anyone was coming because the crows and other birds called in alarm. He got stuck in the bottom with a Mepps, the birds called, he pulled and the Mepps flew up and caught his nose. There he was with the Mepps dangling, the hook over the barb and blood dripping, flying home on his motor bike.'

The lower moor aluminium-sulphate disaster

This poisoned about 60,000 fish, mostly juvenile. The fishing clubs, private owners and the NRA joined in a combination of measures to achieve the recovery of the river. The NRA bought-off the seven licensed netsmen for 3 years. Bag limits were agreed for rod fishermen of four sea trout and two salmon a day with a maximum of four in a week. Whilst they continued to pay rents to the farmers, Bodmin anglers set aside two sanctuaries for 3 years. These sections of the river, where salmon spawn and there are many parr, will remain unfished.

Increased spawning areas 2 miles in length have been made available by clearing silt from the gravel of the redds. In addition, the fishing season has been shortened by 6 weeks, from 1 April to mid-May, to ensure that smolts are not hooked during their passage downriver to the sea. As we spoke, these new dates had been in force for two seasons and would continue in 1991, and possibly thereafter. 'We want to put something back into the river instead of always taking out.' The NRA has installed two Denil fish-passes in the upper river to assist the passage of fish to the spawning beds. 'They work. We know they do. Sea trout are already spawning above these Denils.'

The river at Dunmere

Leaving Ray's house we walked along the Camel Trail, which was once a railway line and has become a foot path. Above the weir in East Wood we met Ralph Hands. He showed us a heavy tube fly which he had designed and aptly named 'The Horror'.

'My father taught me fishing long ago. He always advised me to match the colour of the water with the colour of the fly. This I have always attempted. The things they use to catch fish today give me the shudders. Great pink things like cuttlefish or submarines – yet they catch fish. Well now, I tried to

The Horror, a heavy tube fly designed by Ralph Hands and fished with spinning rod and fixed-spool reel. River Camel.

evolve my fly to fish deep off a fixed-spool reel. The brass tube is in a 'U' shape with the line coming out of the top of the tube at the head and the weight of the lure beneath. There's a bit of a silver belly and a bit of black on top. The wing is guinea fowl. The 'U' shape of my tube ensures that the belly swims underneath; if the tube is straight, which I avoid, the belly will sometimes be on top. This lure is cast up, down, across, and retrieved rapidly.'

Ralph chuckled, then launched into a tale: 'You know Sid's Pool,' he said, looking at Ray. 'Last time I saw Sid, who was a grand old chap, he was at his pool and I said "Sid there's a fish in there." Next time we met he told me that he had caught the fish. I said: "You owe me one now." "Well," said Sid. "There's one right now in my pool." I caught it, a hell of a fish, and do you know what, I heard him laughing at my elbow because the eggs were running out of it and I had to put it back. He was a grand old chap; died 3 years back.'

We went on up the river in the Dunmere area where there is a stone pedestal on which is a bronze plaque:

This monument commemorates the work carried out by Bodmin Anglers Association, winners of the 1987 Benson & Hedges Conservation Award for game fishing waters, in association with *Trout & Salmon* magazine.

On the plaque is a map of the pools at Dunmere, with the note:

Upstream from this site on the river Camel members of Bodmin Anglers Association have created the indicated pools by the construction of weirs to their own design. The structure used is uniquely adapted to the nature of the river bed and the resources at the Club's disposal.

We came across three anglers fishing above the weir. One, Tony Powell, fearsome, black-bearded and jovial, refreshed us from a bottle. 'We've just put one back. 8 lb it was but too red. A few moments ago I lost a clean fish, all of 17 lb he must have been. Look at the hook – ruined it he has.' Tony held up a worm hook, long-shanked, about a No. 6, as curly as the tail feathers of a drake mallard.

Neil Barnett, member of Wadebridge & District Angling Association 6 December 1990

Neil met me at Polbrock Bridge on the Wadebridge Association waters of the River Camel. Aged 19 years, he is a dedicated and innovative salmon angler. From the age of 11 years, Neil came on one of my game-fishing courses for four consecutive seasons. He started with trout – the wild browns of Devon. From my diary:

8 April 1983 River Lyd. James, Neil, Jason and his father. We caught 9 brown trout on upstream wet and dry flies, and cooked the fish at the river on the Abu smoker.

Two seasons later, a sea trout came his way.

Neil Barnett fishing the Wadebridge Anglers' water on the River Camel with a Shad Rap Deep Runner in December.

16 August 1985 River Lyd. Neil Barnett took 6 good browns and a ¾ lb sea trout.

Rod in hand, at a trot, Neil crossed two fields to the Lyd which ran below our house. Throwing a No. 1 Mepps upstream he caught and returned the brown trout, but brought the peal back to the house as darkness fell.

He started to fish the Camel when 8 years old and has always lived close to the river.

'When did you catch your first salmon?'

'Four seasons ago, when I was 15 years old, I was up at Grogley (a piece of water between Bodmin and Wadebridge) in early December. The place was teeming with anglers because there had been a big run of fish. I span up through the river with a silver No. 3 Mepps. I had faith in its attractive qualities, having hooked and lost two salmon. A sea trout took but was returned, it being after the end of their season. I then changed to worm to work my way down the river, popping my bait into the little gulleys under the banks. Pocket money was short in those days, lead was legal and I used a bit cut off a sheet in the workshop, clamping a strip onto the line with a pair of pliers. Today I use 3 Thamesley Sure-Shot SSG split shot. I had on two lobworms, and after a while added two more from my tin to the No. 4 sliced hook. Salmon like a good mouthful – at least four worms. Trotting them down I stopped to talk to another angler and put my rod down on the bank. Suddenly I saw a flash in the water and thought: "Aye-up, there's something there" and picked up the rod.

'After waiting for 2 or 3 minutes I reeled in and found the line had gone upstream, and knew that a salmon had taken my worms. He swirled on the surface and raced off. It took 10 minutes to land; I was in the river – me shaking, heart pumping, salmon leaping. Someone tailed the fish and knocked it on the head with a lump of wood. That fish was a sea-liced hen of 10 lb 11 oz; we smoked the roe on our little smoker and a friend smoked the whole fish because I love smoked salmon. That day I was the happiest guy on the river.'

'Now tell me about the fish you caught with your elder brother.'

'I was about 16 years of age and James was 2 years older. He could drive, so I beat him up to take me to the river; he is not keen on fishing. He doesn't really mind going so long as I dig up the worms.

'We went to Grogley where the water was high and muddy because there had been a lot of rain in the night. It looked like a waste of time, but there might be a chance of a sea trout, it being July, or some eels. I gave him the rod and put on a spool of 4 lb nylon, some split shot, the hook and a worm. The worm spent most of the time in the trees, but sometimes hit the river. After a couple of hours a salmon jumped and some guys who appeared span for it furiously, then walked away. We then became bored, my brother thinking the fish had moved up the river. I thought it was still there.'

'Your brother looks upon you as the expert?'

'Yes, I suppose so, He thinks he knows quite a bit but can't even tie on a hook. Anyway, he caught two eels, and I became annoyed, having to cut out the hook. They were boot-lace eels which we knocked on the head and threw away. The rod was a 9 ft fibreglass made by Acrod and the reel a fixed-spool Shimano bait-runner. Then he had a take and flicked the spool free to allow the line to run. The salmon jumped, he looked at me and said: "Take the rod, Neil". I took the rod, turned the handle to engage the reel, and the salmon took off.

'I got into the river up to my waist; it was safe because I knew the bottom. With the 4 lb line I couldn't hold the fish from going down, so James ran beyond the salmon, splashed the landing net in the river beyond the fish and drove it back before joining me in the river. We were soaked as neither of us had thigh boots, but we squashed half the fish into the trout net, somehow heaved it onto the bank and I sat on it whilst he found a log and bashed it on the head. That fish weighed 7½ lb, but we couldn't make up our minds whether it was a salmon or a large sea trout. At the car we counted the scales in a line from the adipose fin to the lateral line; there were 10 and we knew it was a salmon. My brother spent the next week on the river – he didn't catch anything!'

Wadebridge Anglers have a considerable length of water, mainly on the left bank, but some on the right, on the tidal river below Polbrock Bridge. There, natural bait is prohibited but spinning and fly fishing are allowed. Upstream at Grogley Station they have water where worm and prawn are permitted.

Neil considers salmon take about 6 hours to swim the 1 or 2 miles from the tidal river at Polbrock Bridge to Grogley where, 2 days before our meeting, a salmon of 25 lb had been taken from Station Pool. A salmon of 26 lb had also been landed within the last week and another of 18 lb from the Association waters. Wadebridge Anglers have additional stretches below Penrose and at Wenfordbridge on the upper river where natural and artificial baits may be fished.

In common with Bodmin Anglers, the Wadebridge Association delayed the opening of the salmon season until the middle of May for three seasons, 1991 being the third. This was to ensure that all kelts have passed out of their tidal section to the sea before the season commences, that smolts have an uninterrupted passage, and that a few fresh fish pass upstream. Neil rarely goes after a salmon until July and looks upon the late autumn as the start of productive fishing. November up to 15 December, when the season closes, are the best months, particularly when spring tides flood up the valley at new and full moons.

Little is gained by fishing at high tide, but one or two hours after the peak one should commence fishing as the tide recedes and the river flow predominates. 'Then salmon start to cruise up the river.'

'Can you see them?'

'Yes. Last year I saw eight salmon swim by in half an hour. They moved slowly at the same speed at which you might amble along a rough bridle path. A strong upstream wind pushes water into the river from the estuary – this sometimes brings in fish.'

As we sat in the car, three anglers passed at intervals. all carried spinning rods and large lures: No. 4 Mepps or a long Rapala.

I asked Neil his personal fishing method at Polbrock.

'I like to use a 7 cm Shad Rap Deep Runner if I can afford one; they cost over £7.00. They're a Rapala, made in Finland, which wiggles across the bed of the river. The plug has two No. 4 trebles, one at the tail and the other under the belly; a deep lip below the head makes it dive at once on hitting the water. The one I'm going to use today has a black back, silver belly and red throat. It's the only one I own, but sometimes I find one in a tree.'

Neil has a fixed-spool reel, a Triton Sea Spin 2500 made by Shimano, with a free-running option controlled by a top lever, mounted on a stiff 8 ft Acrod fibreglass spinning rod made by Appleton & Cragg of Wadebridge. The free-running device is useful when fishing the worm, for a salmon must be allowed to move off freely with the bait. When a fish takes the worm, the free-runner lever is flicked up and the spool revolves without resistance; to strike, the reel handle is turned and this engages the drag.

When spinning the Shad Rap, Neil uses 15 lb Maxima nylon, or 20 lb in high dirty water. The bait is tied directly to the reel line which is cut 1 yd above the plug to tie in a swivel. There is thus no reduction in strength in the trace. This arrangement is quick to set up, but not really desirable because snagging of the bait may cause the reel line to break rather than snapping a less strong trace. The river is shallow, making extra weight unnecessary with this deep-diving bait. If fishing a Mepps in summer, he favours small sizes, sometimes as tiny as No. 0 but more frequently No. 1 or No. 2. He does not fit heavier trebles to these little baits but always makes certain the points are sharp. Sometimes the hooks bump on the stones of the river bed, blunting the points, but a few strokes with a carborundum stone restores the needle point. A little extra weight is needed to carry out these lightweight baits when cast; this is provided by a pierced bullet which is slid onto the nylon, and rests against the knot joining the nylon to the wire loop of the Mepps. As with the Rapala, he ties in a swivel about 1 yd above the bait. Thin nylon line is used on the reel spool in summer with these small spoons, the finest being 6 lb BS. Neil is not heavy-handed; when he is fishing for sea trout in summer his nylon trace may be of 12 oz BS when the bait is a single maggot.

When fishing, he casts his bait, Mepps or Rapala, slightly upstream to land under the far bank. The lure is then retrieved in a pronounced curve which is more attractive than a straight swim.

I asked him to say a word on salmon lies.

'I normally find my salmon lies by fishing the river in low water in summer. I look for obstacles on the river bed, depressions in the bottom and where the bank has been washed out below the water surface. Salmon also lie in the slacker areas of deep pools and in front of sandy banks.

'Once I was searching for sea trout, hung my head over the bank and saw a tail sticking out from beneath some tree roots. I popped in six loose maggots and a salmon came out and picked them up. I flicked in some more, but nothing happened. I had no worms, but put on a prawn from my pocket. As soon as this hit the river bed five salmon shot out of the hole and dashed about the pool. I nearly jumped out of my skin!'

'How do you land your fish?'

'I carry a large net of unknown make on a sling on my back. It hasn't collapsed on me yet.'

As we had lunch Neil told me of his most exciting but disappointing experience. 'I was spinning a No. 3 Mepps with a ½ oz weight in heavy water at Wenfordbridge when I was 16 years old. The Mepps stuck in the bottom, but then the river bed moved. The fish rolled on the surface and then shot off downstream. It was huge, I hung on. Down and down and down it went beyond some trees on my bank which could not be passed. The reel whirred; I clutched the rod; my arms ached; I wouldn't give up. Eventually the salmon stopped. All became still.

'Some men arrived on the far side and said they could see it. They shouted encouragement but were unable to help, but gestured that it was a monster. I stayed put, the salmon rested under my bank and there were 50 yards between us. Some men came up my side, took hold of the line beyond the trees and followed it down, sliding the nylon between their fingers. Still the salmon rested. They arrived above the fish, slowly drew on the line, tailed him and slid him up the bank, foot by foot. It was a red cock salmon with an ugly kype. I wanted to keep him but they said it must go back, even though it was the largest salmon I'd seen. We put him in my net and weighed the lot, but the scales only went to 20 lb. When I lifted the fish up by the tail as high as I could its nose still touched the ground. We held it, nose to current in the river; it kicked after a while and moved off like a Dreadnought submarine.'

Writing this account on 9 December 1990, 3 days after our meeting, I recalled seeing two mute swans in the river. 'If they swim up here, we are going to have hard weather; otherwise they stay in the estuary.' He was right. Outside my study, the Dartmoor tors are capped with snow and, upcountry, power lines are down and motorways are blocked.

16 River Teign,
Devonshire

On Dartmoor, 6 or 7 miles to the south-west of the moorland town of Chagford, the north Teign river is formed from small tributaries at 1700 ft above sea level. Two miles to the west of Chagford it is joined by the south Teign. Since 1943 this small river has been a shadow of its former self, following completion of the dam which created Fernworthy reservoir.

The first hunters of Teign salmon may have been men of the Bronze Age, whose hut circles within the reservoir are revealed when the water level falls. Food was essential for survival. There were no split-cane rods for the skin-clad men; flint-tipped spears pinned fish upon their redds, and arrowheads may still be found.

In winter, water overflows the dam but, when the level in the reservoir drops below the lip of the dam in summer, the south Teign relies on 'compensation' water. 'Relies' is too inexact a term: this compensation flow is reduced in times of drought and I have known it to be cut off completely.

The construction of the dam deprived migratory fish of their spawning beds. (In addition to salmon the Teign has a heavy run of sea trout. The catch of these fish ('peal' is the Devon name) substantially exceeds the salmon take.) Evidence that Fernworthy dam cut off spawning areas is to be found in my fishing diary, in the first entry of many made over a span exceeding 40 years.

3 September 1949 Fernworthy reservoir. 8 ft split cane. Four brown trout and one sea trout. Av. ½ lb. Stuart as boatman. Started 6 pm. Wind S.W. Bright. Rose a lot. 4 on Peter Ross. 1 on Butcher. 4x gut.

The following season I took two more, on 20 and 22 April. Thereafter peal died out.

From the junction of the two rivers, the Teign flows east and then south to emerge at Newton Abbot. The length of the river is about 35 miles. The main tributary is the River Bovey, which joins the Teign about 3 miles above the estuary.

Teign is a spate river. So also are its sister Dartmoor rivers, the Dart and Tavy. Their anglers rely on rainfall for salmon fishing, but all yield peal in low water. Their valleys are fair, but the Teign valley is the fairest. Heather, gorse and bracken line the hillsides, which rise to 1000 ft in the upper valley. Mountain ash, or rowan, tempts the gourmet with bunches of red berries in autumn. Rowan jelly is better than redcurrant jelly with venison. Deer are present: roe and fallow follow their secret trails in the woods of oak and pine. Buzzards, sparrowhawks, dippers and kingfishers delight the angler by day. When night has fallen, the otter hunts the river and helps himself to the stocked brown trout of Fernworthy.

As with many rivers in the British Isles, the Teign summer grilse run is greater than the spring entry of two-sea-winter fish. The evidence is in the Fishery report of the National Rivers Authority.

Monthly salmon-rod catches on the Teign

Year	Feb.	Mar.	April	May	June	July	Aug.	Sept.	Total
1985	3	7	10	10	12	6	51	27	126
1986	5	5	30	33	18	24	89	54	258
1987	10	14	17	15	24	15	19	27	141
1988	9	15	22	21	19	78	62	77	303
1989	6	15	17	8	15	12	26	35	134
1990	1	3	13	16	13	12	9	16	83
1991	6	5	8	10	12	14	3	16	74
1992	1	5	2	1	8	9	33	38	97

Roddy Rae 26 September 1990

The Chairman of the Upper Teign Fishing Association, Mike Weaver, suggested that I talk to Roddy about the upper Teign. 'He catches more salmon than most of us.'

We met at the Angler's Rest, Fingle Bridge, Drewsteignton. There fishing licences may be obtained, food bought at the bar and angling tales told and heard. Roddy has fished the river for 8 years and supervises fishing tuition for a local hotel and gillies for anglers on the river. He is also a part-time National Rivers Authority fisheries officer, assisting the full-time staff in anti-poaching patrols and river clearance when required. Roddy therefore knows as much as most and catches more than many although, modestly, he did not say so.

He told me that most of the river is controlled by two Associations: the Upper Teign Fishing Association – down to Steps Bridge; and the Lower Teign Fishing Association – the lower river towards Chudleigh. Both these organizations have long waiting lists for membership. A limited number of day tickets are issued for the upper waters from the Angler's Rest, and for the lower water by Drum Sports in Newton Abbot.

Soon after we met, we looked downstream from Fingle Bridge. It was at once apparent that fly fishing would be difficult due to the overgrown banks. Many branches extend over the water from trees; rhododendrons cut the width of

Leave the trees but trim the branches. There is a pruning saw bolted to the end of this telescopic aluminium pole.

the waterway. The Association is adopting a policy of opening up previously unfishable areas, mainly by trimming bank growth, not by felling bankside trees. Even then, overhead casting from the bank would rarely be possible, but the roll cast, by a wading angler, would enable the water to be covered with a 10 ft rod.

Salmon and grilse runs on the river are occurring later in the season. Spring fish start to arrive in the Association's waters in April, but some are caught in February and March closer to the estuary. If there is high water in May, grilse arrive in small numbers and this entry increases in June if there is good rainfall. Grilse continue to run until the end of the season on 30 September, with a few two-sea-winter fish keeping them company. When I examined the Association's fishing records I was surprised by the smallness of some grilse, even down to 3 lb and 3 lb 8 oz in weight. The Teign is small; a fish in the 'teens of pounds is remarkable. Even so, in early 1992, a salmon of 24 lb was caught on the lower river.

Sea trout appear at Fingle Bridge in mid-May. These are large fish, averaging 2 lb. School peal present themselves in mid-June and continue to fill the river throughout the remainder of the season. The 1990 run of peal was late and disappointing in numbers; the first shoals of school peal pushed in during July, but these groups were small. Roddy estimated that, in the 1990 drought season, their peal catches had been reduced by 75 per cent. John Getliffe, a dedicated peal angler, whose normal catch might be 40 or 50 sea trout, had taken no more than 12 peal at the time of this discussion.

Roddy feels that salmon runs are increasing. 'On a September flood they may be seen in droves at Drogo Pools and in the upper waters.'

On fishing methods, he had this to say. 'From the start of the season on 1 February we are allowed to fish by fly, prawn, shrimp and spinning bait. The worm may be used from 1 June. This worm regulation is enforced by the NRA to save smolts on their seaward migration in spring. These diverse methods suit the physical characteristics of the river which, basically, is unsuited to fly fishing as you can see for yourself. It is very difficult to work a fly on this water, although some fish are taken, mainly by dibbling. Some salmon are taken on long brass tubes of 2½ or 3 in., which in my view is not fly fishing.'

I asked Roddy to describe 'dibbling'.

'Basically, it is rather like loch fishing with droppers, and scuttling a bob fly across the surface. Here they fish in fast water with a heavy tube on the point to keep all steady, and then a smaller double on the dropper to skid across the surface. Others go to the deep pools, put on a heavy tube and work this 'sink and draw'. 'I don't think much of that. We do not lose many fish whilst being played by the free fly becoming snagged; there are boulders, but the river is reasonably free of sunken obstructions.'

We went on to discuss worming, which is allowed on the Upper Teign waters, but is prohibited on those of the Lower Teign Association.

'I supply most of the worms, collecting them at night after rain on the cricket pitch or any area of short grass. If it is raining at the time, so much the better. I find them with a rabbiting lamp as they come out of their holes and couple together to mate. It seems indecent really, when they are enjoying themselves. I wouldn't like it at all!'

I commented that, in Wales, I had been told that worms had to be approached from behind.

Roddy replied: 'I think those Welshmen were giving you a bit of spiel. When I see a worm well out of its hole and grab hold it often clings tightly to the tunnel. If you then let go and then take hold again quickly it will come out easily. I do not think they are sensitive to light. Mine are kept in an old drawer with several layers of damp newspaper on the bottom and damp moss on top. They harden up well in this way if a little water is sprinkled on the moss from time to time. They don't need feeding, and will last for the whole season. We don't use brandlings, just lobworms.'

He explained the worming method. 'I fish them on a No. 2 Drennan carp hook and mount two lobworms. Cast them upstream or downstream on a free line, or with various weights, depending on the river flow. I use a 10 ft 6 in.

Bruce & Walker Hexagraph fly rod with 250 yd of 15 lb Maxima
monofilament on a fly reel. This is a more sensitive outfit than a spinning rod
and fixed-spool reel. A change to fly fishing may then be made by changing
the reel spool. In heavy water, I might use a spinning rod and fixed-spool
reel. At the end of my reel line there is a swivel, below which is a trace of 10
or 12 lb nylon, depending on the water conditions. Generally, a weight is not
needed but, if some has to be added, try a bent paper clip for attachment. The
clip is straightened, then bent through the top ring of the swivel and passed
through a tungsten or lead substitute weight before again being bent slightly
to one side to prevent the weight slipping off.'

He described the fishing methods. 'Worms are usually cast upstream. In fast,
deep water, weight may be added to bump the bait on the river bed.
Sometimes eels take, but this happens more to those who fish a static ledger
system. Some anglers take the eels home to smoke, but others just kill them
and throw them away.'

We discussed prawns and shrimps. 'The prawn and shrimp are used
throughout the river. Prawn is the better method on the lower beats. I feel
salmon take the prawn more freely soon after leaving the sea; on the upper
beats it seems to frighten fish. Perhaps the lower beats have deeper pools
more suited to the prawn. I have found this to be the case on the Wye and
some of the Scottish rivers. Small English prawns are popular, but some
anglers on the lower river, and on the lower stretches of the River Exe, are
using large, berried Norwegian prawns.'

Prawns are mounted with a prawn needle pushed up the body from beneath
the tail. Sometimes a paper clip will be used. A single treble is then placed in
the whiskers; (some anglers use a single hook whilst others rely on two
trebles). Roddy does not consider two trebles to be necessary. When
mounted, the prawn is wrapped around with elasticated thread, or copper
wire if additional weight is required. The tail of the prawn is then broken off
to prevent the bait twisting and swivelling in the current.

Shrimps, preferably magenta in colour, are prepared in the same manner, but
with great care because their small bodies are delicate. Roddy usually mounts
half a dozen the previous evening, often using a paper clip in preference to a
shrimp pin.

To fish both of these natural baits, anglers on the upper reaches favour a 9 ft
spinning rod with fixed-spool reel – a change may then be made to a Mepps or
Rapala as desired. The river does not allow much room to swing the rod to
cast with a multiplier; neither is this reel accurate when flipping out a bait
into a tiny restricted pool.

Roddy had some interesting views on spinning baits. 'By far the most popular
spinning bait on the Teign is the sinking, as opposed to the floating, Rapala.
Jointed bodies of 2½ in. and single bodies of 1½ and 2 in. are used.

left: A No. 4 Mepps cast upstream relieved this 6 lb grilse of freedom in September.

right: Roddy Rae's 10 ft 3 in. Bruce & Walker fly rod with fixed butt extension.
Hardy Zenith 3⅜ in. multiplier reel.

'The Black & Gold is good and, in thicker water, one with a fluorescent orange back and gold belly. As a spate clears to a lovely peaty colour, like a pint of beer, the Black & Gold is a killer. The reason behind the popularity of the Rapala is that it starts moving and diving as soon as it hits the water. This immediate fishing action is essential in our small pools. If a Devon minnow is used, half the width of the pool will be covered before it has formed a swimming arc and is revolving to full effect.'

'The Rapala is my choice but, if using a Devon, I like it to be made of wood, but then a weight has to be added and that does not suit our thin waters. The Mepps is good for upstream fishing, the gold colour being attractive and also the combination of black and gold. A No. 4 is best thrown upstream, and the smaller ones, the No. 2 and No. 3, for the downstream cast. Few Tobies are used. They are a great attractor but also a loser of fish. Tobies are better on a large river.'

We then progressed to salmon fly fishing. Roddy uses a 10 ft 3 in. Bruce & Walker Sea Trout and Salmon rod with fixed butt extension, and a Hardy Zenith 3⅜ in. multiplier fly reel. This outfit will execute roll, overhead and Spey casts and is the right length for the narrow river. Few anglers use a rod shorter than 10 ft or as long as 12 or 13 ft. These longer, double-handed rods find occasional use in large pools, such as Drogo and Preston, in high water.

Floating lines are used almost exclusively. This is because salmon do not arrive until April or May when the water temperature has risen to about 55°F or above. Roddy likes a white fly line which can easily be seen; this colour also helps the beginner to watch the line working and moving on the water surface. To the fly line, he attaches about 6 ft of a braided leader, to which is tied a tippet of 12 lb monofilament. The braided leader goes down well, eliminating skating on the water surface by the fly. The braided section is attached to the fly line by a plastic sleeve and secured by a drop of 'superglue'.

Favoured flies are the Monro Killer and Garry series. Yellow is desirable in heavy water, and black with a twist of silver as the river clears. Flies are dressed as brass tubes with a polythene lining into which a Partridge needle-eye treble may be thrust. Sometimes aluminium tubes are needed in shallow sections of the river. Esmund Drury trebles are in demand as droppers. Shrimp flies bring success.

Roddy's choice on a falling river: 'a tube of 1½ in. and a No. 10 or No. 12 Low Water double as a dropper. The dropper would be a Blue Charm or Hairy Mary.' If allowed only one fly for salmon and sea trout, Roddy's choice would be:

Badger & Orange
Tube: 1¼ in. polythene lined aluminium
Hook: No 10 Partridge outpoint treble
Body: Flat gold tinsel
Wing: Orange bucktail and hair from the tail of a badger
Cheeks: Jungle cock
Head: Black varnish

'In 1989 I had four salmon from 3 lb 12 oz to 6 lb 8 oz in one evening on that fly.'

In spring he carries a tailer for large fish, but this method is not suited to the smaller fish of the summer months. Most of his salmon are taken from the river by hand, being pushed up a suitable beach. If a beach is not available, he will lift a grilse out by the gills, sliding two fingers forward under the stomach into the gills, the fingers pointing forward towards the nose.

We looked at the Association's fishing diary, which is kept in the bar of the Angler's Rest. The smallest grilse I could find was landed by Derek Myhill: '11 August 1989. 1 salmon 3 lb'. Derek also had many more entries.

I picked out a successful night by Roddy on 25 June 1990 when he was peal fishing with Graham Studeley. They took three sea trout between them of 2lb 14 oz, 2 lb 7 oz and Graham one of 3 lb 8 oz.

In the first 6 days of July 1990, Roddy and his client Richard Jewel took five salmon of 5 lb, 7 lb, 4 lb 14 oz, 5 lb and 6 lb 8 oz.

A number of fish were caught by anglers on day tickets. These included a fish of 7 lb 8 oz on 31 August by Peter Reid, and a salmon of 10 lb 4 oz on 13 September by J. Webb, both on Shrimp flies.

Salmon lies were discussed. Roddy considers that salmon lie beside and in front of rocks, not behind. They seldom lie in the main current but rest on either side, although they will follow a bait through the main rush of water to take. In low water with a bright sky, they move to gushing water, but the speed of the flow on the surface may be greater than near the river bed. In such places salmon may be taken on the upstream worm.

The author on Dartmoor.

A hot spot in high water is the tail of Holly Pool. The lies are in front of two or three large rocks, just above the run-off. Salmon negotiate the fast, rough water downstream, enter Holly Pool and take a rest beside or in front of these boulders. They may be taken there on fly, spinner or Rapala. It is not a good pool for the worm in low water, because the flow is too slow.

During a walk along the river, we arrived at a pool named Preston, which is fished from the right bank. The pool curves down to the right with the deep water under the outside left bank. We both agreed that it is best to fish from shallow water into deep water, rather than vice versa, when one would be standing above the fish.

17 The small salmon rivers of Scotland
by Rob Wilson

I am one of those people whose thinking apparatus relies largely on mental images. When faced with the problem of defining a small river, my mental picture was immediate, satisfactory to me, and pleasantly evocative but quite impossible to describe adequately on paper. I am probably correct in saying that we all think we know what a small river is, and equally correct in thinking that no two descriptions will tally in all respects. The picture is further confused by the fact that many small rivers become quite large in spate conditions, whilst many in the big to medium class may easily dwindle in drought to a mere trickle. Large or small, they all differ in character, some dramatically, over their length. There are variations in courses, widths and distance covered, with a bountiful freshness of scenery, but one thing they all have in common is the intensely private nature of their banks. I use the word 'private' in the best possible sense: when the angler becomes a true hunter, his solitude only relieved by the presence of the wildlife of the river, the music of live water in the background, bird calls and the sigh of the wind.

To the lone angler, there frequently comes the gift of a sighting denied to his brother on larger streams, where traffic is more prominent. Such an experience was my privilege when I was a tenant of the headwaters of the Black Water in Sutherland known as the Ben Armine Water. The bottom of the beat is marked by a gated wooden bridge which carries the road onward to the Lodge. On our first trip, the gate-opener spotted a salmon in the narrow pool a few yards below. Curious to see how he would react to our presence on the bank, we slowly approached and off he sidled, quietly and without surface disturbance, into the deep shadow of a ledge and total invisibility.

Next day we allowed the car to trickle down, engine off, and were about to get out at the gate when a movement on the bank above the pool caught the eye. Incredibly there was a wild cat and four or five kittens having a glorious game of 'bouncing'. The mother lay on her back on a flat, dusty platform backed by a small rock face, from the top of which the kits were hurling themselves at her stomach. She was doing her best to ward them off, but the fun was so fast and furious that the odd bomber got through; some found time to have a swipe at mother's tail as they returned quickly to the eminence for another go. A little cloud of dust enveloped the scene and they appeared oblivious to the presence of the car a mere 40 yards away. The playtime went on for a good 5 minutes and then, in a flash, all were gone and the heather hid their going. Some quirk of the wind must have wafted our scent to them.

The proprietor below our beat once had the great experience of watching an otter fishing a long pool below where he sat concealed on a high bank. The water, being crystal clear, gave him a perfect picture of a kill which resulted in a dead salmon being carried off downstream, probably to feed a young family.

I have quoted these experiences with pleasurable recall, but if one had to chose a theme for a work on little rivers one could do no better than use the lesson contained therein – *concealment*. It is worth reminding the pilgrim that salmon are truly wild creatures and, in small rivers, are more easily moved, frightened, or even terrified, than in more lordly streams.

Characteristics of small rivers

Sometime about the middle of World War 2, I was doing a job for one of the fighter squadrons at the RAF station at Middle Wallop in Hampshire. It emerged that one of the pilots was a keen angler and the Test was mentioned. The outcome was a viewing of that little river from the front seat of a Miles Master, together with a running commentary on the best beats. That was as near as I ever came to fishing an English river of that category, for I confess to experience limited to a handful of north Highland waters.

A typical pool on the narrow part of the Forss where the banks dictate the siting of the footpath. It means that the approach must be made from above or below, with a long line, in the hope that disturbance by other anglers is minimal or some time previously.

Small rivers in Scotland

When looking at my list of oft-frequented streams, those with which I have modest acquaintance, and those where I have spent an occasional day, they fall into several categories: little rivers that become big as they descend; burns that grow to little river status; streams that remain true to character as little rivers almost from source to finish. In the first category, I would include the Ben Armine Water, the Halladale, the Upper Brora and the Upper Oykel top beats. In the second category are the Forss, the Tirry, the Kirkaig and the Loth. The streams I know that fall throughout their length into the last category are the Dyke, the Fleet and the Mallart. Such a classification may cause confusion when one remembers that the Ben Armine Water becomes the Black Water and then the Brora, but I would not accept as grounds for disqualification the fact that a little river is part of a much bigger one. The justification for pursuing this argument lies in the need for those switching from a big water to a little one to adjust their entire approach. Failure to do so will guarantee lack of success.

Dyke

If I was asked to name a little river that epitomized all the best qualities of the breed I would, without hesitation, choose the Dyke, itself a tributary of the small Halladale. The Dyke is a gem, a miniature Helmsdale going from a burn, spawned by peat moss and lochans to a meandering stream that has it

The Deergate stream on the Brora has been included because it shows the footpath apparently well back from the river. It is actually about 30 ft above the water but, in low water, every fish in this pool can be frightened by anyone standing in the same place as the dog. Although the panic movement of fish will not show at the height of water shown, one wonders whether we underestimate the danger.

all: cut banks, gravelly runs, pools on bends, heathery banks, grassy banks, rocky stretches and many fishy runs before plunging over a series of falls to join the bigger streams. Sadly it is not now a serious proposition as a salmon-producer, but the potential is still there.

Mallart

The obvious solution is to choose a small river with all the attributes of the Dyke – and salmon! There is no doubt in my mind that the Mallart is supreme. It drains a large, very deep loch. Tributaries are minor except in spate conditions. The fall over the first 5 miles is exactly right for the production of a variety of pools and runs, with plenty of fast water to give good aeration and, although the terrain looks dull from a distance, there is in the watercourse all the variety that tickles the fancy of the angler. It generally holds salmon from mid-May onwards, with constant topping-up in freshets.

The head of the Bridge Pool on the Mallart, with Walter Hepburn tucked well in close to the bridge. At this height, the best lies are in the rough water, centre right of the picture. A closer approach would be very unwise.

The significance of the 5 mile mark is that it is the boundary between two ownerships, and also the point where the river plunges over a double fall. The volume and water temperature at this point largely controls the upward runs. Below the falls, a mile or so brings the river to the foot of Loch Naver.

Above these falls, there are three dead-water sections separated by fast water, but even in dead low water, given a breeze, the slack water can yield well to the correct technique and is frequently the saving of a blank day. I will refer to this important feature more fully later.

Tirry

In my list, I included the Tirry, which feeds into Loch Shin about 1 mile above the dam. I have fished here before and after the dam was built. It was never a prolific yielder before the dam was built but, as an important breeding river, added substantially to fish running the Shin. The Hydro Board, realizing that the salmon lifts were not working as expected, ran a restocking programme from which there was no clear benefit, except in the quality of the brown trout off the mouth. Neil Graesser, who was consulted on the issue, told me a fascinating story. Apparently the descending smolts, when entering the loch, turned right instead of left towards the dam and escape via the lift. They then travelled the 17 miles to the head of the loch along the northern shore line, across the top and then 18 miles down the west shore. How many survived the trip is guesswork, but knowing the reputation of Loch Shin for big ferox and the fact the anything over 1 lb 4 oz tends to be cannibalistic, predation must have been close to 100 per cent. So, we have lost a delightful little salmon river.

Ben Armine Water

Sharing the same watershed as the Mallart is the Ben Armine Water, which flows in the opposite direction to the Moray Firth via the Black Water and the Brora. The importance of this stretch, the fishable part of which is only about 2 miles long, cannot be overestimated because it has several miles of the most perfect spawning water imaginable, with numerous side streams favoured by sea trout for the same purpose. A typical hill burn, it comes down a long valley flanked on the right by a 600 ft ridge and on the left by the long slopes to the double tops of Ben Armine. It grows to river proportions as it passes the Lodge to form rocky pools and ravines, four or five of which are classics.

In addition to the wild-cat story, I have another amusing episode which will probably not endear itself to the present 'green' generation. When visiting the Lodge in about 1928, a request for a toilet produced a silent, pointing finger towards a 'house' straddling the burn behind the kennels. Precariously poised on two railway sleepers, the single-seater was arranged above the stream and there, down through the hole, I saw my first spawning sea trout. It was a good thing that the permanent population of the Lodge was only three!

Formation of small rivers

All the little rivers that I know are young in geological terms. About 10,000 years ago, the entire area was being released from the last ice age which superimposed two effects on the faulting of an earlier age: a carving-out of the glaciated valleys and the raising of some areas as the ice pressure diminished. For Scottish rivers, the significance of the geological features was vital. Without the gravel produced in all the stages of ice melt, there would have been no spawning beds. Without rock faulting, the number of deep refuge pools, not to mention ideal funk holes in these pools, would have been much reduced. In the more open pools, salmon lie, as often as not, in the shelter provided by a large boulder, which has either been carried there in glacial debris and scoured to prominence, or conveniently dropped there when the final traces of ice vanished. The finest example of this phenomenon that I know is in the Scourie area, where ridge after ridge is decorated by the ice-abandoned rocks.

Man's attempts to duplicate these lies by the insertion of concrete blocks, and other means, is not always successful, yet I could quote *ad infinitum* instances of boulders selected by nature and lying haphazardly in a pool, giving good taking lies at various heights of water. In support of natural lies is the repeated story of man-made improvements only being successful after the river has made its own adjustments. The very existence of salmon runs depends on the results of these upheavals and, for the successful angler, the smaller the river, the more attention must be paid to the structure of the river bed.

Features of the river affecting salmon

Apart from the geographical, geological and general features of a small river, the existence of salmon runs is governed by such features as the chemical make-up of the water, the timing of spates, and the frequency and nature of falls and water temperatures. Occasionally, accidental obstacles interfere with the progress of salmon upstream. One instance, which occurred about 25 years ago on the Lower Brora, illustrated the breed's sensitivity to unusual objects in or near the water. Many anglers and tourists will be familiar with that picturesque corner of the Brora where a swing bridge for foot traffic crosses just below a ford for vehicles. The uprights of the bridge were being replaced and sockets were being excavated in the banks. On the south side, some very large, almost white, boulders were dislodged in this process and rolled into the main stream at the head of the pool. It was noted at once that very few fish, if any, were running, and a huge stock built up in the ford pool and in the major holding pool below. Removal of the boulders instantly restored things to normal.

I mention the chemical composition of the water for two main reasons. Currently there is some anxiety in the two northern counties over the proliferation of coniferous woodlands in the bog lands which feed some of the rivers. This may increase water acidity to the point where spawning and feeding grounds become sterile. We already have slow growth from birth to the smolt stage, because of poor feeding, and anything that further reduces the food supply would be most unwelcome. Another reason is of immediate interest to the angler. A spate after a period of drought frequently produces a good run of fish but few are caught. The old gillies used to talk of fish being 'sick'. It is not only rivers that are affected; sea-trout and salmon lochs may also yield little in such circumstances. I believe that hill drainage and rapid flushing after rain of partially dried-up lochans empties a temporarily acidic brew into streams and lochs.

None of the small rivers that I know are true early-season waters, but many harbour, to the spawning stage, the produce of spring runs in the lower reaches. The season therefore starts about 3 months later than at the seaward end, but the timing of the start depends on suitable spates and may vary by some weeks. The Ben Armine Water of the Black Water is typical of a small water vital to the interests of anglers below because it comprises many miles of excellent spawning beds with deep refuge holes. Generally a spate at about the beginning of May brings in fish, mainly early entrants from the Black Water but occasionally a runner straight from the sea. Water temperature does not seem to play a significant part in this particular migration. For fish to enter the Black Water from the Brora, the water temperature needs to be at least 42°F to encourage them over the falls. On the Mallart, passage over the falls is governed by two factors: water temperature and rate of flow. In a full spate, conditions are simply too rough for fish to ascend. A few might go over on the rise but the main run waits for more reasonable conditions. It is seldom that a fish will venture over these falls in water below 52°F. An interesting side light is that, when the whole of the Mallart was in the hands of the Sutherland Estates, the fall pool was cleared of washed stones every spring in order to maintain the depth and give the fish a good start. This clearing has not been carried out for 30 years and yet there appears to be no diminution of catches or apparent stock above the falls. The catches may have been held up due to the many salmon caught by Derek Knowles and his keeper Albert Grant, using their low-water stalking methods and the greased floating fly.

One of the major differences between big and small rivers is that the latter have a far greater stock of resident fish and fewer runners. The small-river angler is thus relieved of the problem of dealing with runners and is faced much more with the wiles of slow movers and residents.

Angling methods

I tried to recall instances of success on a small river by any method other than fly but nothing came to mind, except the usual juvenile adventures with a worm and one notable exception on the Mallart with a 6 ft thread-line rod and a 5 lb line. This is worth noting, not because I had unknowingly sinned in using spinning tackle on that particular river, but because there is a lesson to be learned, a lesson which evaded me for many years to come.

What happened was that I had built myself, by hand planing, a Wanless rod and was keen to try the method wherever the chance offered. Two friends fly fished without really knowing much about the water. They finished the day fishless, although every run and pool was well populated. Eventually I pushed off downstream, well below the stretch allotted to the others, and was uneasily, but analytically, aware that salmon everywhere were dashing away on my approach. Then, from far off, I saw one move independently under the opposite bank. In a dim, intuitive manner, this fish was approached from well below. It eventually chased a tiny spoon twice before grabbing it while it was being swiftly brought downstream past it. Thirty more years were to pass before, on that same small river, I was initiated into the finer arts of salmon fishing in difficult conditions. My experience has been entirely with the fly rod and any literature that has made an impression on me also dealt with various forms of fly fishing.

A. H. E. Wood of Dee and greased-line fame, although fishing big or medium rivers, gave us some idea of the benefits of fishing the fly high and far off. Had he been exposed to small rivers, I am sure that he would have brought his technique to its peak. In the event, he stopped far short of the methods evolved by Albert Grant and Derek Knowles. Between the wars, Doctor Brunton Blaikie wrote of his fishing experiences on the Ben Armine Water and, in particular his success with the floating fly for sea trout. That was entirely about upstream fishing and he made no mention of the need for similar stealth when attacking from upstream. Similarly Hugh Campbell, the highly successful fishing manager of the Cape Wrath Hotel waters, which embraced the lower end of the Dionard river, a classic small water, did not accept defeat easily when conditions suggested that some pursuit other than fishing would be more profitable. He concentrated more on flies and tackle than approach and presentation, and had modest success with hooks down to No. 16 and in particular with trebles of that size with no dressing other than a lick of paint on the shank. All Hugh's flies were fished sunk but, being very light, never went deeper than 6 in.

At this point, I will give an illustration of the success of the wet-fly cast upstream. About a decade ago, my partner Taco Nolf and I were co-opted into a ploy on the Ben Armine Water involving a family of beginners who had rented the Estate and needed instruction. This embraced everything from sorting out their tackle to dealing with knots, the selection of flies and casting.

Before we arrived, one of the juvenile members of the family had already landed a salmon by foul-hooking it in a waterfall, a success that seriously diminished the impact of our teaching. Because we were going to use the Long Pool for casting practice, I chose it as the venue for a demonstration of how easy it was to disturb salmon by approaching via a high bank. It worked out perfectly and two fish went charging all over the place the minute our heads topped the edge, but the effect on the tyros was the opposite of that intended. Excitement ran high. To them, active salmon were catchable fish.

The plan was to reach a reasonable standard of casting and then proceed downstream to the Rock Pool, which would be undisturbed and which we would approach with the necessary circumspection. Things did not work out quite like that. When we got to the Rock Pool, a picnic was already in progress right on the bank and a very small boy could not wait to relate how he had lost a fish in the Round Pool. When asked to give details, he explained that it had tried to get up the waterfall and came off the hook; patently another case of foul-hooking. At this point, we decided that the best prospects for the immediate future lay in joining the picnic, but Taco set off to the bottom of the beat with a trout rod and a No. 10 Kenny's Killer. An hour later he came back with a salmon and two sea trout, an episode that accomplished more than theoretical chat in the conversion of an entire family to a better way of life. But these are simple instances of angling lessons that, in the light of later experiences, were only half learned.

The year 1984 was easily the most significant in my angling career. To celebrate a milestone in the march of time, I was able to rent with friends the Loch Choire fishings, which included the River Mallart. It was only for a week, but what a week that turned out to be: a revelationary week, a week of discovery, and of victory over ignorance and entrenched thought.

Let me start with a typical scenario. You have taken a fishing and, arriving on Sunday, have the whole of that evening to relish the delights to come.
A perfunctory breakfast barely disguises the impatience to be off. Swift decisions are made as to who goes where, and you quickly find yourself at the head of a good, strong stream fanning out 30 yd below into a deep pool.
A little jump off the bank brings your feet onto the pebbly shore and out goes the line.

At the third cast, a fish shows in a joyful leap well down the pool and your progress down to it is accelerated by expectation. Then another splashes noisily in the pool below and hope rises as the cast is lengthened. Speed of retrieve is varied, flies changed and the slow sinker replaced by a full floater, all to no avail. With the water running at about 6 in. and approaching settled levels after a spate, things should be different. What has gone wrong?
Not much, but what is wrong is fundamental.

This was brought out at an early stage when Colin Taylor and I made the vast trek overland to fish the famous Crooked Pool on the same river. The headstream looked perfect and knee boots were good enough to allow us to square up to the stream. Fish were showing regularly from the tail of the stream and for the next 40 yd. We had been flogging away for 20 minutes or so, having changed flies, patterns and sizes umpteen times with nary a look from a fish, when the redoubtable Albert Grant appeared, eyed us with scepticism and announced bleakly that we would never catch a fish like that. From that loaded remark there gradually emerged more contacts with Derek Knowles and Albert, and a picture of fly-fishing techniques that not only explained the aforementioned scenario, but also opened a new area for experiment and thought.

The careful approach

The last section set the scene for disaster in small rivers in medium- to low-water levels, but much of what follows will apply in some degree to all conditions except a flood. One of the most common instructions from a gillie who knows his water is to start well above a holding stream, but what is rarely mentioned is the means of getting there. In many cases, the advice is born of long experience of fish being taken by the rod approaching from upstream, and more or less by accident failing to disturb a taking fish. In the normal, bold approach, fish in a stream are either spooked by the angler *en route* to the head, or by too close an approach from above. Nothing spectacular happens and the departure of the fish is discreet and invisible until it reaches the deeper water. In human terms, the subsequent leap might be construed as a gesture of relief and release from danger. Once that happens, the best move is to find another pool because it might take several hours for the fish to return to their favourite lies. About 2 hours is the shortest time I have been able to determine and this was based on the extreme unlikelihood of a fresh fish having moved in because of very low-water conditions and bright sun.
I mention fresh fish because the reaction of a resident to disturbance or unusual bank activity is quite different from that of a new arrival, particularly if the angler is already in position and may have been accepted as part of the scenery. Of course, if he is flailing about with a flashy rod, waving wet plastic-clad arms or smashing down a white No. 10 line the result will also be fatal.

Some years ago I had a marvellous example of how fresh fish will accept 'lighthouses' and so on, when they are newly arrived; and how, when worried, their departure can be so secretive that a bank watcher would see nothing. I was fishing a little stream not far below Loch Brora at dusk when, at the tail of the Beech Tree, I saw a quick flick of two running fish; moments later one rolled in the headstream about 40 yd below me. I was then aware of a fish moving with great care towards me, dorsal fin and tail visible, but water disturbance barely detectable. My legs were well straddled to give a grip on loose gravel and, to my astonishment, the salmon, somewhere in the 7 lb to 10 lb category, came right through and navigated like an eel for several more yards above me, by which time the water was becoming too shallow for it. So, turning with immense discretion, it came right down headfirst between my legs again and off quietly into the pool.

There is some evidence that bright colours are a deterrent to running fish and, as I mentioned, I know of one case where white boulders after a bridge reconstruction had to be removed before salmon would pass. Small rivers are particularly susceptible to disturbance from anglers because of features such as high banks, tracks and footpaths close to the water's edge and, in canyon situations, the difficulty of casting a fly out unseen. Much salmon-holding water in small streams is never more than a few yards from the bank and, thus, resident fish are susceptible to 'strangers' on the bank, particularly those that appear suddenly, not necessarily in angler's guise. Walkers, cattle and dogs can all cause trouble and I have even had a motorbike destroy the tranquillity of a pool I was about to fish.

Neil Graesser has propounded the theory that the patter of dogs' pads resembles those of the otter. Right or wrong, the fact remains that anglers on difficult waters should leave their dog at home. There are contradictions in the dog saga, notably the oft-repeated anecdote of the frustrated angler confronted by a pool teeming with unco-operative salmon. The story goes that the dog was sent in to wake them up and, minutes later, the rod was bent into a fish. I have no doubt that this happened but I often wonder whether the true answer to this situation is the arrival of a runner at the critical time. My own dog, a springer, never misses a day on a big river and is a first-class angler in that he never relaxes and watches the position of the fly with intense concentration. He has, on more than one occasion, seen the move to the fly seconds before I have felt the tug, but he stays at home, or in the car, on small rivers.

On one occasion, with a springer spaniel who had just reached the age of reason at 8 months and was very steady, I was fishing a pool on the Dyke river from a high bank when the dog saw an old friend half a mile away on the far side. It was too much for him and his header into the pool caught my line; then the hook bit and the reel protested as he sped across the heather. At the backing's end, the hold, which turned out to be a tuft of hair, gave way and all was well.

On the only occasion when I deliberately put a dog into the water, events were not quite what I expected. It was on the Grilse Pool on the Lower Brora, in dead low conditions, and on a warm July evening. The water seemed quite dead, nothing showed, and the midges became aggressive. Then a merganser duck and her brood appeared at the tail with the apparent intention of sailing up the middle of the pool. I put my dog in to scare them off. I don't know what happened to the ducks but the dog was nearly torpedoed and a salmon grounded itself in the utter panic that possessed the inhabitants. The turmoil resembled the chaos of the Faroese whale slaughter. I have a feeling that would be more typical of dog intrusion.

Most river anglers have experience of loch fishing for trout. Some have walked too close to a shallow feeding area and seen trout heading at speed for deeper water. In calm conditions, standing up in a boat has the same effect except that the departure of the quarry goes unnoticed and takers close to the boat seem to vanish. There is every reason to believe that salmon act in the same way, yet I am puzzled by an apparent contradiction: both species can be taken by bird predators. Does the sense of preservation desert them in the face of an attack from above, or does the speed of the strike defeat any evasive action? Possibly we have something like the rabbit-and-weasel situation, where the former usually seems paralysed by fear and makes no attempt to escape when the weasel is close.

There is also food for thought in the oft-quoted remark, applicable to wider rivers, that fishing from one bank produces fish from near the other. There could be simple reasons for this, such as depth, boulder lies, and water movement that allows the fly to fish better from one side or the other, but I cannot divorce from my general argument the thought that fish disturbance plays a part.

Before leaving the subject of spooking salmon by sight, it is worth mentioning the effect of certain sounds. Small, rocky rivers are extremely susceptible to noises made by heavy, nail-shod boots on solid rock, or the clink of an armoured wading stick. Sunday school picnics near good salmon pools should be avoided. There is one such pool on the Lower Brora below a ford, with part of the headstream under a swing bridge. About 30 yd from the bridge, it opens out into a deep refuge not noted for taking fish. On one occasion, not many years ago, I was involved with a party whose returns for the first 2 days fell far below expectations. To be precise, they were nil.

When I arrived there was one rod lashing the head of the stream so close to the water that wavelets were lapping his toes. Standing about on the bank within feet of the water near the head of the stream was a large group finishing off lunch, while two dogs explored the possibilities of snatching a scrap or two

The Ford is probably the best known pool on the Brora. I happened to be passing when I spotted the angler fishing from the north bank. About 20 yd below, and at about the same distance offshore, there is a 'hole' which frequently has a fresh fish in residence. I suspect that this angler was unaware of this and was wading to reach what are also good lies on the far side. If the nearer lie had not been fished the chances are that, from this position, his feet would have sent a clear message of danger to a possible customer.

and sometimes splashed into the pool. At the next pool down, three young men stood shoulder to shoulder, belabouring a perfect headstream from close range, a stream from which all takers had long since departed and were derisively flicking about in the deeper water below. Do not interpret all this to mean that they were having a bad time. On the contrary, all were having the time of their lives, including the two children who presently discovered a new game – jumping off the bench at the waterside with thuds that could be felt 20 yd away. Any salmon angler of experience would be able to point out to them the correct approach. In high water one can commit every sin in the book and get away with it, but in low water, and particularly in prolonged low water, any one of the mistakes illustrated will prove fatal.

I tell the story to draw attention to another possible cause of frightening fish, one which I have never seen mentioned or heard discussed. Thoughts on the subject were prompted by experiences when fishing clear-water lochs in modest winds. The clumsy caster, the splasher and the snatcher rarely catch fish for the simple reason that fish scatter before the onslaught. But, as I mused on this, I wondered whether the sound factor ought to be considered; whether the slack cast for salmon, hastily re-executed, could have the same effect. Even a small fly plucked at high speed must have a whiplash effect. One keeper to whom I mentioned this possibility thought it would sound like a 0.22 rifle shot! Whatever the nature of the sound, it would be a noise foreign to the environment and likely to scare fish.

Wading

People are surely not born with an instinct to wade, but it may be that the act of buying waders, or seeing photographs of someone armpit deep in a mini-ocean, makes them connect fishing with wading. Many anglers seem to be compulsive waders and even read instructions on what to do if they are swept away. Wading, and certainly waders, have a place in tackling small rivers but, on the whole, the principal use of waders should be for keeping the legs dry on bosky banks and when kneeling in damp spots. They are also useful when crossing to the other side. Wade if you must, but always consider the possibility that, by doing so, you are getting well into the fish window. Consider also that, after a period of low water and sunshine, most small rivers accumulate a fair crop of algae and trailing weed which can be dislodged by the feet. This cloud of debris then sails down through the lies, to the confusion of your quarry which is already bemused by one or two leaves and twigs. The salmon is likely to investigate individual small items but not a bombardment of muck.

Nevertheless there are conditions which demand careful wading. A typical example is shown in the photograph on p. 189, which pictures James Holt fishing a pool on the Upper Carron. You will see that the pool is bounded by a rock wall down which the main flow is deflected. There is no cover and to fish

A pool on the upper Carron with James Holt doing a bit of wading to line up with the stream running strongly down the far side. Note how clean the boulders are – no fear of releasing a swarm of flak here.

sufficiently far off the banks would simply mean that the fly would be swept at once towards the near shore. Hence James is narrowing the angle to get the fly to fish by casting down and across. It will be seen that the boulders in and out of the water are clean. This is a feature of that river. There is no danger of releasing a cloud of confusing debris.

Sometimes it is desirable to enter the water well above a taking lie if approach on the bank would be risky. An example of this is illustrated in Derek Knowles' book on the floating fly for salmon, in which a young angler is seen squatting in a niche in the bank of the Rock Pool on the Mallart. This vantage point, almost directly opposite the lie and about 15 yd away, is reached by creeping down the bank in the water, keeping the head below the first horizon of the fish. It is at this pool that Derek has placed a marker on the bank 30 yd above this lie, and has demonstrated that an upright approach beyond it immediately leads to fish flight.

On occasions, the ambition to reach a distant shore with the fly encourages wading when it would be much better to stay on the bank first time down, in order to cover closer lies more adequately. When the remarkable John George Edwards took to gillying on the Brora as his regular profession, he was out on one occasion with his famous namesake, the international caster and champion. The river was well stocked but the great man came off clean. When John was asked afterwards what went wrong he replied that the performance was beautiful, but that the fish were not among the stones on the far bank!

The attack

It will be clear by now that the ethos of my message is the nurturing of the hunting instinct and the suppression of rash impatience. But, once inbued with the right spirit, what is the difference between fishing a small river and a big one? The answer is 'Not much'. With the exception of wading, techniques are similar, apart from the fact that there is little width for the across-stream cast and thus the fly is mainly fishing below the angler. The hanging fly attracts salmon. Oddly enough, I was first shown this method not on a small river but on a very large one, the Spey, where it was executed by choice rather than necessity and usually after deep wading. The fly is cast just to the far side of a stream, held as it sweeps across, and maybe traversed back again by rod-tip lateral movement and hung in the fast water. If a reserve yard or two of line is held in the hand, it can be fed out slowly. A considerable area can thus be searched on one cast. On a small, cliff-confined stream, the method is far better than continuous casting. There is one snag: fish taken on the dangle are notoriously difficult to hook but, if there is any spare line, it can be let go at the critical moment in the hope that the turn of the fish, or a slight belly in the line, will put the hook firmly in the scissors.

The full scope of this method emerged when, for some years, I had the privilege of fishing the lower part of that marvellous river, the Inver, which drains Loch Assynt. Just before the river plunges into its last chasm above the seaward stretch, a series of man-made pools have resulted in dams and groynes vented centrally to produce very powerful, long surges of water. In almost every case, it is possible to walk out to the edge of the races and, starting with a short line, fish them thoroughly without subsequent casts, simply by allowing the current to pull the line from one's fingers and by an occasional mend across. I have taken fish by this method right at the tail of one of these streams when the backing was showing on the reel.

The main differences between wide and narrow rivers arise in periods of very dry weather. A week without rain hardly worries the big river; a fortnight may change the methods of fishing slightly; and a month of drought may still leave a fishable stream. The little river reacts much more dramatically and none that I know can survive a week of drought without changing character completely, unless there is a bit of snow melt coming down. In full flood, most are unfishable at about 1 ft above medium summer levels. In spate, they fish well and no particular attention needs to be paid to stealth other than that demanded by common sense. It is when the level drops to low summer flows that difficulties arise. Warm-weather arid conditions give rise to high water temperatures and it is then that we hear phrases like 'impossible', 'fish right off', or 'a waste of time'. It is then that the majority of anglers either seek other avenues of the sport or venture a cast or two in the fading light of evening.

Not included in that angling majority were the two stalwarts from Loch Choire already mentioned: Derek Knowles and Albert Grant. Their philosophy was that they had 5 miles of salmon fishing and that, in the interests of science and the possibility of extending activities into these difficult periods – all too long in a dry summer – something should be done.

Firstly they established just how close they could get to some of their known taking lies. To their surprise and the incredulity of many experienced anglers, the distances were astonishing. Standing on the river bank about 3 ft above the water, they were visible at 40 yd from upstream and downstream. At one pool on the Mallart, I was able, with the aid of binoculars, to establish that a fish was in residence in a favoured lie at the head. I then had the privilege of watching Derek creep down below bank level, present a floating fly and land a 6 lb grilse. The telling of this story, and particularly the use of visual aids, gave rise to great hilarity amongst my friends. When it was mentioned that the hook was a No. 16 treble, incredulity was replaced by the firm conviction that a bit of leg-pulling was going on.

There is another difference between the big and little river which could be described as the 'work load'. It is quickly impressed on rods who start their careers on large rivers that, given the minimum amount of technical knowledge and expertise, the rest is a question of time and energy. Hard casting and searching hour after hour is often the order of the day, putting the emphasis on endurance and sheer physical fitness. Fishing the smaller streams is much more a contemplative matter, with the quarry being known and the searching reduced.

Derek concentrated on short rods, usually of 9 ft and with a DT6F line, and his little bulky flies were designed to hold a good application of grease. The first of these flies was the Yellow Dolly. We are not all equipped physically for creeping about on rocky river banks and, here, providence in the shape of Albert saved the day, because he developed a technique with long rods for these impossible conditions. Stiff-kneed 6-footers like myself could enjoy the comfort of the vertical stance when directing a fly to a distant target.

I will describe my first outing with Albert in the long hot summer of 1970 when, with wind forecast, he said that conditions might be suitable for taking a fish from the Crooked Pool. This is a U-shaped pool with an attractive headstream, at that time a long stretch of dead water confined by mini-cliffs of peaty soil on the outward side of the bend. Albert was right, a half gale was rippling even the smoothest section and, at one point near a little indentation, a fish showed gently. In the circumstances it may seem extraordinary but, so strongly is Albert's hunting instinct developed that, from then on, all conversation was at whisper level. On previous occasions he had driven his Argocat around the inside of the bend 7 yd from the bank and decreed that no angler should approach nearer to the water than the vehicle's tracks.

I had put up a 14 ft light carbon rod, a DT8F line with 13 ft leader of 7 lb nylon, and a ³/₈ in. tube with No. 16 treble. All – line, leader and fly – had been anointed liberally with solid Mucilin. My instruction was to drop the fly about 6 in. from the opposite bank into the tiny bay where the fish had shown. 'Try to get it right first time' was the advice. I failed. I aerialized a little bit too much line, the fly landed on a tussock of grass on top of the bank and the line remained airborne across the pool. A hoarse whisper from Albert indicated that all was not lost, that he did not disapprove; then followed the order to pull it off gently. The fly came away first time, flopped onto the target area and was promptly taken without fuss or hesitation. The task was then to get the fish out without disturbing the pool. I stayed between the Argocat tracks and Albert wriggled over the edge onto a narrow ledge, from which he tailed the fish before wriggling back almost to my feet and standing up.

We took two fish each that day and lost one before the wind dropped. Albert was using his favourite 15 ft carbon rod and a 14 ft leader but, being more athletic than me, took one of his fish from a crouched position at a point where the bank was very low and he was casting 25 yd downstream. In my case, the casting was almost straight across or very slightly upstream. I might add that the one I lost took on a slow retrieve after an abortive cast. It was not the one I was after and remains one of the very few fish to be lost on a small treble, although later I confess to using No. 14 trebles. So, this is what it boils down to: concealment, the longest possible leader 1 ft shorter than the rod, using a splash-free delivery and everything afloat. Lining a fish is fatal but the direction of the cast is not important; wind and cover making the decision for you.

The purist might ask what one does about rocks, knowing that so many lies are close to surface-breaking boulders. Derek ignores rocks. If a line or leader falls across a rock he leaves it, so long as the fly comes round through the lie. A taking fish will pull it clear. There is an extension of this advice, where a pool lies in flat country, affording no cover of any consequence, and the crouched approach is impractical. It is quite legitimate to allow the line, and even part of the leader, to fall on dry ground, thus enabling the angler to remain outside the danger area. Only two problems arise: the difficulty of aerializing enough line with a big rod and the risk of damaging the hook when lifting-off if there are rocks or gravel. Readers may query the use of the long double-handed rod when any reservoir caster can make the distance single-handed with a relatively short rod. I think the long, light rod has the advantage of the delicacy of the cast and the reduction in the frequency of false casting.

Tackle

I have been a rod-maker long enough to have found out that there are as many preferences as there are customers, and almost as many prejudices, so what I am about to write must have personal flavour. There is no such thing as an all-round fly rod although, amusingly, in the 1960s and 1970s many beginners were deceived by the name of a certain 12 ft rod into believing that it was a general-purpose tool. It was a light ledgering rod, the shortcomings of which were all too apparent when a novice tried to cast a fly.

A common mistake of the novice was to pick a short rod for boat fishing. It was always difficult to convince them of the error of their ways but, on the whole, the veriest beginner sorts it out with the help of tackle-dealers and friends. He usually gets it right for at least one river and one band of conditions and, provided that the rod will accept a range of lines, it is surprising, even in our climate, the variety of conditions with which it will cope. Most serious salmon anglers have at least two salmon rods and a trout rod, and are amply equipped to cover any likely conditions on a small river.

One of my own favourites for many years was a 12 ft 6 in. split-cane rod taking a No. 7 or No. 8 line. It could handle flies up to 1½ in. but was sensitive enough to be gentle on wee trebles and little doubles. Later I switched to a Bruce & Walker 12 ft Silver Stream, an excellent rod in fibreglass but, because I was becoming more and more involved with light tackle, I asked the same firm to consider a similar rod light enough to take a No. 6 or No. 7 line. I still have the prototype. It was first named 'The Brora' but this was later changed to 'The Highlander' because of wider appeal.

On my 60th birthday this rod killed its first fish, a 16-pounder on a very small double. The only fish I ever lost on it was not the fault of the rod but resulted from a pawl failure and a jammed reel. It was thus a natural choice for part of the armoury when adapting to the methods evolved by Derek and Albert. The apparent lack of backbone, noted when tried by some anglers, far from being a handicap gave excellent buffering at the take and on wildly leaping fish. With a No. 7 floater, I used this rod for what might be termed 'general conditions' with the floating fly and also in times of drought, when longer casting and better line control than that afforded by a trout rod were demanded. At that time The Highlander was the lightest 12 ft salmon rod on the market. It could be used single-handed for short periods, rolled beautifully, and yet could deliver a good line into a head wind. It was a paragon amongst rods and one that makes me regret the passing of fibreglass.

The other two rods in my armoury were of the material that superseded all others, carbon fibre, from an American source. At that time the maker's name was Fenwick, but I understand that the ownership has changed hands. From the first batch of 9 ft rods, in two-piece format, one was purchased by Derek Knowles and used almost exclusively for salmon fishing with small floating flies. It played a considerable part in the development of the technique. Sadly it came to a very sticky end when it slipped through a crack into the driving mechanism of an Argocat and was instantly altered from a two-piece to a thousand-piece rod.

Another Fenwick I kept for my own use was assembled with snake rings and a very light, sliding-reel fitting; it weighed exactly 2⅞ oz. The rod worked well with a No. 5 line but was best with a No. 6 and a magnesium reel. It was the first carbon rod I used extensively but it had one disconcerting feature: although extremely sensitive to the slightest pluck or knock, it never transmitted at once the message giving the size of fish hooked. On more than one occasion what I dismissed as a brownie on the take turned out to be a salmon and, to balance, many a good hope proved to be a trout. I soon learned to keep my mouth shut until better evidence was presented. Although I have not kept records of fish lost I have a distinct impression that this rod almost shared the same record as The Highlander in terms of minimal losses. But, as my legs stiffened and creeping and crawling became less attractive, so use of the rod diminished in favour of the 12 footer and the other carbon rod. This was of 14 ft, assembled on three-piece blanks, also from the Fenwick stable, with a fairly robust reel seat and full open rings. It weighed 12¼ oz which is about average for the length. It had a better line tolerance than most, being best with a No. 9 or No. 10, but was quite happy with a No. 8 and would handle a No. 7 once one got out 17 or 18 yd of line. As this was about the minimum I required for most of my fishing, bearing in mind that a leader would be another 4 yd, the rod was ideal for the long-range fishing required on the Mallart dead water, the Sea Pool on Forss, the Junction Pool on the Fleet and the Long Pool on the Ben Armine Water.

It is worth re-iterating at this point that Albert Grant, for similar work, always used a 15 ft carbon rod, an unlikely mate for a ¼ in. tube and a No. 16 treble.

The Junction Pool on the River Fleet, mainly dead water needing a good breeze. The figure on the left roughly marks the distance from the water which might be considered safe but the trees behind prevent the long cast necessary to fish a floater at the far side.

Albert's original came from Northampton and, like my 14 ft rod, could handle a light line. When he first bought it he also used it for spring fishing on Helmsdale and Brora; this could involve flies up to 4 in. long which goes to show the error of being too dogmatic about such things. It is only fair to add that Albert also uses more orthodox lengths when fishing is more normal, i.e. where there is a bit of water with a minimal need for concealment.

Flies

When one lives in the same place as Megan Boyd MBE, one time doyen of traditional, fully dressed salmon-fly tyers, one has to approach the subject with humility. Megan, who made her living from flies from her school days until her retirement in 1989, set a standard of authenticity, accuracy and quality that will probably never be surpassed. She was not an angler. In fact, in the nicest possible way, she thought we were all slightly barmy. She had backing and encouragement from a long line of distinguished mentors, including the redoubtable Mrs Jessie Tyser, who was meticulous to the point of fussiness when it came to fly dressings and sizes, and who firmly believed that the noble salmon should be caught on equally noble flies. Her snort of dismissal when a fish was reported to be caught on 'something I tied myself' was crushing. In the end she came to accept that modern tubes and articulated flies had something going for them. Megan must have a host of customers and friends who helped her in many ways, notably Jim Pilkington and Bobby Gilroy, both well known on Brora and Helmsdale.

The fly known as the 'Pilkington' was not the production of Jim who, to the best of my knowledge, never tied a fly himself. It owed its conception to his brother Stephen, who was also well known in the north and occasionally dressed flies. When the hair-winged tubes were establishing themselves, Stephen grew tired of the advice that he was one colour short. By way of a joke, he decided to end the arguments by turning up with a large hair-wing with nearly all the colours available at that time: red, blue and yellow. It was so successful on Brora in March that he hardly ever used anything else.

Forever associated with Bobby Gilroy will be the simple low-water fly known by two names: 'Gilroy' and 'Megan's'. This was virtually a Stoat's Tail with a light blue throat hackle which, for many years, had been the prime summer fly on Helmsdale. By coincidence, at the time when Megan was producing this pattern, and with the help of Dusty Miller, I had evolved, amongst other hairwings, a pattern with a blue and black mixed wing originally called the Black & Blue but subsequently and aptly rechristened 'The Bruiser'.

Dusty was regular officer in the RAF when I first met him, stationed at Kinloss, and when he wasn't flying he was fishing, and when he wasn't fishing he was tying flies. His quality was faultless, his uniformity awe-inspiring to the extent that it always seemed a sin to sell any and break the symmetry of the immaculate rows in which they were delivered.

Above all, his inquisitive, inventive mind and angling experience were invaluable when discussing new patterns. He was involved with me in attempting to rationalize the proliferation of hair-wing flies resulting from the short cuts offered by tubes and Waddingtons. One of the devices successfully produced with his help was the 'shrunk-on' plastic body for big, articulated flies, originally considered as protection from kelt's teeth but later popular for giving a translucent effect to fly bodies. He was also the tyer who made the first Willie Gunn pattern, experimentally produced with bunched hair and approved by Willie Gunn himself on first sight and then sealed by great success on the river. Within the year, he suggested a trial of the mixed-hair type, which has never looked back since. It is a great one to use where there is doubt about the best pattern to try.

A pattern that will not be as familiar is one that started off, in odd circumstances, as a sea-trout fly. In the late 1960s, the Balnacoil Water of the Brora was tenanted by an American party who were there to catch salmon and did not much bother with the normally excellent sea-trout fishing. Their invitation to two of the Estate employees was eagerly accepted, but presented those worthies with a problem. One had run out of good sea-trout flies. On the subsequent proceedings, there has been some confusion but, if I put it this way, I will not be far wrong. Alistair Mackintosh had the ability and Kenny Burns had the need, and jointly they scraped enough material together to produce what eventually became known as 'Kenny's Killer'. It could well have been the 'Mackintosh Murderer'. After their first night on the Black Water, the tenants came down to breakfast to find 22 large sea trout laid out for inspection, all taken on the *ad hoc* fly. By 10 am, the entire squad was in my shop requesting copies of what was a Silver Stoat's Tail with a yellow throat hackle. As Kenny was the one who supplied the bedraggled sample the name followed naturally. At the time I had a young schoolboy demonstrating fly tying as a holiday job and it was therefore easy to arm the tenants instantly with a supply of proven killers. What they did was to abandon salmon fishing almost completely and, in a week, they killed 200 sea trout at night on this one pattern. Nowadays, I don't think a separate name would be justified, but the pattern is now so well established in the north that its status was a happy accident. It is amusing to record that, within the year, I was told that I had the pattern and the name wrong. A Ross-shire angler offered the information that it lacked jungle-cock cheeks, and that the name was 'Yellow Peril'.
I must say that it is a handsome fly with those additions, but the fact is that Kenny's Killer goes marching on and the Yellow Peril seems to have lost its appeal.

On my early visits to the Ben Armine Water it became clear that the pattern enshrined in the game book and held in reverence by keepers and gillies was the Lady Caroline, a well-documented, low-water fly. This rather drab nondescript pattern reigned long before the Hairy Mary was heard of but is now rarely mentioned. My father's favourite for small rivers was one of the less decorative patterns, the Black Dose, which he always had tied by Megan Boyd. Even the least exotic of the older patterns have been supplanted by hairwings in the form of the ubiquitous Hairy Mary, Willie Gunn, Bruiser and a range of tyings of the Yellow Badger developed on the Mallart. These latter deserve special mention. They are tied by Bert Grant on the lightest possible plastic tubes in lengths down to ¼ in. Aluminium is too heavy because, up to the ¾ in. tube, the pattern is used fully greased. Let me make it clear that I am referring to body length. Hair length for the ¼ in. tube would be barely ½ in., and for the ¾ in. tube about 1¼ in. maximum. An interesting side light on the evolution of the colour of these small tubes is that, when rationalizing the range of articulated flies, one of the successful patterns was christened 'Naver Elver' because the original pattern came from that river. The tying was simple: a plain gold or silver body with a wing of the dark part of a bucktail dyed yellow. This came out in a sort of khaki colour very similar to the Yellow Badger.

A possible weakness of the tiny tube and trebles to match is that one cannot push the eye into the plastic and, in windy conditions, or as the result of a poor cast, the hook may flick around the leader. In practice, the only thing to do is to have an inspection if there is any doubt about the quality of the cast. It is when one tires a little that errors creep in. Failure to extend the back cast fully is the most prolific source of snagged trebles. For these small flies, the hook must be light and strong, not too long in the shank, and with a gape a little greater than the standard Limerick. In my opinion, the Partridge outpoint is supreme and I have yet to see one broken in a fish.

I make that last remark because amidst a host of excuses for losing fish hurled at me across the counter was the recurring one of the broken hook. Now, I have no doubt at all that hooks break in fish, that hooks straighten under load and that trebles flatten under clamped jaws, but I have also thought that such phenomena could be due simply to impact damage before any fish was involved. It is surprising what can happen when a high-speed hook meets an unyielding object, such as a rock, and the anvil does not need to be as hard as stone. Two examples involved the gunwale of a boat and my own plastic-coated jacket when fishing from a boat. In each case, the crack was heard and an inspection showed both hooks broken off at the bend. More minor damage can result in dull points not always readily visible on tiny trebles. A good way to check is to pull the hook across one's thumb nail whereupon any absence of sharpness will immediately become apparent.

One of the most successful developments in the post-war period was the series of dressed trebles produced by the late Esmond Drury. Where they did best in the north was in the bigger rivers, notably the Oykel. Its strong streams with some deep holding water suited these flies and, in the late spring, the larger sizes were excellent. I never had any luck with them on small rivers, even in the smallest sizes, because I think their weight tended to sink them below, rather than level with or above, possible takers. Others may differ in their opinion, but I had my theory boosted when Dr Bradbury conducted me over a nest of salmon pens at the fish farm near Ullapool and at Badcall Bay near Scourie, by courtesy of Dr Marshall Halliday. In the first case, small, active fish of up to about 6 lb took their feed pellets with great commotion, at or near the surface. Single pellets were taken in the same way, but any that drifted deeper than 1 ft or so were completely ignored. At Scourie, in a pen full of 18 lb fish, the single-pellet test produced a more leisurely suck on the surface and anything that sank much below that might never have existed.

To sum up, I have found a strong bias on small streams towards the duller patterns with an occasional hint of silver or gold and light irons and light tubes with small trebles. Once the water reaches the upper 50s F, it is always worth trying the full floater. In impossible conditions, it simply becomes a matter of find, stalk and float the smallest tubes.

Weather

One thing that civilized man has almost entirely lost, unless one includes sufferers from rheumatism, is built-in weather-forecasting ability. Shepherds tell me that sheep have it strongly and that, over and over again, they demonstrate this by retreating from high ground well in advance of a storm. There is no doubt that salmon react, sometimes favourably, sometimes less co-operatively, in advance of weather events. Anglers are often puzzled by the apparent complete disregard of their lures when every feature of the circumstances would suggest success. The answer frequently comes next day with a dramatic change in the weather. This may be the gathering of water-laden clouds from the west, a change in wind direction, a rise or fall in air temperature, or a barometric indication of a pressure change.

I have found that the effects of these fluctuations is more pronounced on lochs than rivers, but there is one change that, within reason, hardly effects loch fishing but could be critical on rivers. That is the alteration in water temperature that can occur in the course of a day's fishing because of winds, sun or showers. Hail stones can reduce water temperature almost instantly and the angler should always be alert, particularly on rocky-bedded streams, for the quick rise which the morning sun can accomplish. If already in the upper 50s F, the size of fly is critical. A drop in water temperature of 2 or 3°F might have little effect, but a rise could mean that a fly one or two sizes smaller might make all the difference between success and failure.
The thermometer should figure as an essential item in the tackle bag.

Wind, at any rate too much of it in the wrong direction, can be a curse on any river, but in low-water conditions, and particularly in stretches of dead water, a good breeze is vital. An upstream wind is favoured by those who go in for backing-up, but otherwise I have been unable to detect any advantage or disadvantage as far as wind-induced ripple is concerned in a variety of wind directions. Mechanically, of course, something like a half gale in one's teeth inhibits good casting. If at all possible, one should try to make the wind work in a helpful way, maybe by changing banks or, as in the case of the Mallart devotees, simply by casting in the direction of the wind, particularly if the fly is a floater. The effects of bright sunlight are often mitigated by a good wind ripple, but nothing can soften the glare of a setting sun shining straight down a long pool.

Yet there is a period near sunset, just as the sting goes out of the light, when fish become alive. It may not last more than a few minutes and I have heard it referred to as 'the evening promenade'. The impression one gets is of hitherto dormant fish cruising around just before final retirement, a ripple here, a splash there, and a good chance of a taker. On many occasions I have known of multiple takes many pools apart, all within a 10 minute period.

Casting to difficult lies

There are occasions when it is almost impossible to get into a good casting position because of the configuration of the bank. There is one excellent example of this on the Ben Armine Water in the form of the Round Pool. This is best described as a large pot enclosed by a vertical cliff on the west side and a steeply sloping, solid rock face on the east. The river tumbles into it via a deep cut and a fall about 10 ft high. It then swells out to a near-circular shape but the main run is down the west side and the exit is on that side too, quite small and running over a rock sill with some gravel. By creeping round on a narrow ledge, I discovered that salmon lie in layers against the vertical face – infernally difficult lies to cover properly from any available angle.

The best apparent approach was to sidle round the sloping slab to get as close as possible to the fall, but little success followed. In this case it was not a question of frightening fish. They lay in a strong flow in deep water and even greater depth was near. Failure was probably due to the fly being pushed outwards far too quickly and there was no way to resolve this problem. However, more or less by accident, instinct encouraged the rod to stay put at the head and an ever-lengthening line eventually hung the fly a matter of feet above the out-flow; and there it was, able and willing, hanging like a late autumn fish almost out of the pool! Not only that but it was found that, once a fish was played and landed circumspectly, and the pool given 15 minutes or so to quieten down, another moved into the lie. On one occasion, my brother and I, taking turns, took four in about an hour, all on the long line and all without leaving the perch near the fall. On reflection, there was an element of luck involved because no fish opted to go downstream when hooked but were played out in the pool itself.

This single-stance situation has a parallel in the Dowlings Pool on the Mallart. This is a canal-like stretch with a reasonable headstream that is quickly lost. The pool thereafter meanders between steep, peaty banks where it is not noted for success by orthodox methods but can be an impressive yielder to the floating-fly technique if the water is undisturbed. On one occasion, one of my friends, who had injured a knee, chose the head of this pool to have a restful day. He took one and lost one, simply by becoming part of the scenery and casting his Yellow Dolly at intervals to likely spots within easy range. One could adapt this technique to other lies by getting into position and waiting for evidence of a fish before casting. There is, for example, a lie above the footbridge on the Forss where I used this method and raised two fish which had shown themselves, and I always felt that, with more time for experiment with fly sizes and patterns, success could have followed.

At this point, it is appropriate to mention that, when fish are 'off' they mean 'off', but, even in the worst possible case, one may sometimes tease a fish into taking a fly – with one exception. Dead water or deep slack water at one side of a major pool will frequently be seen to hold a big fish, always referred to succinctly by a local gillie as a 'big black bugger'. They show frequently but sluggishly and may be in residence for anything up to 6 months. They completely ignore any sort of lure, even when their brothers and sisters are excited into action in a spate. One theory is that they are fish which have been hooked, played out and lost earlier in the season, and which have found a good safe hole and have no intention of again venturing into trouble. No time should be wasted on them.

Epilogue

When the knots have been tied, breaking strains calculated, and the sharpest hook selected, when statistics have been studied and your head is almost bursting with the facts, relax, and, in an evening, midgey drizzle, fish with me.

The following is an article of mine which was published in *Trout & Salmon* in 1985.

Salmon in Lilliput

'You mean that's what it's called, the Piddle?' exclaimed my companion. A vision sprang to his mind, he told me later, of that appealing cartoon: 'Ne buvais jamais d'eau', in which a small boy is pictured relieving himself into a pond.

I confirmed the name of the river, reassured him on the absence of small boys and encouraged him with an account of a 22 lb salmon I had gaffed in 1975 for an angler. The fish had been hooked, played and landed from a pool no larger than a squash court a few miles above the sea where this Dorset stream runs out at Wareham. The lure was an all-black No. 2 Mepps with no additional weight, because the water is not deep.

'All you need to do,' said the expert, 'is chuck the spoon over the other side of the current and let it flutter back to you.' He was right. A versatile man, he dyed his prawns from a lightly cooked, appealing pink to a startling magenta, which proved magnetic to the fish. They were not the large, soft prawns purchased by the scoopful from the fishmonger, for these are soft and soon fall to pieces, but good, small, whiskery, tough ones brought into Poole harbour. He did not rely on luck, being a first-class angler who knew his river well and stuck to practical ways in a small, deep, weedy stream with overhanging trees.

The kit was very simple: just a spinning rod, a fixed-spool reel and 17 lb nylon. The methods he practised suited the small, obstructed pools, into which it was possible to flick a Mepp or lower a prawn, but where a fly would hang up in the trees on every second cast.

Another of the little rivers I have tried is the Lussa on the island of Mull where I fished with my father-in-law in 1971 and 1972. The house we had rented had a mile and a half of one bank of this small salmon spate river and two small floods came down during our July fortnight. We had trout rods and started with the fly but, apart from a few finnock, experienced no success until we read the fishing diary in the house. There was one intriguing entry made 2 weeks before our arrival: 'We might have done all right if a bit more skilled with the worm'.

Whether this had been written by the owner with his uncultivated vegetable garden in mind I do not know, but we certainly dug it over for him, including the corners and every last square yard. They were good succulent worms, wriggly and irresistible. Two did the trick when mounted on a salmon fly hook stripped of the dressing. We had to cast gently, using a swinging motion, or the worms flew off into the bracken. Projected straight across the pool, they sank quite well when aided by a lead sliver pared by a knife from the lead flashing on the roof. We trundled them down over the rocky bottom and the take was gentle – just a slight twitching of the fly line between the fingers indicating the moment to raise the rod. We landed three salmon of between 5 and 7 lb and managed the same the following year. Great fishing on a light 8 ft 6 in. split-cane rod.

And, finally, a small West Country river which runs below my house – the Lyd. Trees are again the problem and, although I have cut them back the space is very restricted for the fly and so I spin. A Mepp is good but the bait on which I rely is the size No. 1 little pink rubber plug called a 'Flopy', which comes from France. This river runs off Dartmoor, down through Lydford Gorge, it falls rapidly to my stretch. A good stream for small trout in the summer months, a full spate is needed in September to bring fish up from the Tamar, branch off into the Lyd and up the valley to my beat which is about 1 mile in length. There are many small pools, few of them more than 4 ft deep when the water is low. After a good rain, I start at the top to fish right down the whole length with the Flopy before working back upstream, covering the water a second time with the Mepp, usually a No. 2 in gold. Each pool is well fished by half-a-dozen throws after which I move. On that small river, in Oak Tree Pool, in 1984, my daughter Lara took an 8½ lb fish on a No. 2 Mepp Aglia Longue – the second salmon of her life.

The salmon usually run by night for the water is shallow over the stickles and I dare say they feel exposed by day. As a result it is not worth covering the beat more than once in 24 hours.

These small rivers require short rods and stealthy initiative to bring success. In tiny pools, with watchful salmon and scary trout, it is the unobtrusive angler, blending with the bushes and moving slowly from pool to pool, who catches the fish.

Game fishing instructors and schools

Register of Experienced Fly Fishing Instructors and Schools (REFFIS)

Chairman: Charles Bingham, West Down, Warrens Cross, Whitchurch, Tavistock, Devon PL19 9LD. Telephone 0822 613899

Secretary: Richard Slocock, Wessex Fly Fishing, Tolpuddle, Dorchester, Dorset DT27HF. Telephone 0305 848460.

REFFIS is the only group of professional instructors insisting on a comprehensive Standard of Facilities and Code of Customer Care for member Schools and Approved Instructors, in addition to the requirements of The Salmon & Trout Association. REFFIS facilities are regularly inspected by Committee Members. Not all REFFIS members teach salmon fishing. A telephone call to the Chairman or Secretary will put you in touch with a salmon instructor. Likewise, information on river and still-water trout instruction will be provided.

In the spring of 1994 The Salmon & Trout Association inaugurated a new instructor's qualification to replace the game-angling qualification previously offered by the former National Anglers' Council (NAC). This is known as The Salmon & Trout Association National Instructor's Certificate (STANIC). All REFFIS members hold STANIC and are members of The Salmon & Trout Association. Further details of STANIC may be obtained from The Salmon & Trout Association Development and Training Officer: James Woolcock, Juniper Cottage, Ingestre, Stafford ST18 ORE. Telephone 0889 270150.

REFFIS approved instructors

Andrew Allen, 1 Laundry Cottage, Syon House, Brentford, Middlesex TW8 8JF. Telephone 081-568 6354.

Charles Bingham. Address as above.

Robert Brighton, 12 Fyrish Crescent, Evanton, Ross-shire IV16 9YS. Telephone 0349 830 159.

John Berry, 17 Cross Street, Barugh Green, Barnsley, Yorkshire S75 1NL. Telephone 0226 382 080.

Simon Cooper, Fishing Breaks Ltd., 16 Bickerton Road, Upper Holloway, London N19 5JR. Telephone 071-281 6737.

Derek Herbert, Parkburn Guest House, Grantown-on-Spey, Morayshire PH26 3EN. Telephone 0479 873116.

Roderic Hall, 78 Wandsworth Road, Knock, Belfast, Northern Ireland BT4 3LW. Telephone 0232 658 220.

Pat O'Reilly, West Wales School of Flyfishing, Ffoshelyg, Lancych, Boncath, Dyfed SA37 0LJ. Telephone 023 977 678.

Thomas H. Pass, 4 Putty Row, Macclesfield Road, Eaton, Congleton, Cheshire CW12 2NP. Telephone 0260 223 472.

Roddy Rae, Half Stone Sporting Agency, 6 Hescane Park, Cheriton Bishop, Exeter, Devon EX6 6JP. Telephone 0647 24643.

Andrew Ryan, Clon-A-Nav Farm Guesthouse, Nire Valley, Ballymacarbry, Clonmel, Co. Waterford, Eire. Telephone 052 36141.

Richard Slocock. Address as above.

Graham Ward, East Anglia School of Fly Fishing, 22 Twyford Gardens, Bishop's Stortford, Herts. CM23 3EH. Telephone 0279 659914.

Duncan Weston, Belvedere, Salisbury Road, Ower, Romsey, Hampshire SO51 6AN. Telephone 0703 814 215.

Simon Ward, 20 Primrose Way, Locks Heath, Southampton, Hampshire SO3 6WX. Telephone 0489 579 295.

Game fishing instruction may also be arranged through the following:

Association of Professional Game Angling Instructors

Secretary: Michael Evans, Little Saxbys Farm, Cowden, Kent TN8 7DX. Telephone 0342 850765.

Farlow's of Pall Mall, 5 Pall Mall, London SW1Y 5NP. Telephone 071-839 2423.

House of Hardy, 61 Pall Mall, London SW1Y 5JA. Telephone 071-839 5515.

Orvis Co., Bridge House, High Street, Stockbridge, Hampshire SO20 6HB. Telephone 0264 810 017.

The Rod Box, London Road, Kings Worthy, Winchester, Hampshire SO23 7QN. Telephone 0962 883 600.

References

Bingham, Charles: 'Beguiled by Hairy Mary's lethal lure' *Sunday Telegraph*, 1990

Bingham, Charles: 'Salmon in Lilliput' *Trout & Salmon*, 1985

Bingham, Charles: 'Spring salmon – spinner and fly' *Countrysport*, 1986

Brunton Blaikie, J: *I go a-Fishing*, 1928

Fleming, John: *Reminiscences of a Local Angler, 60 Years Ago*, 1927

Goddard, John & Clark, Brian: *The Trout and the Fly*, 1980

Gray, L. R. N: *Torridge Fishery*, 1957

Hardy, James L., ed: *Handbook of the Northern Anglers' Federation*, 1957

Knowles, Derek: *Salmon – On a Dry Fly*, 1987

Orton, D: *Where to Fish*, (Biennial)

Pain, C. E: *Fifty Years on the Test*, 1934

Paterson, Wilma, & Behan, Peter C.: *Salmon and Women*, 1990

Righyni, Reg: *Advanced Salmon Fishing*, 1973

Scott, Jock: *Spinning Up to Date*, 1950 (4th edition)

Walton, Izaak: *The Compleat Angler*, 1676 (5th edition)

Wanless, Alexander: *The Science of Spinning for Salmon and Trout*, 1946 (Revised edition)

Index

Page numbers in *italic* refer to illustrations.